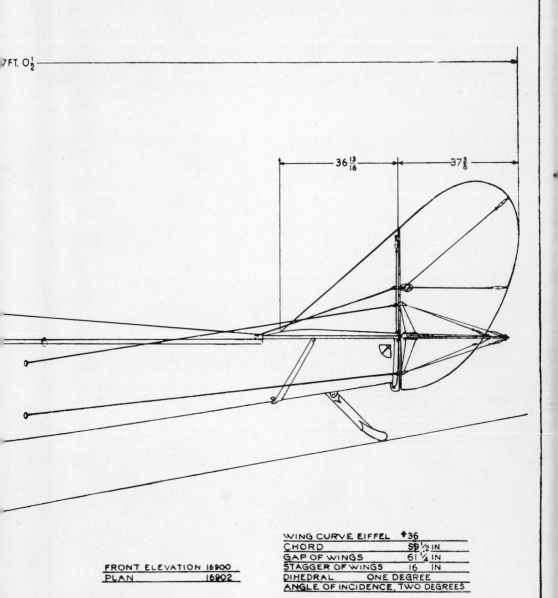

7 FT. 0½

36 13/16   37 3/8

WING CURVE EIFFEL ♦36
CHORD   59½ IN
GAP OF WINGS   61¼ IN
STAGGER OF WINGS   16 IN
DIHEDRAL   ONE DEGREE
ANGLE OF INCIDENCE, TWO DEGREES

FRONT ELEVATION 16900
PLAN   16902

DIMENSIONS ARE IN INCHES UNLESS MARKED OTHERWISE.   LIMITS TO BE WITHIN   UNLESS OTHERWISE SPECIFIED.

						CHANGE	E			ERECTION	MODEL JN4-H	MATERIAL	SPEC. No
K							D			SIDE ELEVATION		HEAT TR. SPEC. NO.	FINISH SPEC. NO.
J							C						
H							B			DRAWN BY	TRACED BY	CHECKED BY	APPR. BY	APPR. BY	SCALE: ¾ IN. = 1 FT.	
G							A	RETRACED WITH CHANGES	H	B.KUCYNSKI	J.LAMBRIX	R.C.H.	J.Daly	J.McN.	IN FL. OF	SUPER. BY
	DATE	FROM	CK.AP		DATE	FROM	CK.AP	12-20-17	1-23-18	1-23-18	1-23-18	1-23-18	16900 — 1-2-18	

BUFFALO, N.Y.   THE CURTISS AEROPLANE AND MOTOR CORPORATION   HAMMONDSPORT, N.Y.

16901

JENNY WAS NO LADY

JENNY

THE STORY OF THE JN-4D

NEW YORK

W. W. NORTON & COMPANY · INC

Was No Lady

by Jack R. Lincke

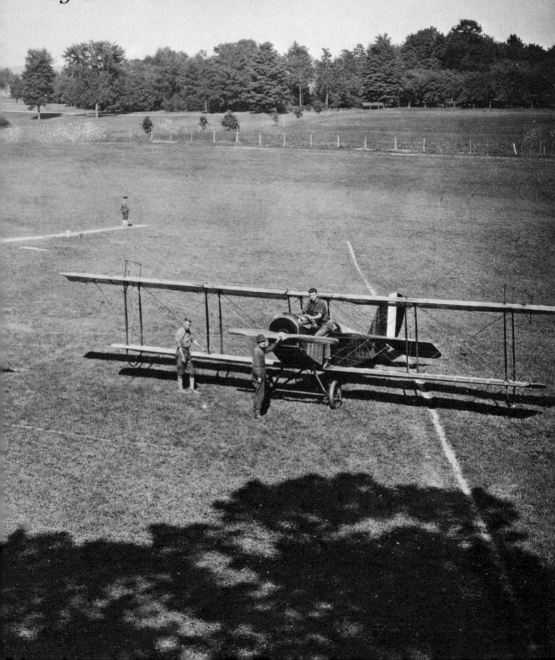

FOR MY DAUGHTER

To you, Mabel, with gratitude
for your loyalty and the
many splendid things I have
learned because of you

CONTENTS

PREFACE

Jenny did a nice, banana-shaped loop, a chandelle, a wingover, a snap roll; then she tried an Immelmann and fell out of it—tried again and just made it. I watched intently.

Right in the middle of a two-turn spin, I heard the first sergeant call out from the rear of the column to my squad leader: "Put Cadet Private Lincke on report for turning head and eyes in ranks." Then to me: "Don't you ever learn, chump?"

I didn't like the emphasis he had put on "Private." This was a low blow. The first sergeant had just taken over my rating after I had been busted over a tangle with regulations. No, I didn't like him; and I wasn't going to like the bull ring I'd have to walk with rifle and full pack because of this gig.

Then the cadet major gave the command: "Pass in review," the band went into "The Stars and Stripes Forever" and sent us on our way to complete evening parade.

Meanwhile, Jenny was trying another Immelmann, and while I stepped all over the heels of the swearing cadet in front of me, gawking at her, she made it, gave up for the evening and started a lazy glide home to bed, her wires humming drowsily in the autumn haze.

This was Kemper Military School. I was fifteen. Jenny didn't know it, but she had me hooked.

At home on the ranch in Montana we had a "handy" foreman, and there was a bond between us—we were always broke; but I had the edge—a herd of cattle. So, without my folks knowing it, I wrote to Vic to sell fifteen of my steers, stick the usual 10 percent cumsha in his pocket and send me the rest. I bought a Jenny.

Since Kemper was in Boonville, Missouri, and the Jenny was in Kansas City, approximately 150 miles away, my next problem was to get flying lessons at Kellerstrass Field as often as I could get there. When I did, I hired anyone who claimed he was a pilot to give me some dual. It is doubtful that many of them could fly—they just wanted an airplane ride and I gave them one right out of a book.

From time to time I did manage to get a bona-fide instruction hop, but not many. By the time I had graduated from Kemper, I had run out of patience and time, so I lashed down my suitcase in the after cockpit, topped off the gas tank and the radiator, then started the 1500-mile trip to the ranch at Whitehall, Montana.

I spent all that day following the wrong railroad tracks and returning to Kellerstrass for more gasoline—scattering everybody and causing panic every time I came in. Finally, darkness put me out of business for the day. Next morning I found the Burlington tracks and was on my way.

It was a grand flight, making it from pasture to pasture and landing every time I could find one close enough to a garage where I could get gasoline. For two nights I slept under a wing, and by the third day I had reached western Nebraska.

Near the Wyoming line the horizon began turning an ominous black—it was a dust storm and a huge one. I continued, and shortly was on its fringe. Jenny started tossing and slewing.

"Dust storm?" I thought. "You just fly in one side and out the other." Instrument flying was unheard of because there were no instruments. Blind flying meant nothing and those who had tried it were dead, so they couldn't tell you not to try it.

"In one side and out the other" was a good theory, but once we were thoroughly wrapped up in the swirling blackness and had lost visual reference, gravity began to choose the side we were going to come out of and we were already in trouble—big, bad trouble. I sensed that Jenny wasn't level, that she was acting queerly—that I wasn't flying her; she was flying me. Then she spun left.

We came whirling out of the bottom of the storm and vaguely saw land. Both my feet went to right rudder just like the book said—stick full forward, wide-open engine, and prayers. Just a few feet above disaster the controls began to bite. The whipping slowed, then stopped. I leveled the wings, got the nose up and was looking for a place to land; just in time to fly through a fence and smack into an alfalfa stack.

The prop splintered, the wings and landing gear went next.

The fuselage and I followed the OX-5 deep into the hay, leaving the tail outside with the other debris.

Nothing is darker, smellier, or more full of strangling dust than the inside of an alfalfa stack. I could hardly breathe.

The engine and fuselage had compressed the hay so tightly I couldn't claw my way out. Fortunately, some of the fabric had ripped off, and by stuffing hay into the cockpits and the fuselage as I worked my way along, I dug a tunnel. Just when it seemed I might choke to death, I got out and scared the hell out of a rancher who had galloped up on his horse and was trying to figure out how to retrieve the body.

My new friend went to his barn, hooked up a team and came back. I crawled through my tunnel to the OX-5, secured a line around it, and the horses pulled it out.

A garage man gave me enough for the engine and the wreckage, for its curiosity value, to pay for a ticket home, and that transaction ended my solo flight.

But, like I said, Jenny had me hooked. This was the start of a love affair with subsequent honeymoons in other Jennys and other breeds of airplanes that led throughout America, much of the Pacific, Hawaii, Midway, Alaska, the Philippines, China, Mexico, South America, Australia, Burma, Indo-China, Manchuria, and Mongolia—for thirty-eight years and fourteen thousand flight hours—and on November 28, 1967, the Jenny affair was rekindled when I flew a reconstituted JN-4D.

If the writing man told the truth when he said, "A woman's place is in the wrong," then everything in this book is Jenny's fault.

JENNY WAS NO LADY

CHAPTER ONE

The Air-going Model-T

Jenny (JN-4D) America's aeronautical "Model-T" in which most pioneer Army, Navy and civilian pilots trained. This airplane became the backbone of the entire United States aviation industry.

The Wright brothers took hold of man's centuries-old dream and made it a gasoline-drinking, breathtaking reality. Then, out of the travail of the first tremendous flight of 120 feet in 12 seconds at Kitty Hawk, North Carolina, on December 17, 1903, and out of the injustices heaped upon the inventors by the American War Department, by the Cabinet, by American plunderers and European pilferers, emerged, eleven years later, the wonderful, ugly, cantankerous, lovable, implausible JN-4D, or, by your leave—Jenny.

This 140-pound aggregate of man's restless ingenuity did for getting around above the earth precisely what Henry Ford's Model T did for getting around on the surface of it.

There are few pilots dead or alive who started flying prior to 1927 who didn't learn in or get most of their experience and their lumps in a Jenny. Her pilots became great names in aviation, such as Admirals William A. Moffatt, John Towers, Victor Herbster, Pat Bellinger; Generals Tooey Spaatz, Hap Arnold, Jimmy Doolittle; and Charles Lindbergh.

The *Aircraft Year Book* for 1919 acknowledges Jenny's preeminence with this observation: "Ninety-five percent of the men the U.S. has taught to fly have touched the controls of a JN-4D." Conversely, 95 percent of those who did, got touched by Jenny and often in the tenderest places.

15

Jenny fostered an epoch in man's life, an epoch that has become a part of immense events which are never static, never without awe-inspiring possibilities, as man rams his pushy nose into corners of those incredulity-inspiring reaches where reality becomes tremendously lost in space—and lost to the comprehension of most of us.

But there had to be a beginning for all of this, and Jenny supplied the first nudges. Without her there wouldn't be an X-15, a missile (for better or for worse), a satellite; nor would we be sonic-booming our way from coast to coast in the time it took to shoe the lead team of a Conestoga, a chore still fresh in the memory of living great-grandparents.

It is not being maudlin to state on behalf of Jenny that she was the most significant airplane, or aeroplane, if you wish to date the term, that America or any other nation has produced. She was a remarkable assemblage of engineering contradictions, achieved at a time when aerodynamics was in the diaper stage and we had to design wings and fuselages as we did our bridges, leaning heavily upon mechanical engineering and hydrodynamics because there wasn't much aerodynamics. Then, when all the harried mathematics were assembled, the guesses and bits of fact were entrusted to craftsmen who created a skeleton made of spruce. This was given form by wrapping it in fabric. An engine was put in front and the ensemble was flown by a man who knew even less about what he was doing than did the people who designed and built the airplane.

Had it not been for Jenny, aircraft manufacturing by the United States in World War I would have been a complete rout instead of only a shambles. Out of the enthusiastic stupidity from August, 1914, to April, 1917, out of the unproductive ego and our fumbling attempts to build for the air war, it was Jenny and Jenny alone who kept us from making utter fools of ourselves; because she was the only military airplane we were able to build in quantity.

After seventeen months of frenetic effort to duplicate 15 models of British and French combat planes, we managed to ship only 125 nervous De Havillands to France. Most of them didn't arrive until May 17, 1918, six months before the war's end. Only 36 flew briefly and unsuccessfully before the Armistice. But more than 8,000 Jennys were turned out during nineteen months of U.S. belligerency. In addition, the Canadians built them for themselves and called their version the "Canuck." We and the Canadians built them for Australia, Spain, Italy, France, and Great Britain. Never in all the years between Jenny's first flight and preparations for the Second World War did America build so many airplanes of one kind.

In the swaddling, starvation years for both military and civil aviation—between the Armistice on November 11, 1918, and late in 1925 when the skies were churned by airplanes—it was chiefly Jenny who flew. The several thousand JN-4Ds that were sold as postwar surplus, plus hundreds dumped in the United States by Canada and Great Britain, became the only civilian air vehicle in quantity for almost nine years. However, they were on a rapidly declining curve, as Jennys were scrubbed by crashes or simply wore out.

Jenny achieved immortality in another phase of her life. In addition to putting more men into the air than any other airplane of her times, she also put more of them underground. In fact, in terms of the total number of men who flew her and the flight hours involved, she probably did in more Americans than smallpox. Those who kept tabs claimed she brushed her teeth with embalming fluid. But in justice to her it must be made clear that the antisocial proclivities of the OX-5 engine, and not Jenny per se, often brought about the untimely demise and the prominence of many men who through the novelty of being killed in an airplane achieved more eminence in death than in life.

The continuing reference to Jenny as "she" and never as "it" or "that" is because airplanes have a feminine, coquettish spirit which is traceable to their genes. Yes, genes. Airplanes were and are feminine because men love them even more than they love a woman. A love affair between a man and a woman may go stale, yet this never happens between a pilot and an airplane. No woman can compete against an airplane for a man's affections, and this is incontrovertibly documented. Jenny was in many ways a sweetheart, even a siren or a hoyden at times. Nonetheless, she was a piquant lover, and, lamentably, she and her contemporary sisters have been responsible for many divorces. Among the shards of hundreds of marriages one could recon-

struct the cause célèbre and find it to be an airplane, of which a
wife became so jealous she strapped on her marital parachute
and bailed out.

As we move through these pages, we are going to kid Jenny as
we do anyone with whom we have an affectionate understanding, because we are enamored of her. Although we will tickle her
foibles, we will always remind her that it is only in fun, that she
was grand.

We apologize to her designers, one posthumously, and tell
them that we do not belittle their accomplishment, rather we
honor it.

In telling you about Jenny, we must also tell you a little about
the kind of aeronautical maternity ward into which she was born,
so you will better understand her. Also, two important aspects
have been consistently ignored in treatises on airplanes. The first
is that all aircraft of a given make and model possess a personality. Second, like people, there are heroes and bums, saints and
sinners. In this history, we are just as interested in Jenny's disposition and character as we are in her pounds, feet, and gallons; in
what she could and did do; and what she could not do no matter
how much her attributes have been enlarged by romanticists
peering through nostalgia-tinted goggles.

As for Jenny pilots, the earlier they were, the more completely
they fitted the category referred to as "characters"; the man had
to match the machine.

A curious and a sad phenomenon of pilot evolution is that as
time has passed pilots have stopped being individualists and have
on an ever-increasing scale eased themselves into a plush mold of
conformity with the large body of workaday feather merchants,
until their more robust inheritances are all but obliterated. They

*Jenny in all her air-borne glory. She did for U.S. aviation what the
Model-T Ford did for surface transportation, trained 95% of our pilots for World War I, flew the first air mail and became the vehicle of
the barnstorming era. Jenny was a composite of two airplanes, one
designed by an Englishman, the other by an American. This Jenny is
being flown by a Cadet-in-training at Rockwell Field, San Diego,
Calif. She is carrying the just-adopted Allied aircraft insignia. (U.S.
Signal Corps)*

have become as kindred as peanut-butter sandwiches. This is what enlightenment and sophistication do to people. Both have a devastatingly leavening effect with which they dilute variety, reduce it to a common denominator, and draw off exact copies like gingerbread men marching out of an oven on a conveyor belt.

In the bygone, rugged times, barnstorming Jennymen often slept under the wings of their ships. Today, the gentlemen pilots of the airlines sleep in posh hotels. It is coffee, cakes, and a 38-24-36 stewardess on the flight deck. Such is the mischief of time and progress, those twin iconoclasts who do not keep their dirty fingers out of our business.

The record of history is frequently sneaky and glossed over, otherwise it might be too lewd or discouraging to read. Only a few have recognized that no person, no thing, could be as foolproof as he, it, or she is painted in a history book. Consequently, we are going to tell the truth about Jenny: her virtues, her vices, her weaknesses, and her strengths. There will be no obfuscation of the fact that there were variations in her virtue, and these are accepted because they make her interesting, for no man loves the saint part of a woman any more than he loves the part that eats.

It was these realizations that prompted me to delve so deeply into the personality and character of Jenny—sans bra, sans girdle, sans makeup—her mores, by your leave—to reveal her as a stalwart and a weakling, a darling and a tramp, a madonna and a bum. But she had a character. Maybe there was more bad in it than good, but it was character and not stultifying conformity.

What has become of this rebellious quality in pilot and plane? It has been abraded into a no-contest pattern because flight has become less and less a joust between man and machine. Now it is instrumented, tower directed, and objective. The only real battle left is between pilot and weather. Set your slide rule correctly, read the manual, and the jet flies itself. The interpersonal thing that used to exist between man and Jenny has been erased by an overwhelming science.

In Jenny days it was not like this. You were the Joe Bananas, the Numero Uno in charge of operations, navigation, aerology, women chasing, bill dodging, repair, and overhaul. If you weren't, Jenny had little use for you and it was a short, hot heat.

A co-pilot? St. Jude, the patron saint of snafued ventures, no matter what your religion, was your man. If he and the incompletely known laws of aerodynamics and the gremlins were on your side, you needed no other helpers. If they weren't, you had a short lease.

No, sir, flying is no longer the intimate thing it once was. While pilots now have vaster dimensional freedom in heights, distances, and speeds, they have left so much below and behind that they lack the grand old Jenny élan and gung-ho.

There was a great stimulation in your courtship with Jenny, and as your affection for her grew so did your jealousy, because the best you ever achieved was a diminutive rapport, never a *ménage à deux*. You learned soon, or not at all, not to make a truce but to maintain a wary neutrality in which you kept yourself well fortified with airspeed and alertness, because Jenny believed in taking advantage of others before they took advantage of her. There were no careless Jennys; there were only careless pilots.

Current aircraft are not the test of derring-do that Jenny was. For instance, now you can nose over in a military trainer and let her rumble for thousands of feet with no qualms about blowing a wing. If you barely lowered Jenny's nose without closing the throttle, the mortician never finished picking the pebbles out of you. This was not only a fact of flying, it was also a remarkable restrainer, and since restraint is a self-applied discipline, it built pilot character.

In the old days when someone said, "Charlie just got it" (meaning he had "bought the lot," i.e., had been killed), the first words another pilot said were "What happened?" even before he said: "Too bad." He might have been the deceased's best friend, but that is what he said, because what had happened to Charlie could happen to him and he wanted to know what it was. If a camshaft broke, you could understand it. If a propeller split, it was not unexpected. But the very worst thing the informant could say was "No one knows. They just found him piled up and dead."

This was spooky. You always figured that if a cylinder head flew past, or for some other reason the OX-5 died, your skill would get you down in operable shape. As for a structural failure, it was not a worry because that was something that happened to the other fellow's Jenny, not to yours; your Jenny was the best that flew.

One element, not too common but well known in these mystery crashes and accepted as an occupational hazard, was that occasionally a pilot would rend his rump on a whiskey nimbus. Another element, far more common, but usually not understood, was that a pilot would blunder into fog or heavy rain and be found dead in a heap. A pattern finally became apparent via the grapevine: the ships were hitting in a left spin. Although no one knew why, this was logical because, when one lost visual reference (and not having instruments), one's senses were unable to distinguish between the centrifugal force of a turn and the pull of gravity; consequently, disorientation set in and a spin was a certainty. Also, almost without exception, inadvertent spins went to the left because of a plane's design.

Then, some pilot would think he had solved this storm hoodoo. If he got into weather, since everyone was dying in a left spin, he would concentrate on keeping his left wing up so that nothing bad could happen. He tried it, overcompensated, and was found dead at the end of a right spin.

This was the essence of Jenny heyday flying. It wasn't more dangerous, it was just more ignorant.

CHAPTER TWO

Birth of a Hybrid

Jenny's design began in England and was completed in the United States as an assemblage of the best parts of two different airplanes.

Jenny started out as a hybrid cosmopolite in 1914. She was sired by a Briton and an American and damned by everybody who flew her. She was an aeronautical Siamese twin inasmuch as a J-model airplane, designed in England by B. Douglas Thomas, was crossed with an N model designed in America by the late Glenn Curtiss.

This airborne mating produced the JN, our Jenny, which combined the best of the J and N crafts and eliminated as many of their bad features as was practicable. As the designers corrected their mistakes and made successive improvements, the alterations were designated by numbers in the model nomenclature. For example, after the first correction, models carrying it were designated JN-1; then came JN-2, JN-3, and ultimately JN-4.

The alphabetical series after the JN-4 marked power-plant and mission changes. The bona-fide Jenny with a regulation OX-5 engine did not go past the Model JN-4D. However, there were so many engine and functional variations that Jennys existed with model identifications running up to JN-4HG. When the meaning of the letters and figures in these was explained to a former Jenny dilettante, now a veteran jetliner captain, he said: "I always thought the 'D' stood for 'Damn the thing.'"

The metamorphosis of Jenny was circuitous because America was behind Europe in the development of tractor-type aircraft, i.e., machines with the engine in front and mounting a propeller which "pulled," in contrast with those which had a rear-mounted engine and a "pusher" propeller. The principal advantage of the tractor which appealed to pilots was that in a crash one didn't get mashed by a forward-hurtling engine, a phenomenon that occurred with such regularity that on February 24, 1914, pusher types were condemned by a U.S. Army board. Because of their hazards, Glenn H. Curtiss made the first move to develop an American tractor airplane. Thus, the amalgam of the Curtiss N and the Thomas J became the first airplane here to have a for-ward-mounted propeller. This also meant the first enclosed cock-pit for personnel, who formerly were surrounded only by hope and wind.

B. Douglas Thomas, one of the world's pioneers in aircraft de-sign, was the prime mover of the Jenny. His influence on it began when he met Curtiss during the latter's inquiries into the pro-gress of European tractor types.

Mr. Thomas was born in England on November 17, 1891. In his teens he became an apprentice engineer with Vickers' Sons and Maxim, airplane builders, whose works were in Erith. For the next four years he was assigned to training in design. In 1912, when he was twenty-one years old, Thomas was employed as assistant chief engineer with the just-organized Sopwith Avia-tion Co., Kingston-on-Thames. He describes his meeting with Curtiss at the Sopwith plant, an event which ultimately led him to become an American citizen and enabled him to indelibly mark U.S. aircraft design with Jenny and his notable Thomas Morse series of military airplanes:

"I was too shy to talk to Curtiss, but I tagged along as one of the party of engineers who were to greet him and answer his questions about tractor airplanes. We were with him half a day.

"I seldom went to London, but that night I did. It started to rain and I ducked into a shop on the Strand. A chap who was reading a newspaper looked up, and I saw that it was Curtiss. He was en route to Russia, where he was to attempt to open an air-craft factory on the strength of an order to build one plane for the government. I was surprised that he remembered my face when he spoke."

Curtiss was impressed by the aeronautical knowledge possessed by the twenty-two-year-old engineer. Since he had to leave immediately for Paris on his way to Moscow, he offered to pay Thomas's transportation if he would come along and continue their discussion. While they were crossing the Channel the basic idea of Jenny took shape. Curtiss commissioned Thomas to design an airplane that would be designated as the J model. Upon his return home, he went right to work, and since the winter of 1913–14 was mild in the London area he worked in a tent in his family's yard.

"I had to make all the drawings, calculate stress data, and specify materials," Thomas later explained. "I was furnished a photograph of a Curtiss OX-5 engine but no dimensions, so I had to do some guessing about designing the engine mount. This wasn't the only drawback; I had to pedal a bicycle on a twenty-mile round trip every time I had blueprints made."

B. Douglas Thomas, one of the fathers of Jenny and of tractor-type, tandem U.S. airplanes. This photo was taken in 1966 after Mr. Thomas had retired from Convair. Born in England, Mr. Thomas was engaged by Glenn Curtiss while on a visit to England. In addition to Jenny, Mr. Thomas designed a long line of "Tommys," i.e., Thomas Morse military airplanes. He is shown here with a large model of a "Tommy" and a smaller one of a JN-4D. (Convair)

Thomas mailed drawings across the Atlantic as rapidly as they were completed, and at the Curtiss plant in Hammondsport, New York, parts were fabricated immediately. No contract had been signed to cover the work and Thomas hoped Curtiss would ask him to go to Russia to manage his plane factory. Instead, in April, 1914, he received a cable typical of the taciturn Curtiss which simply said: "Come on over."

Thomas disembarked in New York City on May 2, 1914, and has lived in America ever since. For a number of years, after his design work on the Thomas-Morse airplanes, he was with Consolidated Aircraft Co., from which he retired in the thirties.

When Thomas reported for work he found his Model J partially built. Curtiss's Model N was at the same stage and carried an interesting feature consisting of midwing ailerons, which were a part of the infringement strategy by which Curtiss sought to evade royalty payments to the Wrights for their basic patents.

Although Curtiss lost every suit brought against him for this determined proclivity, he did not alter his tactics. Using appeals, bond posting and other subterfuges, he continued using infringing ailerons while his lawyers dragged matters out in the courts. In 1917, Curtiss was saved by World War I, when all U.S. aircraft patents were pooled under government auspices and users paid royalties to their holders.

If Curtiss ever believed he had not received sufficient accolades for his aeronautic designs, he could at least be assured that he was renowned as the best aileron thief in the business.

When Thomas went to work, Henry Kleckler was factory superintendent and George A. Page was in charge of production. Assigned as an assistant to Thomas was A. V. Verville, who later became a prominent designer.

The first J made its maiden flight on May 10, 1914, piloted by Curtiss. Later he flew it as a seaplane with a single float. It had wings of equal span, trailing-edge ailerons, and an OX-5 engine.

During the summer of 1914, two modified Js with interplane ailerons, six degrees of dihedral, and the Eiffel-36 wing section were shipped to the Army's sole flight-training unit, the First Aero Corps, which had been established at North Island, San Diego. This Army portion of the Navy's bastion subsequently was designated Rockwell Field. These airplanes were the twenty-ninth and thirtieth purchased and were assigned these serial numbers. They were more successful than they had a right to be at that time. In fact, Number 30 became the fastest thing on wings in the United States during a design evaluation test flight on September 6, when Curtiss got it up to 85.7 mph. This was the equivalent of Mach 3 today. The performance considerably

This is B. Douglas Thomas' "J" Model tractor, designed by him in England and built by Curtiss in New York as fast as blueprints were sent across the ocean. A Curtiss tractor, called the "N" Model, was blended with the "J" and this became known as the JN, or "Jenny." Photo shows the "J" Model which did so well in the first demonstration trials held at Rockwell Field, San Diego. Note skid landing gear and single-unit fin and rudder. (Convair)

exceeded the Army's requirements for a craft capable of flying at 70 mph, of climbing at four hundred feet per minute, and of staying aloft for four hours.

Curtiss also entered his Model N, and, while waiting for competitors to show up, defied the fates by making a flight with the between-wings ailerons blocked to demonstrate stability. A San Diego reporter wrote: "It raced through the air at the terrific speed of 70 miles an hour, practically unguided by the pilot." What the reporter didn't know was that in those days practically all flights were unguided.

The Army found it necessary to cancel the evaluation flights, however, because too few designers showed up with airplanes. Nonetheless, demonstrations continued for fifteen days before an Army Inspection Board.

During subsequent flights, Glenn L. Martin, a pioneer designer, made the best performance by climbing to 4,170 feet and remaining aloft for five hours and fifteen minutes. Bad luck on November 5 removed both Mr. Martin and his craft from further competition when he crashed from seventy feet during a slow-speed demonstration, and suffered severe head cuts. His passenger, Captain L. E. Goodier, had a leg broken. On October 8, Captain H. K. Miller took his future in his hands while he worried Number 30 up to 7,441 feet, establishing a U.S. altitude record. On December 7, one of Curtiss's test pilots (in those days, the pilot was more tested than testing), Raymond V. Morris, flew a Model N to 4,790 feet in ten minutes. On December 16 he reached a speed of 82 mph.

Of such stout stuff were Jenny's parents made. Very soon after these events, the best aeronautical chromosomes of the J and N models were combined into one, with this mutation producing the JN, or Jenny.

Thomas hadn't been at Hammondsport long until he perceived that American ways were not British ways. It was difficult enough to design aircraft with little or nothing to go on except "It looks good, maybe it will work," while assimilating foreign customs and idioms.

Thomas found Curtiss to be an admixture of practical engineer and genius, although not educated in the former. He varied a volatile temper one day with sphinxlike taciturnity the next. Both characteristics backfired during the crossbreeding of the J and N models.

It started when Curtiss blew his stack one Friday because the owner of the factory buildings he had leased was six months behind in his contractual maintenance. Curtiss phoned him and shortly afterwards two Curtiss executives spent an hour trying unsuccessfully to talk the phone company out of discontinuing service because, as a representative said: "Our girls don't have to listen to such language." This ignited Curtiss all over and he yelled, "Why the hell are they listening? Probably selling my engineering and business secrets to competitors. I'll sue the phone company." So with no further pilikia, service was reinstated.

One half of the building which had fused the pyrotechnics, and in which the offices were located, was given over to development work and the remainder to fabrication. Newly designed parts were made in the former, tried out on the Jennys, and if satisfactory, went into production in the latter.

When the staff returned to work Monday morning following the boss's fire fight with the building owner and the phone company, the members were pleased to see that the place had been repainted and presented a bright and shining demeanor. "Good," they said. "We can take off our flak suits." But the respite was short-lived; pandemonium broke out in the development section.

The painters had completely obliterated a series of pencil and chalk drawings of parts which Curtiss, as was his habit, had sketched on two walls instead of having his ideas reduced to blueprints. As a result of this destruction of his graffiti, which covered some two dozen important units of Jenny's skeletal person, production on them was halted for eleven days while engineers used existing parts as models to turn out the production drawings which should have been made in the first place.

Know something? Even this didn't make Curtiss kick the habit.

At this stage of airplane development, mathematical adaptations to the new science were exceedingly nebulous. Progress was based upon trial and error and the experiences of pilots. But progress was soon to receive an impetus.

World War I got going in earnest on August 1, 1914, when Germany declared war on Russia, and against France on the 3rd. Great Britain joined up on the 4th. To say that the United States

Major General Benjamin D. Foulois, U.S.A.F. (Ret.), photographed in 1963 when he was 84 years old (he died April 25, 1967). With him is famed jet pilot Al White, of North American Aviation, Inc. The model is of the Kitty Hawk, in which the first heavier-than-air flight was made by the Wright brothers in 1903. This is the same type airplane in which Foulois later taught himself to fly after only three hours of dual by Wilbur Wright. The airplane in the photograph is the XB-70, initially test flown in October, 1964. (North American Aviation, Inc.)

reacted with electrifying speed and brilliance would be doing history a disservice. In a sort of ho-hum spirit, the government reorganized the First Aero Squadron and its base at North Island. However, this was not a great military feat inasmuch as the unit consisted of only sixteen officers, seventy-seven enlisted men, and eight airplanes. This establishment was under the command of the truly indestructible Captain Benjamin Foulois, who later was to be one of the first to fly a U.S. plane in combat—a Jenny—against Villa's forces during the Punitive Expedition in Mexico.

"Benny" was the third Army officer to become a pilot and never has a military man or a civilian done so as precariously. When the Army bought its first airplane in 1909 the contract with the Wrights provided for training two pilots. Those selected were Lieutenants Frank Lahm and Frederick E. Humphreys. However, Foulois, who was Orville Wright's passenger on the acceptance flight because he was the lightest and smallest officer handy, became so attached to the airplane and the Wrights to him that they gave him three and a half hours of unofficial dual at their own expense. However, he didn't solo.

Subsequently, Foulois and the above airplane were the total U.S. Air Force, with their base located at Fort Sam Houston, Texas. Here, Foulois, still not having soloed, became the first correspondence-course aviator in history. While teaching himself to fly, after each inadvertence he found out what he did wrong in an exchange of letters with the Wrights and then tried to do better next time.

Airplane Number One was rebuilt so many times that before long it bore little resemblance to its original self. Since the Army had allocated only $150 a year for maintenance, the craft was kept flying mostly on Foulois's paycheck. Finally, the venerable wreck was taken away from him and put in the Smithsonian Institution, in 1911 where it has been on display ever since.

Foulois rose from the enlisted ranks of the infantry to commissioned grade and at thirty-eight became the youngest brigadier in the Army. During World War I he served as Chief of Air Service of the A.E.F.

At this point we will digress to establish the first casualties of Jenny, a list she was to expand to jittery proportions before she was retired from the jousting.

The previously-mentioned J model, which flew in the initial North Island design evaluation on June 27, 1914, had to be ditched just offshore in the Pacific on December 21, 1914, because of a power failure. It was piloted by Captain Hollis LeR. Miller, who carried student pilot Lieutenant Frederick Gerstner as observer. After a successful landing, Gerstner started swimming ashore, but became entangled in kelp and drowned.

The first to meet death from a Jenny crash impact was Captain G. H. Knox, Quartermaster Corps. He was killed while a passenger in a JN-2, Signal Corps No. 47, on August 12, 1915, at Ft. Sill, Oklahoma.

The first pilot to die in a crash was Lieutenant W. R. Taliaferro, one of the most skilled and courageous airmen of this early era. He had been designated Military Aviator under General Order No. 39, on September 25, 1913, when a second lieutenant. He was flying No. 30, the second J model delivered to North Island. He attempted a loop at two thousand feet, but upon reaching the inverted position "fell off the top" and was unable to recover before plunging into the bay. His body was found twenty-four hours later trapped under the wreckage in fifty feet of water.

CHAPTER THREE

Jenny Aloft!

The impending entry of the United States into World War I launches Jenny on her career as the premier training airplane which was called upon to perform many missions with different engines which added to her built-in idiosyncrasies.

The European holocaust had been blazing seven months before the United States decided she should have some airplanes. On March 10, 1915, construction was begun at Buffalo, New York, on the "Churchill Plant," named after the doughty Sir Winston. Within thirty days, the 110,000-square-foot factory was operating. Ultimately Jennys were produced at the rate of one hundred per month.

By fall, the first Jenny war bird was completed. It was a historic occasion when on a snowy afternoon at 3:15 work was suspended while the crew hurried outside to see Jenny carefully trundled to the apron for an engine warmup prior to a flight test. Whistles shrieked and workmen cheered—having no conception of the impact this first U.S.-mass-produced airplane would have upon the destinies of men here and elsewhere.

There she stood, new and gleaming, her khaki war color contrasting sharply with the snow. From then on Jenny's personality became enmeshed with the objective of quantity production. So absorbed did she become that at times she believed she was the catalyst and without her there probably wouldn't be a war. She considered herself the sine qua non of her own being.

In the angry years until the Armistice, 6,072 Jennys were built for the United States Government at $5,000 apiece, and more than 2,000 were produced for other governments. In excess of

33

The stalwart JN-4D, America's first warplane, as she appeared following her mutations through the JN-2 and JN-3 to the JN-4, JN-4A, JN-4B, JN-4C—to the ultimate Jenny, the JN-4D. This was photographed at Kelly Field in Texas after we had entered World War I. (U.S. Signal Corps)

500 Jennys were delivered to U.S. flying fields out of 2,317 built after the Armistice despite the blanket cancelation of aircraft orders with its signing. This was a quid pro quo between manufacturers and politicians in which the latter neglected to blow the whistle on Jenny makers when the Allies blew it on Kaiser Bill, enabling factories to go on incubating for several months.

But Jenny didn't get a real impetus until that fateful May 4, 1915, when Captain Schweiger, commanding the German submarine *U-20*, made a decision off the Head of Kinsale, Ireland, that in 13 words would wreck his nation: "Come to course one-six-zero. Speed standard. Ready bow tubes." Time stood still while the orders were executed. Then came the command: "Fire one." With a slight jolt and the slam of compressed air, this and succeeding torpedoes got under way. A few minutes later the *Lusitania* was sinking. Of the 1,198 who became casualties, 124 were Americans. U.S. participation in the war was now inevitable; and Jenny was destined to give hundreds of U.S. pilots a bird's-eye view of the Four Horsemen of the Apocalypse.

Jenny aeries began springing up across the nation until these were in operation: Standard Aircraft Corp., Plainfield, New Jersey; Eagle Aircraft Co., Niles, Ohio; St. Louis Aircraft Corp., St. Louis, Missouri; Sturtevant Airplane Co., Boston, Massachusetts; Springfield Aircraft Corp., Springfield, Massachusetts; Curtiss Airplane Co., Hammondsport, New York (Curtiss soon owned or controlled six factories); Churchill Plant, Buffalo, New York; plants in San Francisco, Sacramento, Redwood City, California. The Canadians built their Jennys, or Canucks in Toronto, B.C.

A JN-4A ready to fly. Note the pronounced dihedral angle of the top wing, i.e., tips higher than center-section. This gave stability, but decreased maneuverability. The highest pylons above the ailerons were part of the wing-bracing system. Aileron cable emerges from side of fuselage and runs diagonally forward to a pulley on leading edge of top wing and then aft to aileron-actuating horn. (Curtiss Aeroplane Co.)

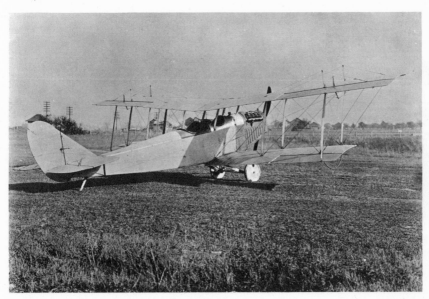

Above

A JN-4A without her "skin." One flew a lot of wood aloft when he piloted a Jenny into the "wild yonder." There was one school of administrative thought that held to the belief that student pilots should not be permitted to see Jenny without her raiment, lest they lose confidence in her ability to remain together under stressful situations. (Curtiss Aeroplane Co.)

Below

Side view of a JN-4A. Note trussing for fuselage. The ailerons were actuated by double cables seen here attached to their trailing edges on top and bottom wings. The half loop under the wing tip took some of the curse out of groundloops. They frequently prevented a wing tip from digging into the turf and flipping Jenny onto her back. In minor mishaps, these prevented wing damage. (Curtiss Aeroplane Co.)

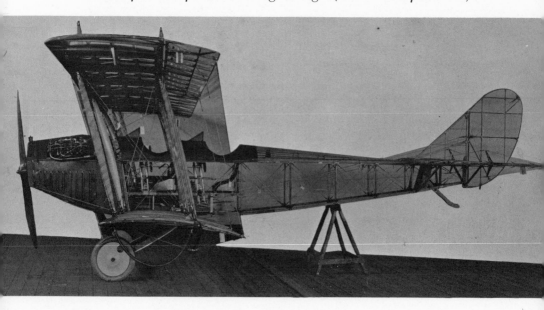

Before going into the meanings of the several model variations of Jenny, her specifications and the more detailed facets of her anatomy, let us first, for the uninitiate, make a general description of her skeletal attributes and appendages.

A spruce framework formed the fuselage, wings, vertical fin, horizontal stabilizer, and elevators. The four landing-gear struts were also of spruce, as were the tail skid and the inter-plane struts. The main control, originally called the "Joyce Stick" after its inventor, was made of laminated wood. Later, this elevator-aileron control became the "Joy Stick," owing to its functions in acrobatics. Now, where used, it is simply called "The Stick." Thus we become increasingly less dramatic as we become more sophisticated.

The woodworking skill that went into Jenny's skeleton equaled the craftsmanship in a Stradivarius and was a wonderful thing to behold until some ham-handed mechanic or pilot had made repairs to it. All components were built on smooth hardwood tables, precisely leveled and trued. Later, rudimentary hardwood jigs became the forerunners of the metal ones used today.

Once the spruce assembly was completed, the whole thing was braced with piano wire, and the structure was locked into an exact position by integral turnbuckles and profanity.

When the wood had been given several coats of varnish, the cotton or linen coverings were attached on the bias to contribute to the bracing, and were treated with multiple applications of nitrate "dope." This compound shrank the fabric to drum tautness and resulted in surprising strength and water resistance. It also went off like a bomb if you dropped a cigarette on it.

With all of the structural amenities completed, the wings and tail were rigged. Never have the world's grandest houris been more carefully trued and plumbed with corsetry, et al., than was Jenny when being gussied for flight. With loving care she was aligned externally between the wings and at other crucial locations with small-diameter steel cables as precisely as a musician prepares his harp for a concert.

Performance? A little. She would do seventy-five miles an hour with full power and some strain when new. But she preferred a less arduous sixty to sixty-five because she flew on the theory that it was better to be a little late down here than a few years early

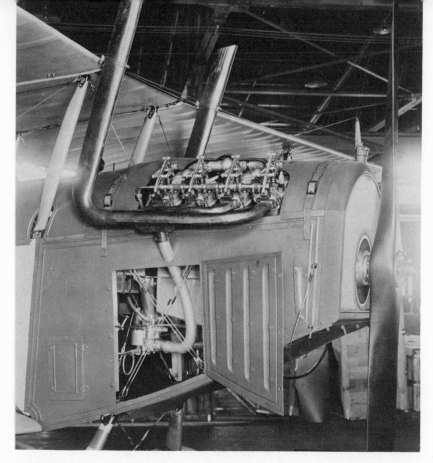

up there. She would land at forty-five mph and climb at two hundred feet per minute if you didn't have a roll of tools in the back end. Her gluey habits after takeoff were notorious. She *might* be cajoled to an altitude of sixty-five hundred feet, but if there was a flyable canyon close by, it was prudent not to be stubborn about those sixty-five hundred feet; you might not have all of them when they were needed. In the sawed-off altitude where Jenny lived, drank her gasoline, and flew, there always seemed to be an argument over the few feet between her and whatever was below.

Jenny's usual OX-5 engine was a water-cooled, V-8, 90-hp son-of-a-gun. Some of the horses were usually limping. Jennymen were divided into two schools: those who hated the airplane and those who hated the engine.

Although later we will go into detailed specifications of the various models of Jenny and explain their basic differences, we must acquaint those who never saw a real, live Jenny with her most outward attributes. To this end, we will now fill in the gaps

Left
This OX-5 installation shows a hot-air tube and muffler assembly which was one of the first attempts, if not the first, to overcome carburetor icing. The vertical exhaust stacks were quite common in Hisso engine installations. Engines were not completely cowled to aid cylinder head and exhaust valve cooling. Note "buttoned-down" engine cowling secured by leather straps. This was a JN-4A model. (Curtiss Aeroplane Co.)

Above
Side view of engine installation in a JN-4A. Note downthrust alignment of the engine, and the remarkable woodwork in the engine bearers and fuselage longerons; also routing in the vertical member seen just aft of the engine and forward of the fuel tank. Rudder bar for directional control is just below the fuel tank. Although a shaky lashup, the craft performed miracles. (Curtiss Aeroplane Co.)

in the experience of those who didn't learn to fly until after 1927, when Jenny was scrubbed.*

Some models mounted an OXX-6 engine, which differed from an OX-5 in that it had two magnetos and two spark plugs per

* Following its inception, Army aviation underwent five reorganizations and name changes. To attempt to correlate them for the period 1907–1926, the era we are studying, would be more confusing than to simply use them interchangeably. These are the changes to date: Aeronautical Division, Signal Corps, created 8/1/07. Aviation Section, Signal Corps, created 7/18/14. U.S. Air Service, created 5/24/18. Army Aviation, created 6/6/42. U.S.A.F., created 7/26/47.

cylinder instead of one. A few variations mounted the horren-
dous Hispano-Suiza, nicknamed the "Hisso," which was crammed
with 100, 150, 200 or 300 hp. Only the most astute birdman could
"dominate all that power." This engine was used in some of the
Navy's versions of the Jenny, called the N-9. It was also used in
the airmail Jennys.

During World War I, Jenny was a principal in many training-
field tragedies owing partly to her aerodynamic inadequacies and
partly to untutored maintenance, but attributable mainly to the
fact that flight instructing was new and those who gave it often
knew no more than the recipients.

There were many Jenny deaths at Kelly and other fields.
Among them was that of Vernon Castle, who left a lucrative entertainment stardom to do his best for his country. He was but
one of hundreds whose experience and tragic ending now let us
fly in greater ease.

At many of the airdromes, cadets were housed in tents—
summer and winter. Barracks building never did catch up. In
fact, when I was an aviation cadet at March Field, California, in
1928—ten years after the war—we lived in tents.

When you ask a World War I Jennyman to summarize his
training experience, he says laconically: "Mud. I froze my butt."

In terms of air handling Jenny was a surprising admixture of
strengths and weaknesses, of coquettishness and faithfulness,
steadfastness and treachery. Although she could on occasion be a
lady she seldom touched the stuff. If you flew her badly, for instance, her innate competitive spirit became aroused and she
fought back. When this resulted in her spinning-in, the thud was
heard in every cadet barracks in America and Canada.

The emphasis upon any of these characteristics depended considerably upon the weather, the breaks, and upon who manipulated her and how deftly—or upon who was reminiscing and how
drunk he was.

It was because of this kaleidoscope of virtues and vices that
much of the nostalgic talk about Jenny always smacks considerably of a special breed who flew by the seat of their pants with no
help from other raiment or the Federal Aeronautics Authority.
Those were the days, veterans say, when you died every time
you flew. It wasn't quite true.

All one had to do to live was either to stay out of a Jenny or approach her and her power plant in accordance with the engineering shortcomings of the era; with a leavening of respect for what you, the pilot, hadn't yet found out. Actually the worst features of the planes were the airy-minded maniacs who flew them. It was only cowards and irreverent cynics who referred to a Jenny and an OX-5 as a bunch of parts flying in formation.

Now that we are up to the flying phase, the reader will recall that an OXX-6 was an OX-5 with two magnetos and with two spark plugs per cylinder. This slightly increased power and was also a safety factor; but it didn't count because it was always a camshaft that broke, anyway.

This kind of thing set up a condition in which forced-landing agility was much better insurance than flying skill. Almost anyone could get a Jenny into the air and keep her there—that is until the engine died; then one's ability to get down was the pay-off. Cemeteries are dotted with Jennymen who, instead of watching for a usable cow pasture, were thinking about their wife's younger sister when a camshaft broke.

Jenny developed a generation of airmen who were fast with a pass at unfamiliar terrain. The dullards dropped out early and have been referred to posthumously as "intrepid birdmen." They weren't intrepid, they just corked off once too often.

Despite her surprises, there were nice things about flying a Jenny. There wasn't much in the cockpit but you, your high tan boots, wind, sand, and a jiggly panel with three or four instruments which you ignored because they seldom worked; and, anyway, they shook so much they made you nervous if you paid them any heed. They really weren't instruments you could sink your teeth into, yet you often did.

Furthermore, you weren't confused at night by today's hundreds of diabolically misplaced cockpit devices, any one of which grabbed in the wrong sequence can make page 1 and a pall of smoke five thousand feet high.

Navigation wasn't so difficult because of the slow speed, provided you had enough sandwiches along to tide you over if your course went awry. If you ran into bad weather en route, you stayed out of it, or you spun-in and died. It was that simple.

When you closed the throttle (cut the gun, to be more pictur-

Above left

This is not an annex to Dante's Inferno; it is a tire-testing machine. It was not difficult to tell which way was up and which down, as well as how to "out fast" if something went awry. The "neutral" was probably for those uncommitted people who refused to be concerned over whether the machine or the tire triumphed. (Curtiss Aeroplane Co.)

Above

Looking precisely like what it was—a cudgel of the Inquisition—this diabolically contrived combination of tail-skid and bungee "firing device" could turn a tail-first or wheels-first landing, or a bump on the field into a series of gallops, and maybe into Jenny kindling. Note routing to save weight. This is a JN-4A. (Curtiss Aeroplane Co.)

Above right

Double Deperdussin controls, commonly called "Double-Dep" are shown with a right-hand throttle installation. The pilot had to fly with his left hand and use the throttle with his right. Note "homey" effect of instrument-panel lights. The gas tank was forward of the pilot, and if it ruptured in a crash, gasoline hurtled onto the engine and invariably exploded. (Curtiss Aeroplane Co.)

Right

JN-4 stick control and right-hand throttle. Rudder bar is at bottom of fuselage and forward of the stick. Wheel at bottom of stick has the aileron cable attached. Ignition switch is at the left attached to the upper longeron of the fuselage. This right-hand-left-hand throttle-stick combination was a "pilot bugger." Note "wall-bracket" lighting for instruments. (Curtiss Aeroplane Co.)

esque) to glide back to earth, you were treated to a dissonant arpeggio. The number of sour notes and the intensity of vibration depended upon which brace cables were loose—and how loose. People on the ground were frequently alarmed by this nagging orchestration, but it lent a thing to Jenny flying that our slick-skinned, no-wires pilots of today know nothing about.

The opportunity shouldn't be neglected to say something about Jenny wheels without brakes. Parking crosswind between other airplanes or hangars was something only a drunk or a fool tried twice. By the same dictum, it was prudent to stay the hell away from all obstructions and from the last one-fourth of the field when landing. Groundloops could be real big in those days and you couldn't check one with a burst from an OX-5 because it had to cough a couple of times before it took. By then, this was the worst thing you could have done because it doubled the speed of the groundloop and quadrupled the damage.

There wasn't a tail wheel on a Jenny; just a skid. Nor were there hydraulic shock-absorbing struts on this or the main gear—just bungee wrapped around the axle and snubbing the skid. If you haven't tangled with this combination you haven't smelled fear. It was our first aeronautical attempt at developing a self-fueling pogo stick and it came close to working. Bungee was like the material in a woman's girdle: it bulged everywhere it shouldn't have and didn't give where it ought to have. It was great stuff for checking a pilot's self-confidence.

A bad approach, a rough landing, or a bump on a field in cahoots with the bungee on the scatter-footed gear could turn into a series of small flights, each one getting a little longer and a little higher with successive bounces until it was hard to decide whether you were still landing or were flying again. If you tried gunning the OX-5 you stuck out your neck, because while it was coughing preliminary to speeding up Jenny to get some lift you ran out of field. Then, as a rule, you parted the kindling and called for another Jenny.

An additional factor that lent considerable variety to Jenny flying was the types and combinations of her flight controls. From the start, Glenn Curtiss developed and used his own wheel-and-shoulder arrangement as standard equipment. This was designed to avoid some more Wright patent suits. In use, the pilot leaned in the direction he wished to bank the airplane, and his shoulders moved a control yoke.

Most early Jennys used the European "Dep," or Deperdussin system. This linked the aileron controls to a Curtiss-type wheel mounted on a pylon. When the latter was moved fore and aft it moved the elevators. Turning the wheel right or left actuated the ailerons. Left and right steering was done with a foot rudder which was pushed in the direction of the desired turn. This was in general use by 1915 and was soon adopted by the Army.

The third configuration, the Joyce or Joy stick, was the same as today's universal-movement stick.

Although Jennys were originally equipped with the Curtiss system, export models had a variety of combinations depending upon what nation's pilots were to fly them. Thus, one might find Curtiss controls in one cockpit and Deperdussin in the other—or double "Deps," or double Curtisses. The confusion was then compounded by adding the stick type in both cockpits or in conjunction with either of the above.

As if these shenanigans were not enough to mousetrap the average pilot, one frequently found the throttle on the right side of the cockpit instead of on the left where it belonged. Later it was settled on the left as a universal installation for all single-engine military, and single-engine, tandem-cockpit civilian aircraft.

The right-hand throttle started many pilots flying with their left hands and controlling the engine speed with the right. Conversely, craft with a left-hand throttle started pilots flying with their right hand. Usually, when a left-hand pilot flew a right-hand airplane, all hell broke loose.

CHAPTER FOUR

Evolution of the JN-4D

Jennys were bought by the British, Canadians, and Spanish for use as trainers for World War I. An outline of the characteristics of the several Jenny models and missions; dimensions and specifications, power plants.

As Jenny reached aerodynamic puberty, like all youngsters she required disciplining. This consisted of no small amount of cut-and-try to bring her disposition more into conformity with the id and the courage of those who flew her. In those times, aeronautical engineering was no less shaky than today's child psychiatry, which, like many Jenny tinkerers, makes more bad kids than good ones.

After each change the pilots said it was a rum go, because the designers tried everything and, if it didn't work, they kept right on trying it.

As Jenny became more capable, more things were asked of her, and it is amazing that, no matter what the impositions were, she absorbed them the way Aguinaldo's coral revetments at Cavite absorbed U.S. rifle and machine-gun fire during the Philippine Insurrection.

Jenny complained little when she was overloaded with engines running up to 350 hp, as well as guns, cameras, embryonic bombing gear, and navigation devices. She wore so many hats it is a wonder she recognized herself, because in startling succession she became a primary trainer, bombardment trainer, photo-recon trainer, gunnery tutor, observation plane and—the saints be praised—a pursuiter.

Jenny fully subscribed to the dictum of Wilbur Wright when

he pointed out to the French Government when it was negotiating for the purchase of one of his airplanes that you could not breed a horse that would excel on a race track and would also be good for plowing. Nor was it feasible to design an airplane that would have both speed and weight-carrying ability. It had to be one or the other—but not both.

Knowing this, Jenny did not want to try to be all things to all men. Like most females, she preferred a limited and well-defined career which she could perfect within her own microcosm and more or less under a single genre. She reasoned that, after all, airplanes were not put on earth to achieve an ideal, only to pursue it, and this she was willing to do within the confines of her seventy knots. But, there was always some Buddha Head with a slide rule who did not see it her way. This made Jenny wonder whether people being shipped to St. Elizabeth's Mental Hospital hadn't been misdelivered to the engineering department.

This undoubtedly accounted for her pugnacious nature because it was only through her own special contrariness that she could protest this hydra-headed existence the engineers thrust upon her. Consequently, slip severely in a turn and she would whip into a spin; approach a stall in a climb and convection might jolt you into a vrille; pull up your nose in a left turn and you were back to spinning-in. Make a rough landing and her bungee made her behave like a bronco. This wild-bore attitude was Jenny's counter-battery fire which she directed at those who tried to turn her into a female Atlas, a process which generated almost endless losing altercations with gravity. If Hegel was right in his thesis of dialectical materialism that everything is composed of matter in conflict, then Jenny was an airborne arena for this battle and the epicenter of the three dirty Ss of aviation in her times: slip, skid, and spin-in.

The basic changes necessary to remove Jenny's "hants" followed a philosophical process explained to the writer by an ancient Chinese in Tientsin: "Every Chinese (and Jenny) has three ghosts; by lighting the right joss sticks, each can be split into two, and if this is kept up long enough, they become so small they no longer matter."

To the grafts upon her body and the delving amid her innards Jenny paid little heed—she simply tightened up her stubbornness

A JN-4B. The vertical exhaust stacks kept some of the soot and smoke out of the crew's face, but this was like taking the candy butch off the day coach: so accustomed were pilots to smelling and breathing the output of the engine that it seemed unlike flying to have it piped away. The wrappings on the landing-gear struts were taut windings of strong cord well varnished to shrink and waterproof the wrapping. This lent considerable strength without adding weight. (Curtiss Aeroplane Co.)

and went right on training pilots and making premature angels, for she was a granite-lapped Ma when it came to teaching beginners how things were.

Changes were made in rigging angles, control surfaces, and control systems to put enough cantankerousness in her, but still leave her docile enough for student handling. In some instances, RAF-6 wings were substituted for the conventional Eiffel No. 36 with which she began life. The British liked this, but very few Jennys were built with those for U.S. use.

As additional JNs were built and test-flown, the engineers began to eliminate their most spastic shortcomings. Ultimately, the JN-4A, a variant of the basic JN-4, approached about the best they were going to achieve with this airplane.

It was soon learned that the handling characteristics could be radically changed by altering the line of the engine's thrust and the dihedral of the wings. The more dihedral, the more stable the craft became and the more difficult it was to manage in acrobatics. Consequently, the large-dihedral JN-4A had ailerons in both top and bottom wings to provide better lateral control. Simultaneously, directional stability was helped by increasing the area of the rudder and of the vertical fin.

By lessening dihedral, designers made Jenny so cranky she was vexatious to fly. With this change, upper-wing ailerons were ample. However, no further changes were made in the horizontal and vertical tail surfaces because of the improvement their enlargement had brought to directional stability. Later, the Canadians altered the empennage construction but not its configuration.

When World War I broke out, a British delegation came to Hammondsport, flew Jenny, liked her, and bought 150 for $750,000. Spain and Canada placed simultaneous orders. Through this impetus, further improvements were made which resulted in the JN-4B. It was much the same airplane as the basic JN-4, but had the new empennage of the JN-4A and some additional but minor changes.

In ameliorating Jenny's waywardness no changes were made in the wing area, but the stagger (distance of leading edge of the top wing ahead of the leading edge of the lower wing) was increased to 12 5/16 inches, and the gap (distance between the wings vertically) was increased to 62 3/16 inches. Dihedral was set at one degree, although some versions had as much as 2 1/2 degrees. The original Deperdussin controls were retained.

The JN-4A differed from the JN-4 as follows:

The dihedral was increased from one degree in the JN-4 to four degrees. Ailerons were installed on top and bottom wings for better lateral control. The engine was mounted with six degrees of down thrust to improve flying characteristics. The empennage was redesigned to provide more fin area and to raise the rudder. The horizontal tail surfaces were given straight leading and trailing edges. The tail-skid springing mechanism was enclosed within the fuselage.

Less-apparent changes were an increase in the lower wing span to 34 feet 8 1/2 inches. This was done by giving it the same pointed trailing-edge tip configuration as the top wing. The JN-4 lower tip, in contrast, was rounded at the trailing edge. Stagger was increased from 10 3/8 to 16 inches. An empennage redesign resulted in a five-inch increase in the JN-4A overall length to 27 feet 3 1/2 inches.

Although the Signal Corps bought only five of the JN-4Bs, many were sold to private individuals and to civilian flying schools which trained Army pilots under contract, much in the same way this was done in World War II. Because of Jenny's almost exclusive role in all phases of civilian and military flying at this time, considerable detail on her characteristics follows:

Wing loading was 5.3 pounds; power loading, 21.16 pounds. Empty weight, 1,320 pounds; gross weight, 1,905 pounds; top speed, 75 mph. at sea level; minimum speed, 43 mph.; rate of climb, 300 feet per minute.

A JN-4H mounting a 150-hp Hispano-Suiza, or Hisso, the ultimate in Jennying. This is a military airplane. Its center section is cut out to provide easier entry into and egress from the forward cockpit. The cutout in the lower wing at the root was for camera work. Note absence of top-wing dihedral, which lessened stability but improved maneuverability. (Curtiss Aeroplane Co.)

Still another variation was the C model built by the Canadians. The "C" was not derived from the fact that it was built in Canada, nor that it was called the "Canuck," but from the fact that it was a modification of the JN-3. (This airplane is covered quite comprehensively in Chapter Eight.)

The most famous of all of the Jennys, of course, was the JN-4D. She was built in the greatest numbers, was the model used almost exclusively in the United States as a World War I trainer and the one which furnished virtually all of the surplus sales after the war. She was also the barnstormer's darling, or nemesis.

The JN-4D resembled the JN-4B more than any of the others, yet it had a different appearance. For example, ailerons were mounted only in the top wing, as was true of the B; the downthrust position of the engine and the shape of the tail units remained the same as in the A. Stagger was set at 16 inches, which equaled that of the A. Yet, the span and chord of the wings equaled those of the B.

Dihedral in the D was one degree and this was used in many As; however, some had 2 1/2 degrees. The most noticeable difference was the cutout in the trailing edge of the top wing at the center section to provide easier access to the front cockpit, and to improve overhead visibility. The trailing edge was similarly cut out on the lower wing at the root on both sides of the fuselage to improve visibility below. These cutouts reduced the total wing area to 352.56 square feet. The gap in the D was reduced to 60 inches. The overall length was 27 feet 4 inches; wing loading, 5.45 pounds; power loading, 21.35 pounds; gross weight, 1,920 pounds; empty weight, 1,430 pounds.

Although the D was doing yeoman work, in an attempt to improve its performance a JN-4D2 was designed and produced as an experimental model. However, the changes, which were slight, provided no betterment so only the one prototype was built.

As war experience broadened, combat-type airplanes increased in performance, some reaching speeds of 140 mph; training techniques improved apace with expanding knowledge. Soon it was realized that an advanced trainer was needed to bridge the gap between the primary airplane and the Spad, Nieuport, Sopwith, and other British and French combat planes Americans were flying. Curiously, Jenny was chosen because of her good conduct and the fact that she was available—and nothing beats a woman who is available.

Designers simply fitted a Model A 150-hp Hispano-Suiza, "Hisso," into Jenny's ash-and-spruce fuselage and called her an advanced trainer. This model was designated JN-4H, with the H meaning "Hisso" and not structural changes. Wing area remained the same and there were ailerons in the top wing only.

Exceedingly little was changed about Jenny's profile except for the nose radiator shape, engine thrust-line set, and engine cowling. The radiator was almost symmetrical from top to bottom and the flat aluminum cowling under the engine used on the D was replaced by a faired Hisso cowl.

The engine added to Jenny's weight. Empty, the H weighed 1,595 pounds (1,430 pounds for the D); and loaded, 2,145 pounds (1,920 for the D); wing loading rose to 6.1 pounds per square foot (5.45 pounds for the D); power loading dropped to 14.3 pounds (21.35 pounds per hp for the D). The last was attributable to the addition of 50 hp while the weight of the airframe remained static.

The more-powerful engine increased the speed to 93 mph at sea level (75 mph for the D); ceiling rose to 12,800 feet (7,000 ft. for the D); rate-of-climb came up to 750 feet per minute (200 feet per minute for the D). Landing speed remained at 45 to 50 mph.

Some Hisso Jennys grossed as much as 2,300 pounds as they were required to assume more duties. These were indicated by letter designations that resemble those used until quite recently. For instance, the JN-4BH was a bombardment trainer with a Hisso, as indicated by the H. B meant bombardment, G stood for gunnery, O for observation; P designated pursuit.

The JN-4HG was a gunnery trainer. The JN-6BH was a day-bombardment trainer. The JN-6HG-1 was armed with one machine gun. The JN-6HG-2 carried two machine guns. The JN-6HO was an observation trainer. JN-6HP was a pursuit trainer mounting a Hisso.

All Hisso Jenny wings were dimensionally identical to the D wings and had ailerons in the top wing only.

Beginning a precedent that plagued military aircraft for forty years, until jet engines provided more power than the airframe

JN–4D

Airfoil section:	Eiffel No. 36

General dimensions:

Wing span, upper plane	43 ft., 7⅜ in.
lower plane	33 ft., 11¼ in.
Depth of chord	59½ in.
Gap between planes	60 in.
Stagger	16 in.
Length of machine, overall	27 ft. 4 in.
Height of machine, overall	9 ft. 10⅝ in.
Normal angle of incidence of panels	2°
Dihedral angle	1°
Sweepback	0°
Angle of incidence, horizontal stabilizer	0°

Areas:

Upper planes	167.94 sq. ft.
Lower planes	149.42 sq. ft.
Ailerons (each 17.6 sq. ft.)	35.20 sq. ft.
Horizontal stabilizer	28.70 sq. ft.
Vertical stabilizer	3.80 sq. ft.
Elevators (each 11 sq. ft.)	22.0 sq. ft.
Rudder	12.0 sq. ft.
Total supporting surface	352.56 sq. ft.

Weight:

Net weight, machine empty	1430.00 lbs.
Gross weight, machine loaded	1920.00 lbs.
Useful load	490.00 lbs.

Fuel	(21 U.S. gals.)	130.00 lbs.	(6.9 lbs. per gallon)
Oil	(4 gallons)	30.00 lbs.	
Pilot		165.00 lbs.	
Passenger		165.00 lbs.	
	Total	490.00 lbs.	

Loading per sq. ft., supporting surface	5.45 lbs.
Loading per hp	21.35 lbs.

Performance

Speed, maximum, horizontal flight	75.00 mph.
Speed, minimum, horizontal flight	45.00 mph
Climb, in 10 minutes	2000.00 ft.
	(200 ft. per min.)

Motor:

    Model, OX–5, Vee, four-stroke cycle, 8 cyl., water cooled.

Horsepower (rated, at 1,400 rpm)	90.00 hp.
Weight per rated hp (total wt., 390 lbs.)	4.33 lbs.
Bore and stroke	4 in. × 5 in.
Fuel consumption per hr.	9 gals.
Fuel tank capacity	21 gals.
Oil capacity provided in crankcase	4 gals.
Fuel consumption per B.H.P. per hr.	0.60 lbs.
Oil consumption per B.H.P. per hr.	0.03 lbs.

Engine bed:	Laminated ash, spruce, ash
Covering for wings, fuselage, control surfaces:	Irish linen or cotton. Treated with 5 coats of dope.

ADDENDUM

Instruments: Stewart-Warner tachometer
Athward level reading from 0° to 10°
Creagh-Osborne compass
U.S. oil gauge indicating 0 to 120 lbs.
Gasoline gauge fitted to tank.
Instrument lights
Total weight of above, plus panel: 26.5 lbs.

Equipment: 17 lbs. of tools; 8-lb. fire extinguisher

Control-surface movement:
    Rudder   30° to either side of longitudinal axis. Corresponding movement of rudder bar is 45° to either side of center-line.
    Elevator   60° i.e., 30° above or below neutral
    Ailerons   1-inch "lead" below trailing edge of wing
    Stabilizer, horizontal   Non-lifting. Cambered top.

See complete assembly and rigging instructions in Appendix.

SOURCE: Curtiss Standard JN–4D Military Tractor Handbook, 1918. Issued by the Curtiss Aeroplane and Motor Corp., Buffalo, U.S.A.

designers can use, more equipment and more divergent mission requirements soon began to reduce the plane's performance, and speed fell to 80–85 mph from the initial 93 mph because of a gross weight that increased to 2,700 pounds.

Further changes added ailerons to both top and bottom wings, in a series designated as JN-6H. Except for this, these were simply JN-4Hs with a larger and balanced rudder. It was the JN-4H that was used to launch the first regular airmail service between New York and Washington, D.C.

From 1919 to 1925 many Jennys were modernized by the Air Service. In this program, the craft were given a steel-tubing fuselage mounting both standard and "beefed-up" wings, with standard and reworked OX-5 and Hisso engines. The steel-tubing fuselage models were designated JNS-1, and in some instances JNS-H, -E, or -I to indicate a particular Hisso model.

CHAPTER FIVE

The Navy Takes a Try

The Navy used Jenny as a landplane trainer and converted her for use as a primary seaplane, designated the N-9. Almost all of the Navy's early aviators trained in these two airplanes. Navy JN-4 and N-9 specifications.

By the time the Navy finished tinkering with Jenny she had been made a part of a gallinaceous farrago: a modified JN-4 to be used in landplane training; and the N-9, in turn a modification of the JN-4, for seaplane training.

These were not the only training aircraft used by the Navy in the World War I era and after. This partly accounts for their relatively small numbers. The overall limiting factor, however, was the comparatively small size of the Navy's air arm during this period. The figures are given on page 75 at the end of the chapter.

It was an odd incongruity of aviation, an activity that later would get people accustomed to accepting the bizarre as normal, that at the outset the Army was decidedly Wright because its first airplanes were Wrights. When naval aviation got under way in earnest, about five years after the first plane was bought by the Army, it became largely Curtiss, mainly because of Curtiss's sales acumen, but also in part because of service jealousies and rivalries. What one liked, the other bum-rapped. Ultimately the companies' positions became intermingled when the two arch foes consolidated into the Curtiss-Wright Co. This was good for aviation, but it did nothing to improve the temperament of the War and Navy departments in their interrelationships.

This filtered down to the ranks in a manner exemplified by the following: when the writer was an infantryman, we used to drink this toast: "Here's to the next war, may it be between the Navy and Marine Corps." Later, when the writer was a naval aviator, we used to drink the toast with the paraphrase "Here's to the Army, may the next war be between it and someone else we don't like." Still later while the writer was in the Nationalist Chinese Air Force, the toast went: "May the next war be between West Point and Annapolis."

It was the Navy's patronage, wittingly or otherwise, that enabled Curtiss to build up his business on wobbly patent purloinment and which furnished the capital for his many legal scuffles with the Wrights. The reader will recall that World War I was Curtiss's greatest business blessing because with U.S. entry in the war he had just come out at the wrong place in the last spastic struggle with purloined patents to continue his enterprises. At long last he had come to the end of his aileron, so to speak, but the government's pooling of all patents for common usage in Jenny and other attempted warplane production balanced his financial wings.

Whether Jenny ever blushed over the realization that she was being laterally leveled by ailerons not rightfully hers is moot. She became accustomed to accepting philosophically all things done

JN AIRPLANES PROCURED

FISCAL YEAR	TYPE	QUANTITY PROCURED	CONTRACTOR
1917 (Jan.)	JN–4B	3	Curtiss A & M Corp.
1918	JN–4	2	Curtiss A & M Corp.
1918	JN–4	3	Curtiss A & M Corp.
1918	JN–4H	30	Curtiss A & M Corp.
1918	JN–4H	6	Curtiss Exhibition Co.
1918	JN–4HG	90	Curtiss A & M Corp.
1921	JN–4H	50	War Department
1921	JN–4H	4	War Department
1921	JN–4H	1	Parris Island
1921	JN–4	11	Naval Aircraft Factory
1923	JN–4H	1	Port au Prince
		201	

A Marine Corps JN-4H (Hispano-Suiza engine) at U.S. Marine Corps flying field, Miami, Fla., October, 1918. The Hisso engine can be identified by the valve cover and exhaust tubing, which contrasts with the exposed valve mechanism of the OX-5, and its different exhaust system. (U.S. Navy)

BY THE U.S. NAVY 1917–1923

DESIGNATING NUMBERS	ENGINE TYPE	HORSE-POWER
A–157 to 159	Curtiss OXX	100
A–388 to 389	Curtiss OX–2	90
A–995 to 997	Curtiss OX–5	100
A–3205 to 3234	Hispano–Suiza	150
A–4112 to 4117	Curtiss OX–5	100
A–4128 to 4217	Hispano–Suiza	150
A–6193 to 6242	Wright 1 (Hispano-Suiza)	150
A–6243 to 6246	Wright 1 (Hispano-Suiza)	150
A–6247	Wright 1 (Hispano-Suiza)	150
A–6316 to 6325	OX–5	100
A–6545	OX–5	100

Above
An N-9 seaplane on the ramp at Pensacola. Capt. A. W. Marshall, whose plane this was, was Commandant at Pensacola with rank of Rear Admiral when the author was a student Naval Aviator. (U.S. Navy)

Above right
This JN-4H Jenny has just landed after a heavy rain at the U.S. Marine Corps flying field, Miami, Fla., October, 1918. (U.S. Navy)

Right
A U.S. Marine Corps Hisso Jenny, JN-4H, at Miami, Florida, flying field. October, 1918. (U.S. Navy)

Below
Uncrating JN-4H Jennys at U.S. Marine Corps flying field, Miami, Florida, October 24, 1918. These are Hisso Jennys, so-called because they mount the Hispano-Suiza engine. (U.S. Navy)

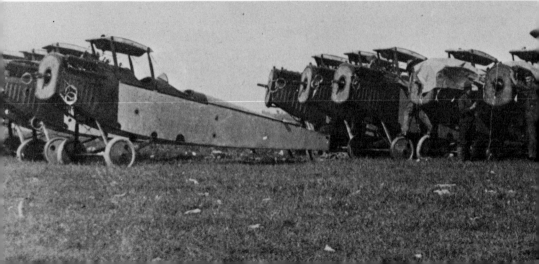

to her not in anger or rank stupidity, although her judgment in this sphere may at times have been subject to question because of her nurtured conviction that all engineers had minds like un- born foam rubber. Because of this, her philosophy never changed: stall her at low altitude and her ailerons gave not a damn whether Curtiss had paid the Wrights for them or not— and the stall began at the point of dispute, the ailerons, just where and when you needed help the most to bring up a low wing and keep out of a spin. Perhaps aerodynamics, abetted sub- consciously by Jenny, was attempting to expiate the economic peccadillos of her designers.

With all legalistic and moralistic quibbling aside, Jenny's ap- proach to life was simple: "Supply me well with that liquor of flight, airspeed, and you won't need my ailerons. If you err, they will err, and you probably won't need them another time."

One can see that there was no time under these circumstances for splitting the hairs of Blackstone; flight was too quick, and when a wing went down, your only counsel at the bar was air- speed and ailerons. If you lacked either, you were guilty as charged.

THE NAVY JN-4

The Navy's first acquisition of JN-4 airplanes was in January, 1917, at Pensacola. This station, formerly a Civil War Navy Yard, had been converted into an aviation school at this time.

When the United States declared war against Germany, the Navy had 38 pilots and 54 trainers, not all of which were Jennys. Between fiscal years 1917 through 1926, purchases totaled 201 JN-4s, JN-4Hs, JN-4HGs; and 510 N-9s.

Tabulations on pages 58 and 59 list the engines carried in these planes and give their horsepower. Tables of specifications for the JN-4 and the N-9, pages 73 through 74, give the salient features of both. It will be noted that there are a number of dif- ferences between the Navy and the Army JN-4s.

JN-4s and others were used in the sparse landplane training given to Navy and Marine Corps pilots. To supplement it, the Naval Air Station at San Diego was authorized to establish a landplane school on December 20, 1921.

In the Jenny landplane course, Naval Aviation aspirants were given fifteen hours of solo flying and had to be able to handle service-type airplanes, the syllabus said. However, with this skittish amount of time, they could not proficiently handle any kind of airplane. They had to make a sixty-mile cross-country flight, hold an altitude of six thousand feet for fifteen minutes and from this height make a dead-stick landing within a fifty-yard-diameter circle, and make two night flare landings. If lucky, the student was taught a little dog fighting and night and formation flying.

THE NAVY N-9

When the Navy looked about for a primary seaplane, its eyes haplessly fell upon Jenny, that lady who seemingly was capable of responding to anyone for any purpose. Shortly after the first one was delivered, it was mounted upon a Burgess float. On the test-flight day, the pilot got aboard, opened the throttle and got the worst water ride he had ever had.

Undaunted, Navy engineers removed the OX-5 and installed a 150-hp Hispano-Suiza. Jenny was still defiant.

The latter disappointment sired a third—the N-9. It did fly, although dispiritedly.

The N-9 was mother to the Navy term "Angel Maker," and many a blue-clad airman is floating around in heaven with the words "Here under the auspices of an N-9" stenciled in gold on his halo.

The N-9 was a Jenny, make no mistake, but one with most of the goodness modified out of her. A comparison between the specifications of the Army's JN-4D and the N-9 will illustrate several differences, most notable among which was the 135.44 additional square feet of wing area needed to lift the float. Instead of a wind-tunnel airspeed of 75 mph, she had a speed of 69. This might not seem much of a change, but made all the difference in the world to the Big Kahuna: Lift = K^y A V^2.*

---

* Lift=K^y A V^2. This was the formula used then to calculate the lift of a given wing. It means Lift of wing=Lift coefficient of the wing, times the wing area, times the velocity squared. In more recent times the formula has been expanded to include one-half the density as follows:

$$\text{Lift} = K^y \frac{1}{2} \theta A V^2.$$

March, 1918. An N-9 taxiing in to seaplane beach at Pensacola. The pilot is taxiing downwind and has his ailerons cocked to assist him in turning left; or to aid the rudder in compensating for a partial cross-wind. (U.S. Navy)

The wedding of Jenny to water was one in which "for better or for worse" was left out. It was clear nothing would be "for better" in this mésalliance, and it couldn't have been "for worse." The following is illustrative:

When Captain J. L. Jayne, USN, was ordered to relieve Captain H. C. Mustin, USN, as Commandant of the Pensacola flight-training school, it was decided to honor him with a welcoming N-9 parade.

On the day of the captain's arrival, the wind was at Force 6 and Pensacola Bay was spooked. Two N-9s stubbed their toes on takeoff and nosed over onto their backs. The third blundered into the slipstream of another, crashed, and sank. One started to vibrate so severely that its pilot headed for home and got to the beach just in time for a split propeller to stampede the reviewing staff with its flying parts. The fifth, under the wary managment of Lieutenant E. W. Spencer, USN, made it around the bay alone and salvaged 20 percent of the occasion.

Had this been a demolition demonstration, or a dramatic plea for better airplanes, it couldn't have been more successful. As a welcoming parade for a new commandant it left some things to be desired. When it was over, the hosts and their guest, to say nothing to the N-9 pilots, agreed that it had been a busy day and it was time to "splice the main brace."

One could almost sense this leavening effect of Jenny upon those who so abruptly discovered what they had to live with. Never one to kowtow, perhaps she sensed some of the hauteur in Navy ways and decided that there was no time like right now if someone had to be put in his place. In any event, she treated the Pensacola salts to a bit of air discipline and the word was soon passed that Jenny's motto was: "Hominem non odi sed ejus vitias"—"I hate not the man, but his faults."

In February, 1917, Lieutenant Francis T. Evans, USMC, defied mathematics and the laws of probability by looping and spinning an N-9. For disproving accepted theory, he received the Distinguished Flying Cross. His feat was later duplicated by Lieutenant E. O. McDonnell, USN, and since this was the first witnessed instance in which the Navy ever followed the Marine Corps, he received nothing.

That Jenny did not always see eye to eye with her mentors was demonstrated by the inheritances she passed on to her offspring, which often manifested themselves in overt behavior. Thus it came about that after the N-9 had run an assortment of Navy braid up the aeronautic mast, it was decided to hold a wind-tunnel clinic to find out why this airplane was so reluctant to join the fleet peacefully.

On October 3 and 31, 1916, the Chief Constructor of the Navy forwarded the blueprints for the Hydro 96-A, nee Curtiss N-9, with instructions to make a model and test it to determine the air-force vectors for various angles of attack; also the range of speed and the coefficient of longitudinal stability to be expected in a full-scale machine. The following excerpt is taken from that report, designated No. 12 and issued March 8, 1917:

The accompanying photograph shows that with neutral elevator the center of pressure steadily travels forward through a small distance as the incidence increases from 2° to 12°, its mid-travel being at about the vector marked 6°.

If the center of gravity is placed within these vectors, the machine

This is the model of the N-9 used in the wind-tunnel stability tests during October, 1916. (Curtiss Aeroplane Co.)

will be inherently unstable, but will have responded readily to the elevator either raised or lowered when the machine is flying at any angle from zero to 8°. But it will not respond when flying at 10° incidence with the elevator at 10° negative, for the vector corresponding to these conditions lays forward of the assumed position of the center of gravity.

If the center of gravity is placed as shown on Plate 1, the machine will, with neutral elevator, tend to nose dive at all angles of incidence; also with the elevator 10° down. But with the elevator 10° up, the machine will have inherent statical stability at all angles up to 10°.

For purposes of stability (and survival) it was decided best to fly the N-9 with the elevator slightly above neutral and with the center of gravity about eight inches to the rear of the point shown on Plate 1.

The lift-drift (drag was called "drift") ratio was found to be well above 8 at medium flying angles, and at neutral elevator it ran up to 8.9 for incidences of 6° to 8°.

Tests showed that a 100-hp engine, turning a propeller at 70 percent efficiency, would drive the craft at 69 mph, and that the whole machine could be supported at a speed of 42 mph and a flying angle of 12°.

The N-9, therefore, in a pilot's terms was a two-speed airplane: (1) wide open; (2) in the hangar. To summarize, she was aerodynamically ruptured.

There were some things students didn't like about Pensacola, where they learned to fly. These consisted of: Pensacola, the climate, Shinny (home-made whiskey), a proliferation of bugs and Florida Crackers, lack of entertainment, shortage of women—and, most of all, offshore winds. The latter necessitated a seaplane approach toward what later became the Squadron One primary seaplane beach, and the cradle of naval aviation.

Student pilots, like bulls in a corrida, do not like to have a fenced-in feeling, namely landing directly at buildings that an airplane cannot clear on short notice. So, when the wind came off the land and a student wing came in from its daily escape from the N-9s, it was too much at the end of a trying day to have to make a final approach directly at a sea wall extending ten feet above the level of the bay, made of huge stone blocks backed up by several miles of terrain and topped by hangars thirty feet high.

A student named Pete found himself looking down the muzzle of just such a cocked gun one day when he completed his solo flying. When he closed the throttle to glide in to a landing, he was riding an old adage which states: "A nervous pilot lands hot." Pete was nervous and his glide was hot. As the seawall, hangars, *et al.*, loomed bigger and bigger, Pete decided he'd had enough so he "pried" his N-9 onto the water. However, with so much excess speed, it ricocheted. As Pete contemplated this the obstructions grew taller, so on second bounce he hit the throttle.

While the engine was taking its two complimentary coughs, a sailor in the tower atop what was called the "Storm Cellar" blew his anxiety down the tube to the offices of the Squadron Commander, the Exec, Chief Flight Instructor, and the Engineering Officer. "Sir," he said in good nautical fashion, "run like hell, an airplane is coming aboard us."

Naval aviators who have spent much time around student pilots are never ones to ask, "What did you say, sailor?" They simply hit the deck like infantrymen and their desks were their fox holes.

Pete had plans other than tangling with such formidable opponents as hangars and the Storm Cellar, he thought, but the engine changed his mind and the stingy-winged N-9 refused the jump. Just then the formation reached the seawall and luckily

the engine was two inches above it when the impact came. This sheared off the main and wing-tip floats and deployed the propeller.

The N-9 then bellied onto the concrete apron between the hangars, glanced off the Storm Cellar, leaped a street and a railroad spur, then continued ashore. A company of Marines lining up for pay call heard the approaching ruckus; and it wouldn't have done any good to shoot at them; the bullets would have been late.

Still relatively intact, the N-9 crossed a sandy stretch, howled across another street, slammed its nose through the post-office wall and came to a stop under the stamp window.

The postal crew hadn't hung around to find out what was coming, but when the first lady clerk cautiously walked back through the rear door and peered into the lobby at the shambles of an airplane, Pete arose from the cockpit and said: "Any mail for Ensign Davidson?" He then found the drinking fountain and with his wet handkerchief revived the young lady.

N-9 ENGINE INSTALLATIONS

The N-9 was a many-engined (one at a time) affair with a record of two principal power plants and at least four experimental

Above
August 13, 1918. An N-9 rigged for gunnery with a flexible Lewis machine gun on a Scarff ring in the after cockpit. The protuberance just ahead of the top wing is a radiator. The chap in the cockpit is appropriately dressed for flying in an N-9—in a swim suit—and this is the way crews often came home. This is Pensacola Bay with Santa Rosa Island in the background. (U.S. Navy)

Below
November 25, 1926. N-9s ready for inspection at Pensacola. Although eight years had passed since World War I had ended, these precarious craft were still in service, training naval aviators, Marine and Coast Guard pilots. The site was the Primary Seaplane Beach. This was the cradle of Naval Aviation and it was here that all student pilots did their worrying about "check rides," "ups" or "downs," "bilging." There were seldom deaths from primary seaplane crashes, but there were lots of accidents, some so ludicrous they taxed credulity. (U.S. Navy)

It is really flying and an N-9 at that. Note the skid fins on the top wing; also the ample top-wing ailerons which extend considerably beyond the trailing-edge of the wing. (U.S. Navy)

installations. The former consisted of the Navy-designated OXX, of 100 hp, and the Hispano-Suiza Models A and I, of 150 hp. The latter mounts were the Hall-Scott, Aeromarine U-8-D, the K-6 and K-12, in the 100–150-hp classification. Inasmuch as only test airplanes were fitted with these last four power plants, they are mentioned merely for the record.

Of the 510 N-9s procured from the Curtiss and Burgess companies and assembled from spares, all but 35 mounted the Curtiss OXX or the Hispano-Suiza engines. The reader will note in the tables of specifications an N-9H model which differed from the N-9 only in that it was fitted with a rear-cockpit 80-pound Scarff ring for mounting a Lewis machine gun.

The following data give the quantities of N-9s delivered to the Navy or that were assembled at Pensacola out of spare parts. Also listed are the blocks of serial numbers assigned to them; and their power plants:

QUAN-TITY	SERIAL NUMBERS	YEAR DELIVERED OR ASSEMBLED	POWER PLANT	MANU-FACTURER
30	A–96 to A–125	1917	OXX	Curtiss
34	A–201 to A–234	1917	OXX	Curtiss
30	A–342 to A–371	1917	OXX	Curtiss
6	A–2385 to A–2390	1918	OXX	Curtiss
30	A–409 to A–438	1918	OXX	Burgess
30	A–999 to A–1028	1918	OXX or Hispano	Burgess
40	A–2351 to A–2390	1918	OXX	Burgess
20	A–2391 to A–2410	1918	OXX or Hispano-Suiza	Burgess
240	A–2411 to A–2650	1918	Hispano-Suiza	Burgess
ASSEMBLED FROM SPARES AT PENSACOLA				
15	A–6528 to A–6542	1922	Hispano-Suiza A	
10	A–6733 to A–6742	1923	Hall Scott, K–6, K–12 Aeromarine U–8–D.	
15	A–6618 to A–6632	1923	Aeromarine U–8–D	
10	A–7090 to A–7100	1926	Aeromarine U–8–D	

With respect to the foregoing data, the Bureau of Naval Weapons, Department of the Navy, through Eric Collins, director of the Legislative and Technical Information Division, makes the following explanation: "Sources of information were the individual aircraft history cards for each craft; the Bureau of Construction and Repair's Monthly Progress Report of Aircraft Construction, and the summary compilation of aircraft procured from 1911 to 1939."

The first N-9 fatality was Lieutenant jg., Spencer T. Alden, Ft. Wayne, Indiana, May 4, 1918, at NAS Bayshore, Long Island. Next was Ensign Charles C. Craile, St. Louis, Missouri, May 10, 1918, at Norfolk, Virginia; and Pay Clerk Robert H. Monteith, August 24, 1919, at Seagirt, New Jersey.

Although the records of the first Navy JN-4 fatalities are unclear, it is known that the following Marines were the first to perish in this type of airplane: Private Edgar B. Lloyd, U.S.M.C., at Lake Charles, Louisiana, January 17, 1918; 2nd Lieutenant Louis C. Beauman, U.S.M.C., at Miami, Florida, March 23, 1918.

A roster of the 1656 naval aviators who received training in or instructed in the JN-4 and in her water-borne counterpart, the N-9, reads like a list from Navy Valhalla. Their ranks include such stalwarts as those mentioned on the first page of Chapter One and also: T. G. Ellyson, John Rodgers of trans-Pacific fame; G. DeC. Chevalier, W. D. Billingsley, J. M. Murray, H. C. Mustin, R. C. Saufley, Albert C. Reed, Marc A. Mitscher, William M. Corry, and many more.

The Marines are represented by: A. A. Cunningham, W. M. McIlvain, David L. S. Brewster, Roy S. Geiger, Edmund G. Chamberlain. That there are not more is due only to the very small size of Marine Corps aviation in this period.

N9–H * U.S. NAVY (MODIFIED JENNY)

Airfoil section: RAF–6

General dimensions:

Wing span—upper plane	53 ft. 3¾ in.
lower plane	43 ft. 0⅜ in.
Depth of chord, both planes	5 ft.
Gap between planes	5 ft.
Stagger	0 ft. 9¹³⁄₁₆ in.
Length of machine, overall	32 ft. 7¼ in.
Height of machine, overall	10 ft. 8½ in.
Normal angle of incidence of panels	4 deg.
Dihedral angle, upper and lower panels	0 deg.
Sweepback	0 deg.
Angle of incidence, horizontal stabilizer	0 deg.

Areas:

Wings, upper and lower	488 sq. ft.
	(including ailerons)
Ailerons (each 28¾ sq. ft.)	
Horizontal stabilizer	28.7 sq. ft.
Vertical stabilizer (fin)	7.7 sq. ft.*
Elevators (each 11 sq. ft.)	22.0 sq. ft.
Rudder	12.0 sq. ft.
Total supporting surfaces	558.4 sq. ft.

Weight:

net weight, machine empty	2,040 lbs.
Gross weight, machine loaded	2,550 lbs.

Useful load:

Fuel	(29 U.S. gals.)	179.5 lbs.	
Oil	(5 gals.)	37.5 lbs.	
Pilot		165.0 lbs.	
Passenger		165.0 lbs.	
		547.0 lbs.	547.0 lbs.

Loading per sq. ft. of supporting surface	5.2 lbs.
Loading per RHP	17.5 lbs.

Performance:

Speed, maximum, horizontal flight	78.0 mph
Speed, stalling	38.0 mph
Minutes to climb:	10 min. to 3,285 ft.
	14.4 min. to 5,000 ft.
Service ceiling	7,000 ft.

Engine:

Kirkham—K6	150 hp at 1,750 rpm
Endurance, full speed	1.7 hr.

---

* The reader will note that the N-9 had slightly more than twice as much fin area as the JN-4. This is due to the addition of "skid fins" near the upper wing tips to provide more keel area.

* Same as N-9, except as noted on page 71, where it is explained that this version mounted a Scarff ring over the after cockpit for flexible gunnery training.

JN–4: U.S. NAVY

Airfoil section: Eiffel No. 36.
General dimensions:

Wing span—upper plane	43 ft. 7⅜ in.
lower plane	33 ft. 11¾ in.
Depth of chord, both planes	71½ in.
Gap between planes	61½ in.
Stagger	16 in.
Length of machine, overall	27 ft. ½ in.
Height of machine, overall	9 ft. 10⅝ in.
Normal angle of incidence of panels	2 deg.
Dihedral angle, upper and lower panels	1 deg.
Sweepback	0 deg.
Angle of incidence, horizontal stabilizer	0 deg.

Areas:

Wings, upper and lower	353 sq. ft.
	(including aileron)
Ailerons (each 17.6 sq. ft.)	35.2 sq. ft.
Horizontal stabilizer	28.7 sq. ft.
Vertical stabilizer (fin)	3.8 sq. ft.
Elevators (each 11 sq. ft.)	22 sq. ft.
Rudder	12 sq. ft.
Total supporting surfaces	454.7 sq. ft.

Weight:

Net weight, machine empty	1,467 lbs.
Gross weight, machine loaded	2,017 lbs.

Useful load:

Fuel	(31 U.S. gals.)	191.9 lbs. (6.19 lbs. per gal.)
Oil	(4 gals.)	30.0 lbs.
Pilot		165.0 lbs.
Passenger		165.0 lbs.
	Total	551.9 lbs.

Loading per sq. ft. of supporting surface	5.7 lbs.
Loading per RHP (lower than standard JN–4D due to higher hp of Hispano engine)	13.5 lbs.

Performance:

Speed, maximum, horizontal flight	93. mph
Speed, stalling	44.4 mph
Minutes to climb:	11.9 to 5,000 ft.
	63.2 to 10,000 ft.
	10.0 to 4,350 ft.
Service ceiling	10,525 ft.

Engine:

Hispano-Suiza	150 hp at 1,450 rpm
Fuel consumption	14 gals. per hr.
Endurance, full speed	2.25 hrs.
cruising speed	4.3 hrs.
Range, full speed	209 mi.
cruising speed	268 mi.

NAVAL AVIATION IN WORLD WAR I

		APRIL 1917	NOVEMBER 1918
Aircraft on hand	Flying boats and seaplanes	51	1,865
	Landplanes	3	242
	Nonrigid dirigibles	1	15
	Kite balloons	3	205
	Free balloons	1	10
Personnel	Officers ° (pilots and nonflying aviation officers)	48	6,716
	Enlisted men	239	30,693
Forces abroad	Aircraft	0	570
	Officers and enlisted men	0	18,000

Forces abroad: 20 patrol bases in England, France, Italy; one each in the Azores, Canada, British West Indies.

Operations abroad: Aircraft on patrol and bombing attacks logged 791,398 nautical miles. This does not include flights operated with Allied units.
Dropped 126,302 pounds of bombs on German submarine bases and on targets ashore.
Of 25 German submarines attacked, 12 were sunk or damaged.

Operations in U.S.: Aircraft patroling from 12 coastal stations logged 2,455,920 nautical miles.
Training flights from advanced and three primary flight schools totaled 10,949,340 nautical miles.

° The Navy trained 1,656 pilots during the war.

CHAPTER SIX

Pancho Villa and Jenny

*Jenny was the first American airplane to enter combat which
occurred during the Punitive Expedition against Pancho Villa
in Mexico.*

With considerable reluctance, because she knew she was not yet
ready for it, Jenny became the first U.S. airplane to fly in anger
—and the first to militarily draw blood—which unfortunately was
ours and hers. This all happened in Mexico during a rhubarb our
Army would just as soon *o-l-v-i-d-a*.

The prologue to this *comedia trágica* opened in 1912 in that
wispy era when running for Presidente de México was synonymous with running for one's life. In quick succession, political
campaigns and their incidental gunfire fatally rejected the following aspirants for the honor of occupying that uneasy seat:
Francisco Madero, Vice President Suárez, Venustiano Carranza;
Generals Huerta, Reyes, Orozco and Díaz.

Then, charging onstage astride a big black *caballo* came Pancho Villa, whose objectives were never quite codified and whose
contributions to his country's stability had much the same effect
as extinguishing a fire with *dinamita*. But, despite his ambiguous
platform, he did quite well for himself and drove the United
States nuts until he, like many a Jennyman, got overconfident.
This happened at Parral on July 18, 1923, then Pancho too became a posthumous patriot—at least to some.

Because of the inability of the Mexicans to come to some or-
derly meeting of the minds, and the always-present possibility of
their imbroglio overrunning the banks of the Rio Grande, it was

decided by the United States in the spring of 1915 to throw Jenny into the breach—so some JN-2s were ordered to Browns-ville to patrol the border.

Jenny thus began gingerly edging toward conflict. Gingerly is the right adjective because her misgivings were shared by her pilots and by the mechanics whose near-impossible task it was to get and keep her airworthy. So obvious was the predicament that Captain V. E. Clark, following an inspection of the JN-2s during July, 1915, wanted to condemn and destroy all of them.

Wind-tunnel tests were made in August, 1915, in conjunction with the Navy by Naval Constructor Hunsaker, who reported that the JN-2 was statically stable over the entire flying range, but was dynamically unstable longitudinally for angles of 12, 14, and 15.5 degrees. The model tests also proved that, among other bad characteristics, the planes were laterally unstable at these high angles both statically and dynamically. In other words, when the angle of attack got big like a thoroughly intoxicated woman Jenny was clear out of control.

Hunsaker objected to the wing design. He also recommended a large, broad tail to improve control. Jenny agreed. Upon re-ceipt of the report, the Chief Signal Officer summoned Glenn Curtiss to Washington to discuss Jenny's aberrations, and it was agreed that new top wings, stabilizing fins, rudders, and OXX en-gines would be sent to Brownsville and to Ft. Sill as replace-ments.

From October 7 to the end of the month, tests were run on both the original and the modified JN-2s. The results showed that, in efforts to fit them for the rugged Mexican service, they had gained two hundred structural pounds. Consequently, the craft were again modified and turned into JN-3s. This increased performance and made them more usable—up to a point.

Then Villa, El Jefe, erupted on March 9, 1916, and the fan was not big enough to catch all the military eggs he threw into it. His first toss sent a thousand man cavalry force to raid Columbus, New Mexico. Seventeen U.S. taxpayers who came out to enjoy what they thought was a drunken show were too slow when they found otherwise and achieved immortality as clay pigeons for Pancho's *bandidos*.

On March 10, Brigadier General John J. ("Black Jack") Pershing was ordered to assemble twelve thousand troops and start protecting the border states from this marauder.

The 1st. Aero Squadron of six Jennys was ordered to Columbus for duty with the Punitive Expedition. The planes left Fort Sam Houston at San Antonio, Texas, on the 13th of March and, after a series of flights that were adventure enough, reached their destination two days later with all hands convinced they should have remained in the infantry, cavalry, artillery, *et al.*

The aviation participation in the expedition was ineffectual, despite more than enough heroics on the part of the personnel and on the part of the Jennys, which had been flying for almost three years and were the remnants of government bungling, innumerable crashes and rebuilding.

Because of piecemeal Federal policies, resistance to aviation by other service branches, niggardly appropriations, failure to learn from the European air war, and lack of vision, which should have foreseen at least some of the airplane's military capabilities, America had made little technological progress.

The performance failure of the JN-2s was only one of the matters which focused attention on the needs of aviation. At length, on March 31, 1916 (two years after the war had begun in Europe), an urgent Deficiency Act by Congress gave the aviation section of the Signal Corps $500,000. Then, on August 29, Congress became convinced that somehow we were likely to get into the war, and appropriated $13,281,666 for military aeronautics, with an additional $600,000 for flying fields.

It may be observed here that what was then a huge appropriation would not today pay for one jet bomber, and the $600,000 wouldn't pave one jet runway.

When the Punitive Expedition staff drew up war plans, the Jenny doctrine called for observing the enemy, maintaining surveillance over our own advance parties, and carrying dispatches to direct artillery fire.

In the ensuing months, while attempting to implement these tours de force, pilots walked back from forced landings and crashes just about as many chancy miles as they flew. The Jennys were not in good condition when they arrived, nor were they designed to withstand the natural adversaries they were meeting. For example, the dry air softened the glue and caused the wood

layers of the propellers to delaminate. As soon as a plane returned from a flight, the propeller had to be removed and placed
in a humidifier to preserve the viscosity of the glue holding it together. Another propeller would then be removed from the humidifier and attached to the engine's crankshaft when it became
that plane's turn to fly again.

In reality this was only a parade-ground air force and most as-
suredly it could not surmount mountain elevations up to twelve
thousand feet, nor could it cope with the climate and the long
distances to be flown.

Villa was a staunch airplane advocate. In fact, he seemed to
have a shrewder appraisal of its tactical and strategic worth than
most of our Congressmen and not a few of our Army staff officers. A number of Americans flew in the employ of the rebel.
Among these were: Farnum Fish, Eugene Heth, Howard M.
Rinehart, Floyd Smith, Mickey McGuire. The Mexican Jefe had
at least one Christopherson-Curtiss pusher, a Martin T, one lone
JN-3, and two new Wrights, which he usually based at Monter-
rey. His outfit had a fully-equipped airplane-repair shop in a railroad car.

At a late stage of the campaign, tired of Mexican food, fleas,
dirt, and the tenuous hold a bandit pilot had on his life, Howard
Rinehart flew one of Villa's Wrights from Matamoros, Mexico, to
Brownsville and left for home. He asked General Funston to do
what he could about returning the airplane and ultimately this
was done. When the writer asked him many years later what had
prompted him to "defect," he said, "The last two bullets through
the lower wing."

To Farnum Fish goes the historical accolade of being the first
American to shed blood in aerial combat, albeit flying for the
wrong side. To Jenny goes the unsolicited distinction of getting
him into his predicament, and sharing his wounds.

Fish (a Villa pilot) was making an observation flight covering
the disposition of hostile Mexican government troops. On the
way home, he inadvertently flew low over some of his own forces
which he had been warned to avoid. The *soldados*, not knowing
he was on their side, cut down with massed rifle fire, and not
only Jenny but Fish too was hit. A bullet entered the rear of his
thigh, commonly referred to as the "butt," came out the fleshy

part near his torso, then clouted him in the shoulder. He immediately turned toward the rear of Villa's lines and, approaching in a long, flat, partial-power glide, landed and fainted from loss of blood. As soon as he had healed up, he hit for his home in Los Angeles.

Carranza (government) was not outdone by Villa. He also had aircraft. Charles S. Niles, an employee of the American Moissant Aircraft Co., sold several planes to him and became his chief of air service. Other Americans who flew for the government forces (good guys) were Lawrence W. Brown and the Solinos brothers.

The first reconnaissance by Jenny deep into hostile country was made March 16, 1916, by Captain Dodd with Captain Foulois as observer. They walked most of the way.

On a subsequent, and typical, flight made over the same route, Jenny felt like a shuttlecock in a badminton game when the planes ran into "Swiss-cheese" air, downdrafts, miniature whirlwinds, updrafts, and violent gusts, one of which slammed Lieutenant F. S. Bowen around so much he broke his nose on the cockpit cowling. They also ran into snow, hail, and rain.

By the end of March, 1916, it was obvious to even the most unreconstructed enthusiast that the squadron's six Jennys were incapable of effectively performing their assigned tasks. The low-powered engines with high-power loading and the limited rate-of-climb with a military load made it impossible to fly safely even in the vicinity of mountains, let alone over them. The wear and tear engendered by trying to do these things limited operating the craft to no more than an hour or two a day.

Exhibiting a rebelliousness that prompted these airmen to defy the moment and their future, they tried bucking the establishment. On April 3 the New York *World* published their indirect protests in an article by a Mr. Utrecht, a news correspondent. The material severely criticized the squadron's equipment and appealed for more powerfully engined planes capable of carrying a greater useful load and with better performance at altitude.

Utrecht, undiplomatically, quoted officers by name (probably in violation of confidences expressed in bull sessions) as venting the criticism and had Foulois saying that pilots risked their lives as many times a day as they flew and were not given equipment needed to do their work with reasonable risk. When the general

was asked shortly before his death in 1967 if he said this, he re-
plied with a grin: "Young man, you wouldn't be trying to get me
called up on the carpet again, would you?"

Lieutenant Dargue was quoted as saying: "It is nothing short
of criminal to send the aviators up under such conditions as we
are meeting."

The article cited the inability of Jenny to negotiate Cumbre
Pass, where Dodd and Foulois ran into meteorological mischief
that not only prevented their climbing enough to clear the peaks,
but almost destroyed their airplane and forced them to abort
their mission and stagger home as best they could.

Utrecht concluded his dispatch by saying the aviators blamed
officials in Washington (who else?) for their inability to perform
in a military manner.

Anyone who has tried it can attest to the fact that staff officers
are touchy when they are called bonkers. After Utrecht's piece
came out, there was, to be sure, an investigation. Foulois did
yeoman work in getting his officers and himself off the hook; and
at the conclusion of the hearings, believing they had to do something to somebody, the staff revoked Utrecht's press accredita-
tion for not submitting his copy for censorship.

On April 7, 1917, Jenny made her last tired and brave flight of
the campaign, and it had every hair-raising Wagnerian element
(and some it didn't need) to make it a grand finale to this tamale
opera. As General Foulois expressed it recently: "That was the
God damnedest flight I ever made."

In this brannigan, Dargue with Foulois as his observer in one
Jenny, and Carberry with Dodd observing in another took off
from San Geronimo for Chihuahua City, with duplicate dispatches for the U.S. Consul, Marion H. Letcher.

By prior arrangement, Dargue and Foulois landed south of the
city, while Carberry and Dodd landed on the north side. This
was probably ordered by the Dirty Tricks Department because it
was plainly evident that someone expected someone in those two

*Captain Benjamin Foulois, a few days before he left for the Mexican
border with the U.S. Punitive Expedition sent to keep Pancho Villa
on his own side of the line. (U.S. Air Force)*

planes to get killed, so the message was sent in duplicate under the theory that at least one of the four pilots might deliver it.

As soon as the Jennys were down and had discharged their dispatch bearers, Dargue was ordered by Foulois to take off and join Carberry's plane. However, as he started up, four mounted Rurales opened fire.

When Foulois, who was on his way into town on foot, heard the shooting, he ran back and managed to stop it, but was arrested and taken to the city *cárcel* followed by an entourage of several hundred jeering, rock-throwing men and boys. Word of the aviator's predicament was taken to the Consul by an American bystander (in the movies he's always wearing a dirty white suit and is so drunk he can't help).

After a siege at the jail, Foulois managed to get in touch with Colonel Miranda (good guy), chief of staff under General Gutiérrez, military governor of Chihuahua. The latter sprung Foulois.

In the meantime (those were all mean times as far as Jenny was concerned) Dodd had made it to the Consul. During his absence, supposedly friendly Carranzistas hurled threats at Dargue and Carberry, burned holes in Jenny's wings with cigarillos, slashed the fabric and removed bolts and nuts from both airplanes.

Carberry * managed to take off before too much damage was done and fly to a U.S. smelter about six miles away. Dargue † finally made it amid a hail of rocks, but had flown only a short distance when the whole top section of the fuselage blew off, damaging the stabilizer and forcing an immediate landing.

Dargue was soon confronted by another mob. He stood them off with his .45 automatic, but was almost out of ammunition when an armed guard was sent to his rescue by General Gutiérrez. Repairs were made, and on the next day Dargue and Foulois left Chihuahua at 0530 through a threatening mob and got back to San Geronimo.

* Colonel Carberry, U.S.A.F., Ret., passed away in Arcadia, California, on November 13, 1961, at the age of seventy-four. He graduated from West Point in 1910, studied with the French Air Service and during World War I was chosen to select air fields in France for U.S. use. In 1915 he held a world altitude record of 11,690 feet. He wrote extensively for military publications.
† Major General H. A. Dargue was killed when his airplane struck a mountain in the Sierra Nevadas near Bishop, California, December 12, 1941.

This was the battleground and these were the warriors who first flew in combat for the United States. The airplane on the right is an early version of the JN. The one on the left is a Curtiss model, which had the ailerons mounted between the wings in an effort to avoid a Wright patent suit. The photo was taken on January 11, 1917, at Black Butte Volcano in Mexico during a search for two crashed pilots: Bishop and Robertson. Left to right: Lieutenants F. P. Lahm; C. C. Culver; H. A. Dargue; a civilian, A. D. Smith; and Lt. C. C. Benedict. (U.S. Air Force)

Where today could you find such a variety of hostilities in so few days in the same war?

One by one the six Jennys had crashed and had been repaired until they barely held together—and their crews wished for a windstorm that would give them an excuse to cut the tent guys and have done with the machines. By April 20, 1916, one month and five days after starting the campaign, only two JN-3s were left and just before they were condemned to destruction, these splinted warriors were heard to mutter: "Sine pennis volare haud facile est"—"It is difficult to fly without feathers."

Thus ended Jenny's first service under Thor, and if it was less than a thundering success, remember, she was beaten before she started. It was only the indomitable will of Foulois, of his pilots, and of Jenny that let an impossible task be performed as well as it was performed.

The sacrifices were not without value because the remnants of the failures landed where they belonged—in the laps of Congressmen and Army staff officers who, under the rebukes that followed in Black Jack Pershing's reports, for the first time became cognizant, not of the shortcomings of Jenny, but of themselves and U.S. military aviation policy.

CHAPTER SEVEN

World War I and Mass Production

*The United States entered World War I very inadequately pre-
pared in aviation, and she failed in her efforts to build copies
of Allied combat aircraft. Overly ambitious aircraft production
plans floundered. Jenny alone was produced in adequate quantities. Liberty engine, De Havilland fiascos.*

It was a slightly hebephrenic aeronautic maternity ward into
which Jenny was born.

The United States had been doing a constantly increasing
business with all belligerents from the outset of World War I.
We insisted before the world that we had a perfect right, and
would exercise it, to trade with whoever wanted what we had
and would pay for it. Before long we had our greatest financial
stake in Britain and France owing to the former's naval blockade
of Germany, and our "loyalties" tipped in their direction.

Despite the phenomenally profitable hardware and grocery
store we were operating for the combatants, it seemed not to
occur to many in Washington that we couldn't maintain this lucrative "neutrality" indefinitely. Consequently, we did nothing to
ready ourselves for what was inevitable under the circumstances.

It was not until May 5, 1915, nine months after Europe blazed,
that 41 of the initial Jennys ordered for the First Aero Squadron
were delivered and accepted. The remaining seven were shipped
June 21. Upon receipt of these, the lot was assigned Signal Corps
serial numbers 41 through 48. They cost $63,284. Later, they
were moved to Ft. Sill, Oklahoma, and on July 26, after a series
of crashes, were modified to JN-3s.

Nothing was done about intensifying training or experimenta-
tion by the government. There were a few minor flurries, such as

87

those at Ft. Sill between September 7 and November, 1915, when a JN-2 was used in an attempt at aerial photography with a camera developed by Arthur Brock. But nothing substantial was done to lay the groundwork for an air force.

From November 18th to the 26th, 1915, the only squadron cross-country flight since the creation of Army aviation was made by the First Aero Squadron from Ft. Sill to Ft. Sam Houston, Texas; it was a distance of 439 miles with an average flight of 62.3 miles per day. Six JN-3s were flown in this hegira by Lieutenants J. E. Carberry, F. S. Bowen, C. C. Chapman, R. Rader, T. DeWitt Milling, and Captain Banjamin Foulois. Their passengers were: Captain T. S. Dodd, Lieutenants H. A. Dargue, E. S. Gorrell, W. G. Killner and R. H. Willis.

On November 1, 1916, the First Aero Company of the National Guard was organized and called Aviation Detachment, 1st Battalion, Signal Corps, National Guard of New York. Soon afterward it was designated as First Aero Company. The organization had four officers and four hundred enlisted men. Their aircraft consisted of a JN-4 and a Thomas, each mounting an OX-2, 90-hp engine. Next came a Sloane with a 125-hp Hall-Scott, a Sturtevant with a 140-hp engine, and an old Wright plane.

In the fall of 1916 an event took place that was later to have a disruptive effect on our World War I participation and would ultimately jar the Air Service to its longerons: the flamboyant, sometimes arrogant, and usually bellicose Major (later General) "Billy" Mitchell began to learn to fly a Jenny. He was a regular Signal Corps officer and had been ordered to aviation duty in the office of the Chief Signal Officer. Mitchell took his training at the Curtiss school, Newport News, by flying on weekends. He had several instructors, including Victor Carlstrom, Stewart W. Cogswell, James M. Johnson, Walter Lees, and Victor Vernon. Captain T. De Witt Milling also gave him some dual on December 16, 1916.

Mitchell was soloed by Lees, who said of his pupil: "He was very erratic. One day he would be okay and the next, lousy; and I just happened to catch him on one of his good days (for purposes of soloing him). He made two perfect flights that day."

Thus Jenny unwittingly contributed her share to a blowup that prompted Foulois, when heading our aviation in France, to re-

Brigadier General William ("Billy") Mitchell, bellicose advocate of air power who, contrary to widespread public opinion, was court-martialed not for his views, but for his unbridled attacks upon all of his superior officers who disagreed with him. He just missed a court-martial while in France during World War I. The aircraft is a V.E. 7 and the photo was taken at Bolling Field during an air tournament— May 14–16, 1920. (U.S. Air Force)

quest that his job be given to Mitchell, who wanted it so much he seemed determined to get it even if he had to wreck our Air Force and World War I along with it.*

By January 1, 1917, three months before we declared war on Germany, the aviation school at North Island, San Diego, was the only place where officers of the regular Army were given flight training. Thirty-five had been graduated and assigned. Eight were still awaiting duty posts, and 51 officers were under instruction. The field was staffed by 240 enlisted men and it had

---

* On December 17, 1925, Mitchell was found guilty by court-martial, not for his ideas on advancing aviation as many would have us believe, but for his slanderous and insubordinate attacks upon those in the civilian government and in the military branch who didn't agree with him.

32 aircraft, all but a few of which were Jennys. During the previous year, 68 JN-4s had been delivered.

In a history of Rockwell Field written by then Captain "Hap" Arnold, later General of the Air Force, he states that, in a circular sent to various branches of the Army seeking pilot candidates, the following admonition was included: "If you expect to be married or are in love, don't take up aviation." The reason, obviously, was Jenny's refusal to share her men.

Arnold's monograph contained another passage so indicative of the times that it rates preservation: "Post Headquarters, Rockwell Field," it started out, and then said: "Effective this date, horses will not be hitched to any part of an airplane." This was sensible enough, but why was it issued?

In those khaki-clad times, only young officers in the grade of lieutenant and junior captain were accepted for flight training. Consequently no aviator had enough rank to command anything larger than his own ego. To provide brass of sufficient weight and luster, nonflying majors and colonels were put in charge of aviation activities. If anyone knew of a better way to touch off fratricide, he didn't step one pace forward.

In those days officers of staff grade were mounted, so at every kind of Army establishment there were horses, and this was true of Rockwell. The horse in our small drama was named Major and the nonflying officer who rode him was a major and was in command of much that happened at the field, but he did not sit well with his contemporaries.

During an inspection, the major tied Major to the propeller shaft of a parked Jenny. He could be excused for not knowing more about his mount, which he had just that week received from an artillery battery.

Major (the horse) was a veteran Red Leg and nothing else was as military, as proud, prancing, and beautifully dedicated to his calling as a long-service artillery mount. In a review, he never missed a beat of the band and the way he kept all four hooves in cadence was a thing to behold. This is a thrill unknown to today's military landlings, who go to war in their brontosaurs (thunder lizards): the steel-flanked and -shod tanks.

Major might have tolerated the smelly military property to which he was attached had not the post band begun practicing over near the disturbed area in which the Navy and the Army mixed no better than sea water and O.D. paint. Major loved nothing on earth so much as a review with caissons rumbling, guidons flying, harnesses snapping, the cadence of the march, and the bugles—ah! those bugles. Just about the time the band practice got Major's adrenalin jumping real hard, a bugler blew "Assembly" for a guard mount, with not the ghost of an idea of what he was about to cause. To Major that call superimposed upon a military march meant only one thing—"*Achtung*," "Assemble." But he had that damned cloud-hopping airplane tied to him.

The halter rope wasn't long enough to permit him to turn his rump to Jenny and pull, so he moved around sideways and hit her a few belts with his hind hooves. Fabric, former ribs, gussets, and fabric bits erupted in a blizzard from the left lower wing, but Major was still tied. He faced his captor and began to back and pull, first gingerly and then with determination. In a moment Jenny jumped her chocks and followed him. Across a corner of the landing field they went, with Major orienting himself by the band and the bugler's calls, which were taking him in a Navy direction.

If Major had not been so patriotically intent and had looked behind him it wouldn't have happened. But he didn't and it did. He backed over an embankment and he and Jenny went ass over empennage into Spanish Bight in a confusion of flailing horse and airplane.

The line by which Major was moored parted on the way over the side and enabled him to slip his lashings and swim for the beach. When he gained solid ground, he continued on in search of a parade. But Jenny, alas, drowned.

There was a sequel. Animosities engendered by this and the nonflying major brought about the first court-martial of an aviator. It wasn't an admirable proceeding and resulted in the victim's retirement one grade lower than he otherwise would have held. He died at quite an old age in California in 1965.

When we entered World War I on April 6, 1917, little or nothing aeronautical was on hand in planes, airdromes, curricula, or instructors in flight, maintenance, and overhaul. Most important of all was a lack of experience that would indicate what was needed. We had never trained an aviator for combat—only for survival—and there was no one here who knew what kind of instruction was necessary to train radio operators, aerial photographers, gunners, mechanics, and other ratings. Most ironical of all, however, was that, because of our prolonged business dealings with Germany, the Allies had barred our observers from their airplane factories, training establishments—and from the front. We were caught with our military shorts showing and our aeronautical flaps dumped.

In March, 1917, there were only 12 firms capable of building aircraft, and their total 1916 production was less than 400, many for civilian use. When we declared war, the Aviation Section had only 131 nonflying administrative officers, pilots, and student aviators; and 1087 enlisted men. We had 227 aircraft, 93 of which were Jennys; and most of the others were classified as bad ideas. None were combat types. The industry had delivered only 68 JN-4s out of 366 ordered in 1916, which included Burgess-Dunnes (so stable you couldn't turn one even if you got it to fly), L.W.F.s, Martins, Standards, Sturtevants, and Wrights. This wasn't enough of a foundation upon which Gilbert and Sullivan could score a drum flourish, and they were certainly shaky openers for the European poker party.

A group of officers headed by Major Foulois drafted a program calling for 22,625—we repeat, 22,625—airplanes and 44,000 engines, plus 80 percent spares (not much confidence in the pilots) or, in lieu, 17,600 more airplanes. We did not produce a minute portion of these.

Simultaneously, the Chief Signal Officer, Brigadier General George O. Squier, head of the Air Service, appealed to the nation to "put the Yankee punch into the war by building an army in the air; regiments and brigades of winged cavalry on gasoline-driven horses."

Regrettably the regiments and brigades of flying horses turned out to be only gassers.

To give the reader some conception of the undertaking Jenny was expected to fodder, we must have a measure of its scope. On June 18, 1917, Secretary of War Baker, in a fifteen-day bulldozing operation, wrung from Congress a $640,000,000 appropriation for General Squier's petrol-sipping cavalry. President Wilson

Jenny en déshabillé, *just the naked facts. Seldom did one see the lady so stripped. In this view of a JN-4A, we see the intricate woodwork that formed the skeleton. To manufacture the wings, tail group, and fuselage, then rig each so everything remained true and aligned was no small feat. Weight per engine horsepower was so high that every extra pound was a flight penalty. (Curtiss Aeroplane Co.)*

signed it on July 24. This was the largest single amount for one purpose that had ever been authorized. But, as governments are wont to do from time to time, the Aviation Section didn't get a dime until we had been at war three and a half months—time that was as precious as life itself.

Indicative of the magnitude of the effort is this sidelight: on July 28, 1917, the North Elmwood plant in Buffalo began to produce Jennys. This facility was built in ninety days at a cost of $4,000,000. It covered seventy-two acres, with thirty-one of them under a single roof. It became the world's largest airplane factory—about a year late.

In due time, Long Island had eighteen airdromes in action,

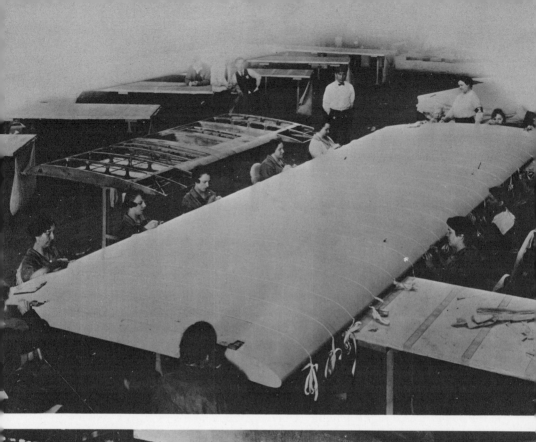

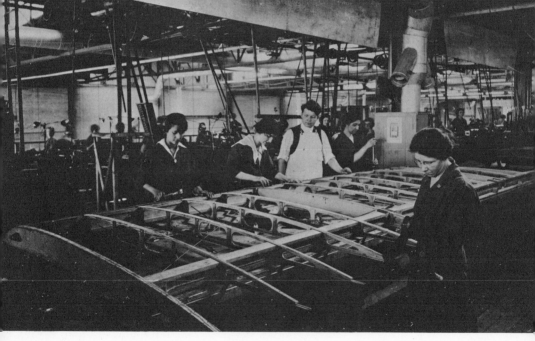

and by late 1917 there were twenty-seven training fields.

In August, the Aviation Section obtained approval for the creation of 345 combat squadrons, 45 construction companies, 81 supply squadrons, one repair squadron, and 26 balloon companies. Of these, 263 squadrons were to be in Europe by June 30, 1918, and most of the rest were to be assigned to training fields here; a few units were going to Panama, Hawaii, and the Philippines. It didn't happen.

By the spring of 1918, the aviation program was in grave disrepute. Production had not got off the ground; in fact, it wasn't even getting light. As a result of investigations, there were castigation and a sweeping reorganization of the entire Aviation Section of the War Department, which while failing to produce aircraft had produced a surfeit of confusion of calibers among its big shots.

On May 21, President Wilson created the Bureau of Aircraft Production and the Division of Military Aeronautics. He placed them under the Secretary of War and transferred aviation to them from the Signal Corps. The former was given full jurisdiction over production of planes, engines, and support equipment.

On May 24, the War Department got around to recognizing these two agencies, but failed in the important requisite of ap-

Above
This is an assembly line? Yes, this is an assembly line—and more lined than assembled. Here we see the mother, or perhaps the grandmother of World War II's Rosie the Riveter; what Rosie did with a riveting gun these ladies did with needle and thread. If production was not frenetic, at least it was serious as the demeanor of these patriots illustrates. When Jenny's wing was completely stitched, the fabric was wet with water, which shrunk it tightly over the framework; then it was dried and given several coats of dope, which made. it even tauter as well as providing a water- and air-tight surface. (Curtiss Aeroplane Co.)

Below
These ladies' raison d'être is to produce wings—not to fraternize. After going through the training department of the Curtiss Aeroplane Co., they were put on the production line, where Jenny, being a lady too, was given the feminine attention of lots of her peers. (Curtiss Aeroplane Co.)

pointing an Air Service Chief to coordinate and run them. This bungle swiftly became intolerable, and on August 27 President Wilson appointed the hard-handed John D. Ryan, former president of the Anaconda Copper Co., as Director of Air Service with the added rank of Assistant Secretary of War, to provide the needed authority to crack heads. Crack he did. While this gave aviation high-level representation it may have inadvertently prevented the formation of a separate Department of Aeronautics, for which there was a critical need.

The gargantuan appropriation (for those times) of $640,000,000 (which doesn't much surpass the Foreign Aid money we gave Egypt for bathtubs for camel drivers in waterless regions) along with the cross-eyed, extravagant production promises of early 1917, obscured the fact that the U.S. aircraft industry couldn't produce 22,000 planes during the first twelve months of the war or in any other twelve months. This was the first emergence in America of a later burgeoning federal philosophy patented by Roosevelt and nurtured by Kennedy and Johnson that, if we rub a thing with enough money, the act per se will take the place of reason and ability; a process not unlike trying to put milk back into a cow.

Unstampeded Americans suspected from the start that the nation's gravest aeronautical defect would be an inability to design and mass-produce combat aircraft. Neither had ever been done here and we didn't have the technical knowledge or the research facilities, despite the fact that the airplane had been invented and brought to practical reality in this country fourteen years earlier, when not a nation in Europe had made the slightest progress toward heavier-than-air, powered flight.

In addition, America didn't have the engines of the required reliability or low weight per horsepower. Starting about five years before the outbreak of hostilities, the best engines came from Europe, but when the war began, none of the belligerents could spare any.

Meanwhile, amid the confusion, Jenny wore a sly Mona Lisa-type smile because despite all of the hugger-mugger in the War Department, in our government, in the aircraft-design lofts, and in the factories, she was rolling out the doors in a steady, smug line for use at our rapidly multiplying training fields.

No whistles, cheers, flags, or speeches marked Jenny's nose-to-tail emergence for war; nay, she went ignominiously in crates from factory to flat car to airdrome, because had we undertaken to flight-deliver her she probably would have wiped out the U.S. Air Service right here on the home front.

It is interesting to examine the cost of airplanes in the 1917 period in contrast with today's multi-million-dollar fighters and bombers:

JN–4A through D	$5,500.00
JN–4H (Hisso engine)	8,042.61
Thomas-Morse (S–4B)	7,750.00
Standard E–1 (trainer)	6,975.00
S.E. 5 (British)	7,442.00
Spad (French)	10,242.00

After a mission to Europe headed by Major Raymond C. Bolling had returned and reported, Washington officials realized the hopelessness of continuing our efforts to build combat aircraft. Every European model we attempted to duplicate ended in a nonflying shambles. Here, the United States made her first and, for all time to date, worst industrial fiasco.

But we had good, tried, and relatively true Jenny and we could always turn to her for a strut on which to weep. We would continue to build her, we decided, but we would buy pursuits mainly from the French because of the ascendancy of the Spad, that wily little squirmer loved by the Allies and despised by the Germans.

In August, 1917, the French agreed to build for us 6,000 combat airplanes, chiefly Spads with some Nieuports and Breguets, plus 8,500 engines, to be delivered by July 1, 1918. In addition, the British were to sell us substantial numbers of their fighting aircraft.

Aeronautical design knowledge, spurred by combat needs, advanced so swiftly that it was impossible to standardize war planes for long. The British and the French developed more than fifty types in four years, the Italians in excess of thirty and the Germans, twenty-five. Americans flew nine combat types, all bought from our Allies. This reiterates Jenny's stellar role, for without her our production score would have been swabbo.

For home-front consumption a story was released which stated that the Liberty engine was designed in a few days by two engineers who were locked up in a suite in the Willard Hotel in Washington and told they couldn't come out until they had a successful power plant.

The truth was that engineers from four other nations, as well as many from the U.S. Bureau of Standards and from other public and private agencies, did a large amount of work on the Liberty. In excess of a thousand changes were made before it was provisionally accepted for flight testing. It certainly was no colossus.

The writer flew these relentless contraptions at March Field in 1928. They were mounted in World War I leftover De Havillands, classified throughout the Air Corps as "flaming coffins." If the "benzine board" of check pilots didn't get you, chances were the Liberty–De Havilland anti-people combine would. A cadet flying a Liberty-D.H. always felt like a fugitive from the law of averages.

Cadets were covertly told that if they were curious about a parachute jump, it was all right to get out and walk if you used a D.H. and questions asked at the investigation would be short ones. The cadet who did this would smugly announce at mess that night: "I got my D.H.," as though he were René Fonck saying: "I shot me four of them damn Fokkers this morning."

This was not destroying government property. It was preserving government people.

After the war, the Liberty in eight- and twelve-cylinder models remained in use for a decade. In addition to it and the OX-5, we produced a few Hall-Scotts, Hissos, Lawrences, Sloanes, A7As, Bugattis, Gnomes, and Le Rhônes.

The last two were rotary radials, that is, the entire bank of five to seven radially-disposed cylinders went one way, the propeller went the other and there was no peace in between. You didn't dare close the throttle on either of these because if you did it caught fire. When making a letdown for a landing—and, believe me, this kind of landing was a letdown—you left the throttle at wide open where the engine always flew, and slowed your glide by shorting out the ignition with a button on top of the throttle lever. Ever since, student pilots and other girl impressers have

Nothing came apart as willingly as a De Havilland airplane. Popularly called the "D.H.," they were better known among Army pilots as "Flaming Coffins," since even minor crashes resulted in explosions and the cremation of the crews.

Here we see Capt. Lowell H. Smith, of around-the-world flight fame, and Lt. John P. Richter receiving fuel from another D.H. in the first complete pipeline refueling in flight. On August 27, 1923, these same two officers set a continuous air-refueling flight record of 37 hours, 15 minutes, 14.8 seconds over a course of 3,293.26 miles of circling flight above Rockwell Field, Cal., and vicinity. This feat triggered a long succession of both military and civilian refueling flights. One of these, carried out by the Army, began on January 1 and ended January 7, 1929. The aircraft was a Fokker C2-3 Wright 220. It was flown by Major Carl (later General) "Tooey" Spaatz and Captain Ira C. Eaker over Los Angeles. The flying time was 150 hours, 40 minutes, 15 seconds. (U.S. Air Force)

been blimping their throttle, trying to sound like World War I aces.

These engines did not use good, sane, clean lubricating oil in their crankcases—but castor oil. Every flight was good for at least three trots to the latrine after breathing that smoky laxative. Moviegoers viewing World War I air pictures have never understood why, immediately upon landing, the pilots jumped out of their airplanes and ran like hell—they were heading for the biffy.

Elliott White Springs, one of our top aces, with twelve victories, and one of the grandest individuals in World War I or thereafter, told the writer that every time he took off on a combat flight behind a Le Rhône or a Gnome he had a bottle of paregoric and bismuth in one pocket of his flying suit and a bottle of cognac in the other to offset the sickening effects of that latrine-oriented lubricant the engine consumed and belched in his face. He took alternate swigs on the way upstairs until he had decided which was making him feel the better, and finished it as he went about his lethal business.

Starting in the spring of 1917, as has been noted, the aircraft industry expanded feverishly and at times haphazardly in an effort to do the job. But the narrow point of our capabilities provided a poor balance for the top-heavy technical problems. By January, 1918, slightly more than nine months after our war entry, monthly engine production was a seriously inadequate seven hundred and aircraft output was the same—six hundred of them Jennys with the rest experimental types, including the antagonistic D.H.s.

Ironically the War Department was the first to slam the door on its own tail when on February 21, 1918, eleven months after going to war, it announced that the first U.S.-made combat planes were en route to the front, implying that this was five months ahead of schedule. Actually, only one D.H. had been shipped from Dayton and it didn't leave Hoboken until March 15 (three weeks after it was supposed to have left) and it didn't fly in France because it was soon on the bottom of the ocean off the Azores, where it and the ship carrying it had been put by a U-boat.

The first American D.H. didn't fly in France until May 17, 1918. This must have tickled Jenny no end because her first place on the production line was still secure on all counts.

Disclosures that the program was still failing, contrary to War Department claims of success, led to presidential and congressional investigations. A committee headed by Charles Evans Hughes, former Associate Justice of the Supreme Court, strongly criticized the indecision, delay, and defective judgment involved.

A production reorganization in the spring of 1918 shifted emphasis to De Havillands (despite their general worthlessness) from Jennys, of which there were now enough, except for replacements. This boosted D.H. output from 15 in April to 1,907 in October, one month before the war's end. If this appeared to be an improvement, it was simply that the chaos was better organized.

An OXX-3 engine, blood brother of the OX-5, since both had the same camshaft, the prime source of Jenny bloodletting. The carburetor is at the lower left, the propeller hub is at the right and there is trouble all over the thing. Note the plumbing and the myriad of hose connections that could break and cause engine failure. (Curtiss Aeroplane Co.)

102

MODEL	BUILDER	MONTH OF FIRST DELIVERY	NUMBER PRO- CURED
JN–4	Curtiss	6–17	603
JN–4A	Curtiss	11–17	1
JN–4B	Curtiss	6–17	5
JN–4C	Curtiss	6–17	2
JN–4D	Curtiss	11–17	1,404
JN–4D	Canadian Airlines	9–17	680
JN–4D	Fowler Corp.	5–18	50
JN–4D	Howell & Lesser	5–18	75
JN–4D	Liberty Iron Works	4–18	100
JN–4D	Curtiss	5–18	450
JN–4D	Springfield, Mass., Corp.	4–18	585
JN–4D	U.S. Aircraft Co.	3–18	50
JN–4D–2	Curtiss	6–18	1
JN–4H	Curtiss	1–18	402
JN–4D–2	Liberty Iron Works	10–18	100
JN–4HB	Curtiss	4–18	100
JN–4HG	Curtiss	4–18	427
JN–6HB	Curtiss	7–18	154
JN–6HG	Curtiss	7–18	560
JN–6HG –2	Curtiss	10–18	90
JN–6HO	Curtiss	10–18	106
JN–6HP	Curtiss	10–18	125
		Total †	6,070

° Speeds given are theoretical engineering speeds at standard atmosphere and at sea level. Jenny couldn't have cared less about these and plodded along according to the specification speed for all OX-5 models, which was circa 75 mph. With the Hisso 150-hp engine, the fastest models would do about 80.

† The discrepancy between the total of the 6,070 above and the more than 8,000 that were built is accounted for by those delivered to Spain, Australia, Great Britain, and France, i.e., approximately 1,930 Jennys. Also, Canada built 2,900 Canucks in Toronto, which are not included in the above, bringing the grand total to more than 10,900.

PROCUREMENT

MISCELLANEOUS DATA	ENGINE TYPE	HORSE-POWER	TOP SPEED,* MPH
Revised wings, tilted engine	OX–5	90	75
	OX–5	90	75
Level engine, minor changes	OX–2	90	75
RAF–6 wings, experimental	OXX–3	90	75
Cut-away top wing	OX–5	90	80
Built at Toronto	OX–5	90	80
Built at San Francisco	OX–5	90	80
Built at Sacramento	OX–5	90	80
Built at Sacramento	OX–5	90	80
Built at St. Louis	OX–5	90	80
Springfield, Mass.	OX–5	90	80
Built at Redwood City, Calif.	OX–5	90	80
Revised controls	OX–5	90	82
Same as 4D, but with Hispano-Suiza engine	Hisso	150	93
Built at Sacramento	OX–5	90	83
Day bombardment trainer	Hisso	150	93
Aerial gunnery trainer	Hisso	150	90
Day bombardment trainer	Hisso	150	79
Dual control, one machine gun	Hisso	150	80
Single controls, 2 machine guns	Hisso	150	80
Observer trainer, single controls	Hisso	150	80
Pursuit trainer	Hisso	150	85

Besides the 8,000 Jennys, we built about 200 of types other than D.H.s. All were experimental models or unusable copies of Allied war planes. In fact, the D.H.s were unfit for war, too, and required extensive modifications to make them suitable for anything besides scaring pilots.

Engine production from July through November 9, 1918, totaled 16,808 as follows: 240 Gnomes, 1,298 Le Rhônes, 451 Lawrences, 2,250 A7As, and 11 Bugattis. We also finished 8,458 OX-5s and 4,100 Hissos for Jenny. The latter were of 100, 150 and 300 hp.

Although attempting to establish rigidly accurate figures on Jenny production is like trying to nail a handful of jelly to a wall, the following tabulation appears to be the most reliable of the data supplied by the War and Navy departments, the Signal Corps and the U.S.A.F.:

CHAPTER EIGHT

The Canadian Method

We trained pilots under a system copied from the Canadian R.F.C. Requirements for flight-training candidates. Forty airdromes built. Seven universities conduct ground schools. Qualifications for Junior Military Aviator and Military Aviator.

Let's see how Jenny fared, here and abroad, right after our entry into World War I.

With but 1,218 officers and men, 227 miscellaneous airplanes, and only 3 flying fields operating in April, 1917, it was necessary to expand this 150 times to attain pledged goals.

It was decided to have three phases of training: ground and primary flight instruction in the United States, and advanced training in Britain, France, and Italy, where combat aircraft and combat-wise instructors were available.

A group of staff officers was dispatched to Canada to inspect R.F.C. training at Borden and at Toronto. Out of this inspection emerged a plan under which the Canadians would get us started immediately by lending us facilities and personnel for summer operations in their country in exchange for access to fields we would build here before winter set in.

We were to duplicate Canadian methods with nine fields in the United States. Hiram Bingham, a Yale professor, was commissioned in the Signal Corps to establish ground schools at M.I.T., Georgia Tech, Cornell, Ohio State, Princeton, the universities of Illinois, Texas, and California. The original course was for eight weeks, but this was lengthened to twelve. Twenty-five cadets entered each school every week. By July 1,600 pilot candidates had enrolled.

More than 38,000 men volunteered for flight training between July, 1917, and June, 1918. The ground schools admitted 23,000 and graduated 17,500. They were taught theory of flight, enough physics and mathematics to understand the former, airplane construction, map making, photography, gun sighting, bomb dropping. Infantry close-order drill was given along with considerable physical exercise. At the end of two months exams were given to determine who was to receive flight training.

Meanwhile, the Aircraft Production Board had been setting up the first 9 of an ultimate 40 flying fields. These were standardized, one mile square, and laid out to handle two squadrons of 150 cadets apiece, as well as instructors, administrators, enlisted men, shops, and hangars for 72 Jennys. Each unit cost approximately $1,000,000.

On July 17, 1917, the first cadets to train in America (classes were training simultaneously in Canada) received dual instruction at Chanute Field, Rantoul, Illinois; Wilbur Wright Field, Dayton, Ohio; Selfridge Field, Mt. Clemens, Michigan.

In a War Department treatise titled "Present Practice of Accepting and Training Aviators," we learn:

Candidates for commission as flying officers must be at least 19 years old and preferably not over 30 [ouch], although in exceptional cases, older men of pronounced athletic attainments who have spent most of their lives outdoors, in the saddle, mountain climbing or in actual flying, may be accepted. [The linking of mountain climbing

Above
May, 1918. Kelly Field, San Antonio, Texas. From the cities and the farms, the mansions and the wrong side of the tracks they came— determined to "make the world safe for democracy." (U.S. Signal Corps)

Below
A class receiving instruction in map and terrain reading. Height of dummy Jenny fuselage above map simulated altitude. Mosaic aerial photos are mounted below the fuselage. In this era, officers wore boots for dress, and the Army had to issue an order banning the wearing of spurs in aircraft because they poked holes in the fabric. However, years later spurs made a comeback when it became necessary to equip jet pilots with a modification of them, so that they could lock their heels into an ejection seat before making a high-speed bailout, preventing their legs from wrapping around them like pretzels because of the air blast. (U.S. Signal Corps)

and flying was apropos because those who essayed mountain flying usually had considerable experience in mountain descending, if their legs were intact.]

It must be remembered that the flying officer is not an "aerial chauffeur," or an "exhibition flyer." He has been more accurately described as a twentieth-century cavalry officer mounted on Pegasus. [Here come General Squier's oat-burning gassers again.]

All candidates are enlisted in the Signal Corps or its Reserve. This will actually hold them for the period of training [like a bear trap] which covers the course at the school of Military Aeronautics (ground school) at one of the eight universities and at flying school up to passing the tests for Military Aviator,* or Junior Military Aviator.* If they pass, they are commissioned. If they fail to qualify for commission and are released, this does not exempt them from the draft.

Like the Germans, they were determined to get you either in the air or on the ground.

From the time of starting ground school and until the cadet was commissioned or washed out, he was a private first class, and drew $100 a month and 60¢ a day ration allowance, which paid his bill at the cadet mess. At Pensacola in the thirties when the writer was a student naval aviator, the pay was $54 a month, classes lived in dilapidated barracks, had no uniforms, and ate in the crew's mess, which was the worst in the Navy. This was fourteen years after World War I and was often referred to as an era of retrogressive progress.

To continue the War Department publication:

Graduates of schools of Military Aeronautics are sent to aviation schools for training in flying. The course of study's time span depends in large measure on the weather, the supply of spare parts [the crackup rate was terrific] and to a man's ability. It can not be pre-determined as to length. Some men pass their test and qualify for commission at the end of one month, others require longer. [In World War II, the flight course lasted approximately twelve months.]

Those who have had previous experience in flying usually require less than others, unless their former instructor has confirmed them in bad habits. It occasionally takes longer to correct bad habits than to teach new candidates who never have had flying experience. [This is as true today.]

In general, candidates received forty to fifty hours of Jenny time and then were shipped overseas for further training. Issou-

* See end of chapter for qualifications.

This Kelly Field instructor should have been and probably was saying: "The most cogent advice I can give you about propellers is to keep your neck out of them. No one, but no one, has ever won an argument with a propeller. They're like horses. One end is more dangerous than the other. Even if you have no regard for yourself, let these props alone. There's a shortage." (U.S. Signal Corps)

don, France, became known as the "home of the million-dollar guard" because for a time it was filled with "high-paid" (by Allied standards) U.S. pilots who had no planes to fly and were assigned to guard duty to keep them out of mischief.

Eventually there were sixteen U.S. flight schools overseas. By November, 1918, these could give "final refresher" and pre-combat instruction to two thousand pilots a month. More than eight thousand Americans received some form of pilot and observer training in France, with an additional five hundred duplicating this in England and Italy.

Since Jenny was good enough for fledglings, but not good enough for war, the primary task of these establishments was to take over where she left off, to give the lads experience in the foreign craft in which they were to joust with the Hun. This added, although meagerly, to the paucity of their flight hours, that elixir of life in air combat.

Thus was General Squier's engined cavalry curried, gassed, watered, and tuned to fight anyone similarly handicapped.

To rate its just-trained pilots, the grade of Junior Military Aviator had been created by Congress on July 18, 1914, and published in War Department Bulletin No. 35, issued August 4, 1914. The act made provision for a qualifying examination covering the general adaptability of a candidate, flying, airplanes, aeronautical motors, meteorology, navigation.

May 18, 1918, Kelly Field, San Antonio, Texas. "Today we're going to review everything you've had to date. Now remember, you have to use more right rudder in right turns, and for the love of Mike, don't pull that nose up in left turns. I DON'T WANT TO GET KILLED! *If you make out all right, I'll put you up for a solo check." (U.S. Signal Corps)*

The first Army board convened to examine applicants for rating published the following requirements: "The candidate will demonstrate his flying knowledge by operating a machine in a triangular course without landing. The minimum length of any leg to be 20 miles. He must make a straight-away cross-country flight of at least 90 miles without landing and for a half hour remain between 2,500 and 3,000 feet, to be registered by a recording barograph." He was also required to make such starting and landing flights as the board might designate.

Above
May, 1918. Kelly Field, San Antonio, Texas. "All right, I'm going to solo you. Take off, circle the field and stay within gliding distance so you can make it if the engine quits. Taxi back after the landing and I'll tell you what you did wrong." (U.S. Signal Corps)

Right
May, 1918. Silhouette targets on the machine-gun range at a training field. Emphasis was placed upon deflection shots, i.e., enemy crossing at right angles to your line of flight. These were the hardest shots to make and still were in World War II. (U.S. Signal Corps)

There was nothing in this to cause Jenny any apprehension, but it did put a strain on the neophytes.

On March 30, 1915, there was issued a document titled "Memorandum for the Adjutant General of the Army," in which it was directed that a general order be issued which would cover the scope of the written examination to be given for the Junior Military Aviator rating. The text will be of interest to military pilots who have trained since the thirties and to civilians who began flying after the present system of examining and rating aviators was begun by the civil government in 1925:

The examination under the subject of aeroplanes will be both theoretical and practical. The theoretical examination will be of such a nature as to develop the candidate's knowledge of so much of the theory of aerodynamics as is essential to the intelligent operation, care, and repair of machines. The practical examination will include the actual making of repairs and adjustments.

The examination on aeronautical motors will be both theoretical and practical. The theoretical questions will develop the candidate's knowledge of the theory of internal combustion engines. The practi-

cal examination will consist of not only questions regarding the care, repair and operation of the aeronautical motors now in use in the Signal Corps, but he will be required to make repairs and adjustments in order to indicate his familiarity with the types of motors now in use.

The examination on the subject of meteorology will be theoretical in character and take up questions of the general laws of the atmosphere and air movements as applied to aviation.

Navigation of the air will be covered by both a theoretical and practical examination. The theoretical part will cover the candidate's knowledge of the theory, while the practical part will be an actual demonstration of his ability to make an extended cross-country flight under different conditions of weather and a report covering his observations during the flight.

After one or two examinations, this office will be in a position to make more definite recommendations based on the experience gained in the examinations for the future issuance of a subsequent General Order on this subject.

Signed, Brigadier General George P. Scriven.

Prior to passing the Junior Military Aviator test, a pilot received a bonus of 25 percent of his pay and allowances for whatever rank and length of service he held.

After being rated, a pilot received the rank and pay allowances of one grade higher than that held by him under his line commission, provided he was not higher than first lieutenant. While on flying duty he received a bonus of 50 percent over the pay of his grade and length of service under his line commission. This, of course, was to attract pilot candidates—despite the high casualty rates.

There were provisions for training a small number of enlisted pilots, and if one of these or a commissioned pilot was killed in line of duty, his next of kin or whoever he might designate received one year of pay for his grade and length of service.

To be rated as a Military Aviator, a candidate had to have served for three years as a Junior Military Aviator. In both examinations, since there were no textbooks at the time, candidates had only to make 70 percent to pass their written tests.

The requirements for Military Aviator rating were issued under Circular 10 by the Chief Signal Officer of the War Department on October 27, 1913, and were the guidelines for rejecting or commissioning Jenny pilots during World War I:

The following requirements for a Military Aviator, effective January 1, 1914, having been approved by the Secretary of War, are published for the information and guidance of all concerned:

(1) Make a cross-country flight over a triangular course not less than 100 miles in perimeter with two intermediate landings; this flight to be completed within 48 hours after the start, the same machine being used during the flight.

(2) Make a straight-away cross-country flight without landing, of at least 60 miles, over a previously designated course; return flight to be made either on the same day or on the first subsequent day that the weather permits.

(3) During the flight prescribed in (1) and (2), the candidate shall remain at least 1,500 feet above the terrain.

(4) Make a flight during which the machine shall remain for at least 30 minutes at an altitude between 2,500 and 3,000 feet above the terrain. This requirement may be accomplished during one of the cross-country flights if practicable.

(5) Execute a volplane [they meant *glide*] with the motor cut out completely, at an altitude of 1,500 feet, the motor to be cut out when the aeroplane is over the landing field, and on landing cause the aeroplane to come to rest within 300 feet of a previously designated point.

(6) Reports will be submitted giving the main military features observed during the flights made under (1) and (2).

(7) No tests will be made with passengers. Time of arrival at and departure from the various points may be attested by military or civil authorities; if none of these are present, by the aviators involved.

(8) The candidate will then be examined theoretically and practically on his ability to read maps; his knowledge of the compass and how to steer thereby; his knowledge of the aeroplane, i.e., what constitutes safe construction; how to make the ordinary repairs to an aeroplane; the action of the machine under ordinary flying conditions, covering the points on the action of the controls, how the angles of lift on the wings change in making turns, how the pressures change both on the main planes, rear elevator, and vertical rudder; and what

constitutes safe flying as far as gliding, banking, etc. is concerned.

He will be examined on his knowledge of gasoline motors; carburetors, the most common troubles that occur to motors and how to correct them. He shall be able to make simple repairs, dismantle and assemble motors, and shall show a thorough knowledge of all motors in use at the school.

He shall be examined in meteorology and topography in so far as they relate to aviation.

CHAPTER NINE

Flying by the Numbers

Flight-training manuals used by the U.S. Army.

The following naysaying Army manuals on how to fly an airplane were as good a guide to ruin as one could find and they were the Alpha, Bravo, Charleys of Jennying in the 1917–18 period. They are reproduced verbatim with the exception of interpolated flippancies. But remember, we do not deride; this was an embryonic stage and it is a wonder so many survived the embryo to flap their wings in the headlong skies of La Belle France.

There are minor duplications in the several manuals. These have not been deleted because to do so would detract from the originality and completeness of each. These have been out of print for fifty years.

In some of the instructions, pilots will notice misconceptions of things that happen in flight. However, they will also perceive a surprising amount of material that is as applicable now as then. Watch for peculiarities in the instructions for handling the controls in "Learning to Fly in the U.S. Army"; also notice the continual admonition to keep an eye searching for a forced-landing field and always to expect engine failure. Mariners had their Lorelei, Samson had his Delilah—and the OX-5 had its camshaft.

To be calm, it appears that the only military things left out here are the Plattsburg Drill Manual, mess call, and Lincoln's Gettysburg Address. It is possible that remembering the procedures was more fatiguing than the flying:

STARTING INSTRUCTIONS

The order of starting is as follows

1. Pilot to Rigger: "Everything all right?"
2. Rigger: "All correct, Sir."
3. Pilot to Machinist: "Everything all right?"
4. Machinist: "All correct, Sir."
5. Machinist: "Switch off?"
6. Pilot: "Switch off."
7. Machinist: "Gasoline on; air closed?"
8. Pilot: "Gasoline on; air closed."

The Machinist now rotates the propeller

9. Machinist: "Contact?"
10. Pilot: "Contact."

The machinist now swings the propeller and stands clear

11. Pilot: Waves hand sideways.
                             [This could mean flies; "I've changed my mind"; or we can assume the engine is off and running.]
12. Air Mechanic: Pulls blocks away from wheels.
13. Pilot: Looks at Senior Non-Commissioned Officer, or Mechanic.
                             [We now have five characters in the cast.]
14. Senior Non-Com, or Mech: Looks to see if all is clear for ascent and no other airplane is descending. If all is clear, he salutes.
                             [We do not know where the band is.]
15. Pilot: Waves hand in fore-and-aft direction. This is the signal for everyone to stand clear without a moment's delay, and is especially meant for the Air Mechanics at the tail end of the fuselage.
                             [Sort of like letting a bronc out of the chute at a rodeo.]

16. Pilot: Waves hand in a fore-and-aft direc-
                                    tion.
17. Air Mechanic: "Stand clear."
                                    [With this warmup, it may be con-
                                    jectured that upon the final com-
                                    mand, everyone ran like hell.]

This appears to be the final act of this farewell tableau and perhaps by now the pilot has dashed off into the wild blue and is on his way yonder. May we hope that at his destination there was a suitable retinue properly schooled in a receiving ballet to turn him around and point him toward home with the OX-5 and Jenny contributing to a happy denouement.

(*The Curtiss Standard JN-4D Military Tractor Handbook, 1918,* cont.)

HINTS ON FLYING

Right-hand Tractors

1. Look over the machine in a general way.
   [Since appearances depend upon which side of the eyeballs you are on, and since Jenny looked good to herself, she cared not a damn how she looked to anyone else. However, the admonition to just take a "general way" look probably stemmed from that school of thought which believed that a real sharp scrutiny might raise too many doubts in the mind of that nervous, ambitious bundle of doubt, the student pilot.]
2. Test motor for revolutions.
3. Be sure controls are working properly.
   [It was very easy for a mechanic to cross the cables leading from the stick to the elevator, so that when "up" elevator was applied, Jenny dived. Messy.]
4. Start off directly into the wind.
   [You'd never make it if you didn't.]
5. Watch your direction carefully and counteract with right rudder the machine's tendency to turn to the left, due to the propeller's air blast striking the left side of the fin more forcibly than the right side.
6. After attaining a few feet headway, raise the tail with controls and keep it in this position to prevent machine from leaving ground until it is well past its minimum flying speed, at the same time watching your direction carefully.

If your course permits keep your machine on the ground until its maximum ground speed is reached; then very easily and smoothly, take it off the ground. By following the above plan of a high-speed takeoff a large degree of safety is assured, for if engine trouble develops soon after, you have surpassed the machine's minimum flying speed and you have a good chance to pick a landing spot that would not be possible if the takeoff were made at slow speed, for the machine would immediately start sinking on loss of power and also lose its controlability to a large degree.

7. The most dangerous place for engine failure is just after leaving the ground.

8. When once underway it is advisable to attain a safe altitude as soon as possible, and it will be found that the best results can be

Kelly Field, San Antonio, Texas. Best known of all U.S. World War I flight schools. This photo was made after the war had ended. Planes in foreground are pursuits. Twenty-four Jennys are visible in the distant background. (U.S. Air Force)

attained by a high-speed, low-angle climb rather than a slow-speed, large angle. A steady, fast climb is the best for all purposes. [Including survival.]

9. After a height of not less than *800 feet,* a turn can be contemplated. It is advisable to reach a higher altitude if possible, but do not attempt one lower unless necessity demands to miss obstructions or to play safe on a certain forced-landing spot in case of engine trouble.

10. Never forget that the engine may stop, and at all times keep this in mind and plan on a safe landing place within gliding distance of wherever you may be. [And hope you never run out of cow pastures.]

If you are still on the climb and wish to make a rather short turn,

nose the machine over until you are flying level so as to keep the speed high. At the same time bring into play the rudder and ailerons in the correct proportions and in the proper directions to give a smooth, even turn. A large, easy turn with little bank is more to be encouraged than a short, sharp one using a steep bank, for if banking is not properly done either skidding or sideslipping develops, both of which, if carried too far, are very dangerous. At no time let your machine attain a high angle of climb, for in so doing you are encouraging it to stall which would necessitate considerable altitude to recover from safely.

At all times remember that although you are controlling the actions of the machine it has a considerable amount of stability itself, and be a little free with the controls rather than stiff and rigid. [How tight is loose, sir?]

11. Do not at any time jerk the controls, but be firm and steady and above all smooth in their operation. This forms a quiet and confident mind which is invaluable in flying, also it reduces the strain on the machine to the minimum.

13. Once a safe altitude is reached your anxiety diminishes, for with height there is safety; but remember to keep within gliding distance of a landing place.

14. Directions of wind here enter into the gliding possibilities of your machine, for although at all times you go the same rate of speed through the air your relations with the ground change with the wind, so if you have to glide into a wind you cannot glide as far over the ground from a given point as you can if the same wind were behind you.

    You will also notice by flying in a side wind that in order to keep a straight course over the ground the machine must be swung around into the wind on an angle depending on the velocity of the wind. This is to offset the drift of the machine.

15. Drift must also be counted on in making turns, for by side drifting the horizon appears to be moving in the opposite direction, which is very apt to mislead one as to his actual turning from the result of the rudder.

    [This was a chimera and wouldn't happen unless you were not sober, or if you were "long long."]

LANDING

16. When within the correct distance for a glide of medium velocity to your contemplated landing place, shut off the engine [which

A Jenny, JN-4D came a cropper at Kelly Field, Texas, November 23, 1918. The cause was OX-5 failure and—you guessed it—a camshaft broke. (U.S. Air Force)

introduced a calm before the thud and blunder of the landing] and nose machine over to the proper gliding angle and head for the field in a direction to bring you directly into the wind.

If you find you are too close to the field and your machine is developing excessive speed, start "S-ing" to reduce your speed as well as altitude. If you have considerable altitude to spare an easy spiral may be executed, but neither of these should be tried unless you are perfectly confident of their success. The best way is a long, straight glide into the field, and it gives one a fine chance to judge distance and wind.

17. Never glide down too flat for your speed falls off and you settle instead of glide down. In so doing your controls become inactive to a large degree [In other words, you are stalled, and for a student, keeping Jenny out of a stall was like trying to put an oyster into a parking meter.] and this must be avoided in all cases. A strong blast must be on the controls in the correct direction at all times to have the machine sensitive to their movements.

When you have glided toward the field and are still about 50 feet from the ground you should start leveling off, but gradually allow

123

the machine to glide down within about six feet of the ground where the final leveling off begins. At this point the machine is skimming along, neither rising nor falling, until its velocity wanes, then as it sinks you increase the wing's angle to the air so as to bring the lift again up to the weight of the machine for its loss of speed. As speed lessens the angle should be increased more rapidly until the machine is flying in the correct position for landing at its minimum flying speed. At this point the machine should be just grazing the ground with its wheels and tail skid. Only practice will perfect landings, for it is only a combination of good judgment of distances and speeds.

18. In making turns you will notice the marked tendency of the machine to *nose down* on a right-hand turn and *climb on a left one*, the latter not being so noticeable as the former. These peculiar actions of the machine are caused by the gyroscopic forces of the revolving propeller and must be compensated by the elevators to keep the machine level. In banks of over 20 degrees the rudder and elevators begin to exchange their proper actions with one another until the vertical is reached, when the change is complete. This must be clearly understood, for to expect the elevators to control the horizontal balance of the machine when on a steep bank and the rudder to control the direction of the same might end disastrously.

19. The most common danger at present to new students is the spinning nose dive or tail spin. [That climax of crises, *la descente en vrille*, as our French companions in arms called it.] Although it is

Above
May, 1918. "Okay, I'm going to solo you. After takeoff, fly straight ahead toward those trees on the horizon, turn left when you clear the field, make your next turn crosswind, and when you are in position, cut the gun, turn onto your final approach and land. Watch out for other airplanes. Keep that neck swiveling, AND DON'T MAKE DAMN FOOLS OUT OF US." (U.S. Signal Corps)
Below
May, 1918, Kelly Field, Texas. Jenny has him in her clutches now. If all goes well, he will win the battle of wits; a wrong guess, however, and he'll win a halo. Contrary to the movies, soloing is not a fright-riddled experience, but one of relief over getting that swearing, pounding maniac of an instructor out of the front cockpit. For the instructor it is not a carefree occasion. He wonders if his judgment has been correct, if he has imparted enough skill so the lad won't pile up. All during the flight, these gremlins keep needling him. (U.S. Signal Corps)

Left
May, 1918. Kelly Field, San Antonio, Texas. "Now where the hell did he go, damnit?" (U.S. Signal Corps)

Below
This was a low-altitude collision which miraculously did not kill the cadet pilot, who is the same one shown in earlier photos in this chapter with his instructor prior to, during, and after his solo. The crash occurred in the summer of 1918. (U.S. Signal Corps)

not dangerous to the man who knows how to get out of one, it is very wise for the beginner to stay well away from the possibilities of having the chance to see if he can get out of one. [The same advice applied re getting caught in a married woman's boudoir.]

There are several ways of getting started in a spin but *excessive* banking with considerable rudder *seems* to be the foremost way of all. In turning, the nose falls due to stalling or *some other cause* and a spin results.

In a spin the ailerons and elevators are useless, for the air blast strikes them from the side instead of straight on. The only available control is the rudder, and this is your best friend. All the possible rudder should be put on in the opposite direction than you are spinning even if you have to put *both feet on one side of the rudder bar*. [Keep loose, stay calm, and charge!]

Remember to hold that rudder and keep the motor going full to supply all the possible air blast. This is the only remedy and if you have enough altitude you have nothing to worry about. [And if you don't, you won't have long to worry.]

The centrifugal force of the revolving machine must first be stopped and this takes place somewhat slowly, but as soon as you feel the rudder acting you will feel the elevators and the ailerons regaining their control, whereby you can complete the work started by the rudder and regain your proper balance.

Despite Thoreau's observation that "The mass of men lead lives of quiet desperation," one perceives from the above *urgentissimo* that in Jenny flying the per-capita boredom among pilots was small.

Above
Cadet is placed aboard the ambulance. This was a collision, and the cadet in the other Jenny was killed. Such scenes were not uncommon on the busy training fields. The causes of crashes were numerous, and few were due to structural weaknesses. Most resulted from incomplete maintenance, engine unreliability, and inexperience in conducting flight operations. (U.S. Signal Corps)

Below
Out of the hospital and all healed up, except for some corrective nose surgery, the cadet has decided to try it again. According to War Department records, few cadets asked to be transferred after they had been in a crash. (U.S. Signal Corps)

Learning to Fly in the U.S. Army—1917

(From U.S. Army Manual)

1. The dual-control system of training used in this country differs from the French method of starting the pupil out alone to try his wings. [In this anarchy, training-plane throttles were blocked to prevent their being fully opened. After classroom instruction, the student, alone in the airplane, taxied along the field trying out the controls, while a shouting, perspiring instructor ran alongside and told him how things worked. When the instructor got tired he unblocked the throttle and the student either became a pilot or a casualty. This was called the "surprise" method, because everything that happened was.] It enables the instructor to keep a constant eye upon the pupil's control manipulations and to correct them instantly whenever they are in error before any damage is done.

2. As soon as the wings bank up, the lift force is no longer all vertical and therefore may not be enough to support the weight of the machine. To offset this, have plenty of motor power for speed in a bank, and *do not try to climb while banking*. It is better to bank too little than too much; too little results in skidding which may be easily cured. Too much results in *side slipping inward and if the tail surface is too great, a spiral dive may result—so look out for overbanking*.

3. To come down, throttle down the engine and push the lever *softly* forward until the proper gliding angle is obtained. The reason for throttling down the engine is: first, that you do not need its thrust when you are *coasting* down because gravity [the old equalizer] furnishes the necessary velocity [and the jolts]; second, if you glide or dive with the motor wide open, high speed will result, placing strain on the machine especially on the moment of leveling out again; third, at this high speed [it couldn't go to 100, or the wings would peel off] the controls become stiff to operate.

4. Maintain the proper gliding speed to within 5 mph of what it ought to be [but what ought it to be?]. The revolution counter will indicate what the speed is [but only of the engine, i.e., rpm]. Arrange [that's a folksy way of putting it] to come onto the field facing directly into the wind. In landing against the wind, you are copying the practice of the birds.

[Most instruction then was for the birds, anyway.] When you come to within 15 feet of the ground, pull the lever *softly* back until the machine is in its slow-flying position. Hold the lever at this position of horizontal flying. No further movement of the lever is necessary except to correct bumps for which purpose it should be held lightly for instant action.

5. The aileron control must be used here to keep the machine level and it may be necessary to operate the rudder after touching the ground [it was usually going like bicycle pedals on a downhill run] in order to avoid swerving. [This was the understatement of the war, considering the groundlooping proclivities of Jenny.]

6. In rolling after landing, keep the tail as close to the ground as possible without causing undue bumping so that the maximum resistance of the wings may be presented to the air and the machine slowed up rapidly.

7. Landing is one of the hardest problems in aviation and it is difficult to learn because it is done at such high speed [40–45 mph].

The Following Are Examples of Bad Landings

[If we accept the literal definition of bathos as "a ludicrous descent," then the following landings were the purest bathos.]

1. The pancake results from allowing the machine to get into its rising position when it is landing. There will be a perpendicular bounce [a call to arms by the bungee] and on the second bounce, the running gear will break [good timing].

   In order to get the machine out of the pancake, open up the engine [but, don't fail to provide for the two preparatory coughs before anything happens] to keep the machine flying, put the machine into a flying position, then throttle down and land. [Provided bumps on the ground didn't antagonize the bungee, this might work, but it usually turned into a disconcerting series of skips and bounces.]

2. Another type of pancake results from bringing the machine out of its gliding position at a point too far above the ground when the machine will drop due to lack of speed and break the running gear. [Somehow, one always got back to breaking the running gear.] To avoid this, open the motor full (cough, cough), thus regaining speed and flying position, afterward throttle down and *re-land*. [Here we go for another gallop into the airdrome fence.]

3. A third type of bad landing results from failure to turn the machine out of its glide at all so that it glides straight downward until it touches the ground. [There was only one of these to a student because few, if any, lived to make this one again.] This is the most dangerous case of all bad landings. To cure it [if you can still move], open the engine [cough, cough] after the first bounce, regaining flying speed before the second bounce, then re-land.

4. If at the moment of landing the rudder is turned causing the machine to swerve, or if the machine is not level, a side strain will be placed upon the landing gear and the wheels will buckle. [This in turn broke the running gear and brought the situation full circle.]

Thus ended the lesson.

August, 1917. Training field, Memphis, Tenn. A cadet on final approach for a landing. A group of cadets and instructors watch in the background. Fields were set up wherever the terrain permitted. This one was alongside a dairy. Cows often got onto the landing field and halted flight operations. (U.S. Army Air Corps)

It should not be assumed that these disasters were common only to cadets. Nay, they occurred also to graduated pilots and instructors. Jenny believed that there was nothing too good for these people and that's what she gave them equally since she had no class consciousness. Like she always said when in a philosophical mood: "Millionaires and bums taste alike to a flea."

The foregoing guide to getting along with Jenny was a reflection of the aerodynamic doubts which plagued her and of trying to determine which was the Ying and which the Yang, or the zig and the zag of life. Being a prototype she had to decide whether she wanted to be the head of a rabbit or the tail of a lion. Since she chose the latter, she had to live up to it, and although as a rule she was right in what she ordained, her victims were of the

opinion that she was a little rough in the way she expressed it:
"Violate my edicts and I'll clobber you."

The following was compounded by Roger Janus, who did a
long stretch on the rockpile of flight instructing in Curtiss
schools and was a civilian Jenny instructor for the Army
throughout World War I.

SUGGESTIONS FOR FLYING STUDENTS

The first thing for the student in aviation to learn and the last
thing for him to forget is that aviation is a serious business.
There is a strong tendency for familiarity to breed contempt in
this, as in any other hazardous occupation, and we must be constantly on our guard against this state of mind.

Flying looks so easy that almost every student is well provided
with delusions and confidently expects that the few difficult
points will, on account of his exceptional ability, be mastered in
a little or no time. Fortunately, only a few minutes in the air are
required to take this out of him and make him perfectly tracta-
ble. [Since Jenny dealt so much with psycho-ceramic would-be
pilots, she was convinced that there would be no stupid people if
everyone was an idiot and that we were working assiduously toward this goal.]

The student must put himself absolutely in the hands of the
instructor. He must constantly impress upon himself the necessity
of keeping cool in a pinch, such as a *forced landing*. [That t-h-i-
n-g broke again. Despite the OX-5 bullying the student with its
implied threats, so did it bully Jenny off the field, over the fence,
and across the (low) hills.]

There have been rare instances of the student clutching the
controls and taking them away from the instructor with disas-
trous results. But this will never occur if the student has the
proper point of view and is on his guard against such an emergency. [Want to bet?]

The capable airplane pilot keeps a multiple of things on his
mind with very little effort. [Like: How am I going to pay my
bills? Is there any booze in the apartment? Wonder if I'll score

*This was a line-astern bombing formation in which cadets were
drilled before leaving for France. This photo was made near Rockwell Field, San Diego, Calif., on May 11, 1918. (U.S. Signal Corps)*

tonight. How am I going to get this rear-cockpit monkey off my back?] But the student should not concern himself with too many things at the same time. If his attention is not concentrated on anything in particular and he depends upon a hazy process of absorption it will take him much longer to become proficient. To illustrate, on his first trip or two he should devote his entire attention to the elevator, learning to keep the machine at a given angle indicated by the instructor. As soon as a little proficiency has been acquired with this control, he will begin to use the aileron control, either stick or wheel (Deperdussin) until he can keep the machine flying nicely in a straight line. This training will require about six trips.

Correcting Propeller Torque.

By this time the student will have noticed that one wing has a tendency to stay lower than the other. This is caused by the torque or turning tendency of the motor. When the machine is turning a right-hand propeller, it will be the left wing which has a tendency to dip, but only a very slight pressure on the wheel will be sufficient to correct this, and keep the wings level. This torque effect is in accordance with Newton's law of motion which states that when any force is in operation, there must always be an equal force operating in the opposite direction. Hence, when the motor turns the propeller to the right, it exerts an equal tendency to turn itself to the left. Going a little further, this force is the side action of the pistons on the cylinders. In every explosion of a right-hand motor a strong pressure is exerted on the left side of the piston.

The sum total of these forces to the left is equal to the force exerted in turning the propeller, and they comprise the torque of the motor. This must be counteracted by the ailerons unless some other provision is made for it. When the machine is gliding with reduced throttle, this force disappears and the wings stay level of their own accord.

It will also be noted that the Curtiss JN-4 has a tendency to steer to the left when flying under power. This is caused mostly by the draught of the propeller. When the propeller passes through the air, it pushes the air behind it and also gives it a whirling motion. In this and many other machines, the rudder is slightly above the line of the propeller shaft which puts it in the upper part of the draught. The whirling motion of this draught

*May, 1918. Rockwell Field, San Diego, Calif. Jenny could be beauti-
ful in her own element, freed of ground restrictions and completely
on her own. However, unless there is a hole somewhere, this cadet is
going to have a hard time getting down. Blind flight was unknown at
that time, and if one got caught above clouds, he had to fly until he
found an opening to get through, or he simply closed the throttle,
nosed down, and hoped. (U.S. Signal Corps)*

causes it to pass across the tail of the machine from left to right.
It is the pressure of this air on the left side of the rudder which
makes the machine tend to turn toward the left. The left aileron
being carried slightly lower than the right to compensate for the
torque also causes a tendency for the machine to turn to the left,
but this is not as strong as the effect from the draught.

Making Turns

During the course of these first half-dozen lessons the student
will get somewhat familiar with the feeling of the machine while
making a turn. Now he will begin making turns and circles himself. It takes more speed and *more power* to fly a machine in a
circle than to fly it straight [the low performance, lack of reserve
power, plus high drag accounted for this] and the smaller the

circle [with its steeper bank], the more speed required to keep
the machine from losing altitude.

In the early days of flying when it took all the power available
to keep the machine flying straight, it was necessary to allow for
a considerable loss of altitude when making a turn and the operation was dangerous. [The Wrights had to slightly dive their
turns when they first made them at Huffman Prairie, near Dayton, in 1909–10.]

Now when we have a good amount of reserve power [like
maybe 10 mph] things are quite different, and a good machine
will be able to maintain its altitude on a circle unless it be one of
very small radius. On large turns it is quite safe to permit the
machine to climb, but for students, practicing turns of moderate
radius, it is best to keep the machine flying horizontal, that is,
neither descending nor climbing.

Supposing now, we wish to make a left-hand turn with a JN-4
going about 70 mph and describing a circle of about 100 yards
radius. The proper amount of bank for this will be about 20°.
[This turn would require approximately 50 seconds for 360°. A
jet fighter banked at 20° and flying at a true airspeed of 1,750
knots would require about 26.5 minutes to complete a 360°
turn.] To make the turn the student will gradually move his
rudder to the left, and at the same time start the bank with the
ailerons. In this way, the rate of turning and the banking will increase gradually, steadily and in the proper proportion.

Above
May 13, 1918. These two Canucks collided in the air as they leveled off for a landing. The crash occurred at Taliaferro Field, Hicks, Texas. Both cadet pilots survived. (U.S. Signal Corps)

Below
Jn-4Ds on the line at aviation school, Mineola, New York. 1918 (U.S. Air Force)

Air Service Radio Mechanics School, Post Field, Ft. Sill, Oklahoma. Pilot and observer wearing intercommunicating telephone. The plane is a JN-4D. The photo was made in 1917 and this pair had telephones for inter-cockpit communication. Yet through World War II, 27 years later, primary flight instructors had nothing better than a speaking tube, although good communications were essential to proper instruction. (U.S. Air Force)

When the machine is turning at the desired rate, stop the movement of the rudder and only use it further to keep the machine turning at the same rate. About this time it will probably be necessary to bring the aileron control back to about its neutral position to preserve the angle of bank, as the machine banks of its own accord. Machines differ greatly in the amount the ailerons must be used on the turn, and the same machine will act differently under different wind conditions [this was a fallacy] so no fixed rules can be laid down. [This was part of the system of "not telling them everything," or "mixing them up a little," in order to preserve some of the mystery so the gurus would always have the edge.]

The student need not be the least alarmed if he has to use the ailerons twice as much one day making his turns as he did the day before. [He ought to be because nothing of an aerodynamic nature

140

could cause this, nor could air turbulence. Although the latter might make him use them twice as often. He probably was developing the "twitches."]

Stalling

If you try to make the machine climb at too great an angle, it will have to expend so much of its power in lifting vertically that an angle is eventually [like in a few seconds] reached at which the machine will be slowed below its flying speed. If held at this angle the machine will no longer climb but will begin to settle. This is a dangerous condition as the controls have very little effect and a bad puff may upset the machine [and roll it into a spin]. However, the condition is easily recognized by the limp feeling of the controls [they could get as loose as a bowl of noodles], a wobbly feeling in the whole machine, and a laboring of the motor.

Keeping out of this predicament was insurance that couldn't be bought with anything except experience and caution because airspeed, like happiness and poverty, is something that can't be bought.

Slipping

When the machine is not correctly banked, it will side slip. If the bank is too small the slipping [they meant *skidding*] will be outward. This is not dangerous [nor is it dangerous in contemporary aircraft]. If the bank is too great, it will slip inward and downward. This is dangerous. [It would not be today, unless greatly exaggerated and during a turn as low as perhaps one hundred feet or less. Anyone numb enough to slip inadvertently so extremely would have no business flying anyway, and would probably kill himself in this or some other way quite early and thus solve his slipping problem.]

When the machine is slipping [skidding] outward, it is corrected either by banking more or making the turn larger [or using less rudder]. When slipping downward, give less bank or make the turn smaller [or use more rudder]. A pilot should be able to tell when he is banking properly by the feeling of the machine, but may never acquire this ability. [Those who didn't probably weren't around too long. Men with lead in their britches were soon eliminated because Jenny couldn't abide people with an insensitive derrière who couldn't fly by the seat of their pants.]

A spirit level will tell the truth, and often the wind can be felt coming in sideways when the machine is slipping [or skidding]. [This method became extinct along with the demise of open cockpits.] Mention has been made of settling on turns. This is quite different from side slipping. A machine will never side slip if it is properly banked, though it may settle badly. This settling must be anticipated when flying at low altitude.

Rising and Landing

After 12 lessons, about half of the instruction time, the remaining 12 will be occupied in learning to take the machine off the ground and to land it. Landing is the great bugbear of the students, and is doubly difficult because even the slightest mistakes are very noticeable and the penalties may be severe. [In fact, at that time, with those airplanes and *that* "running gear," this was one of the most prevalent sources of the poorlies.]

There are two methods of landing, referred to as the slow, or tail-low type; and the fast, or tail-high landing. The slow kind is the one which should be learned by the student, as it is the safest and the only practical way for landing on rough ground or in a small field.

Start into the field on an easy glide. Begin to bring the nose up when about 30 feet from the ground and continue to draw in on the elevator very gently. This must be timed so that the machine is level when it gets about four feet above the ground.

By this time flying speed is dropping and the machine is settling rapidly. At the same time the elevator is being brought back firmly, causing the tail to drop, and speed to fall considerably. The great angle of incidence [actually *angle of attack*] of the wings keeps the machine from dropping too rapidly. It should alight on the wheels and tail skid at the same time. In this position it makes the shortest possible run, with the exception of a pancake.

In case a forced landing is necessary in a small or rough field, the machine should be pancaked. That is, carry out the method described above, except do it a few feet further from the ground. The machine will settle heavily and the landing gear may be damaged, but the speed will be reduced, lessening the danger of running into some ditch or obstruction. Remember, never run headfirst into anything [like making a pass at a colonel's wife when you are a lieutenant]. In case of trouble this is absolutely the most important thing to remember; switch off the motor to avoid the possibility of fire, and do anything rather than run into anything solid. If the machine is brought down tail first, or on one wing the chances of serious injury are greatly lessened.

In making a tail-high landing the machine comes into the field faster and is brought to the ground by gliding level until it settles and runs on the wheels only. In this case the tail is kept up, which keeps the machine from bouncing. [Rough terrain and that belligerent bungee could bounce a Jenny over a barn no matter what kind of landing was made.] Care must be taken not to let the tail drop until flying speed is entirely lost, as it is very easy to glide into the air again and then fall to the ground with a thud.

Getting off the Ground

In taking the JN-4 off the ground, great caution is necessary. It must be kept straight from the start or trouble will follow. There are two factors which tend to turn the JN-4 to the left. First, it being a right-hand tractor, the motor torque presses down on the left wing and wheel causing a greater resistance on this side. Second, the rudder being above the line of the propeller shaft gets more blast from the left. At the same time the tail skid is digging into the ground so that the tail does not respond readily to the rudder as it does when the skid is clear of the ground. Hence, the student must be on his guard to prevent turning. A good precaution is to start out with the rudder bar a little to the right and the wheel [when Deperdussin controls were used; or *stick* when this type was installed] banked a little as if for a right-hand bank. This will offset the turning tendencies. The student will also notice that as speed is gained, the rudder seems to become more and more alive [like a snake] under his feet.

Suggestions as to Air Conditions

There are in circulation a number of rules and notions as to the proper way to maneuver when *puffs* and *bad air currents* are encountered, but these are very likely to be misleading as few people really know much about the inner workings of the atmosphere [according to pilots, meteorologists still don't know what they're doing].

There are some points, though, which are well enough understood to be dealt with here. One bit of advice always holds good and that is: "Do not fight the wind any more than you have to." [This must have been added to the manual by Don Quixote.]

A machine will frequently get a boost, that is will rise rapidly for two or three seconds without any change in angle. This may be caused by air that is actually traveling upward; or by air that is traveling at a different velocity from that out of which the machine has

Above
A formation flight of cadets near Payne Field, West Point, Miss., in a diamond pattern. August 10, 1918. (U.S. Signal Corps)

Above right
2nd Lieutenants William V. Macurdy and Albert R. Meyers, flying this Canuck, No. 440, left Barron Field, Texas, at 10:30 A.M., November 14, 1918, to make a time-of-flight test with a full tank of fuel. They crashed at Handley, Texas, approximately 12 miles east of Barron Field at 12:10 P.M. Both officers were killed. The cause of the crash was never determined. (U.S. Air Force)

Below right
Jenny's burdens knew no end, and here we see two mechanics "bombing-up" a JN-4D. What was lacking in caliber was made up for in enthusiasm and optimism. A crude bombsight, consisting mainly of a sighting bar, provided rudimentary practice in bomb dropping. (U.S. Signal Corps)

just passed, causing a momentary greater velocity of the machine with respect to the air. [The holes in this reasoning are readily apparent.] The machine will also rise when passing into colder air [colder air is usually descending unless it is being underridden by an air mass]. In any of those cases, there is no cause for anxiety [if you were numb-minded enough to ignore dangerous downdrafts, or sinkers, on the lee sides of mountains which have fatally trapped many light low-powered airplanes].

Exactly the reverse will cause the airplane to drop rapidly. This is rather an uncomfortable feeling at first, but one gets used to it and the machine is perfectly safe. There is no necessity for heading down, or anything like that. On this account though, it is never safe to pass over any object with only a small margin of clearance, as one may be dropped directly onto something. When an airplane passes into the hot smoke of a chimney, it will drop with great suddenness, although the column may be rising rapidly. Then it is no longer air but a mixture of light gases of very poor supporting power. So do not try to take the lightning rods off any chimneys.

Some people fancy that when they are flying into the wind and wish to lead around so the wind is behind them, that they must make a wide turn and give themselves time to pick up velocity. [Nothing could have been farther from fact.] They get this impression from the fact that when heading into the wind they are going slowly over the ground and when they turn around they will be going very rapidly with respect to the earth.

As a general rule, the stronger the wind the more numerous and the stronger the internal movements in it and the more we will notice the difference between flying into the wind and with it behind. [Not so.]

Above
Denton Field, Texas, August 19, 1918. "Well, Colonel, sir—you see— it was like this. That clown in the other Jenny wasn't looking where he was going. I tried to take evasive action, but the ! #@%$ ° came aboard me. . . ." "The INFANTRY??????!!!!!!—Oh no!—anything but THAT!" (U.S. Signal Corps)
Below
A line of Hisso Jennys (JN-4H) getting a runup prior to the day's operations. Note mechanic standing by tail of each plane. His job was to bear down on top of fuselage to prevent the tail from rising when the engine was run up to full power for a checkout. When this happened, and it often did, if the crew wasn't alert, the propeller bit into the ground and shattered. Anti-ground-loop skids can be seen under the near wing tip. (U.S. Signal Corps)

It is generally stated that a machine will climb better when headed into the wind. This is more often true than not. [The inaccuracy of this is apparent to the greenest novice.] But there are times when the machine will climb better with the wind on its tail. [Same misconception as climbing "upwind."] Do not get the idea that you cannot climb unless headed into the wind or you will often go to unnecessary trouble.

When flying within a few feet of the water with the wind on the tail in winds of 30 mp or better it will be very difficult and sometimes impossible to climb. [Untrue.] This condition is caused by the rolling motion imparted to the air by its friction against the water. This rolling motion increases with the velocity of the wind and may be a source of great danger. It is easily avoided, however, by keeping at least 50 feet and preferably higher above the water when the wind is behind. [The writer has routinely flown Navy patrol, observation, torpedo, and training seaplanes from a foot up to ten feet off the water —while headed upwind, crosswind, downwind in velocities ranging from five to seventy mph with no unusual effects noted.]

It is not well to keep a machine climbing at its maximum angle when in a strong, puffy wind because it has little reserve speed then and if the angle is suddenly increased by a puff, the machine will be in a bad position to combat a second puff if such should be encountered. [Things were certainly touch and go—touch the wrong angle and away you go.] The same reasoning holds good when making a sharp turn in a steep bank. The machine is more easily put into a dangerous position. These warnings are only of importance while still near the ground—say within 1,000 feet. After good altitude has been attained, and there is plenty of room to straighten out, many precautions can be neglected by the skillful pilot.

Not the least important feature of flight is strategy. You will be well repaid for looking ahead and avoiding complicated situations. It is much better to keep out of trouble than to be clever at getting out of it. [No lieutenant who has made general will go along with this.]

When flying in bad country, study local conditions and map out your flight in your mind so as to keep within reach of good landing grounds. Look far ahead, and also look behind. [This is contrary to the advice from that ancient relic of a baseball pitcher, Satchel Paige, who said: "Don't never look back; Something might be gaining on yuh."]

Although they are not described in any of the quoted manuals, it would be an inexcusable omission not to mention Jenny acrobatics. Even the most astute who had been flying much-faster and infinitely more-agile combat airplanes found it advantageous to perfect acrobatics in a Jenny, since she depended to a much greater extent upon airplane-pilot rapport than was true of other types.

Remember, parachutes were not in vogue then, so if you didn't give a damn, you could make loops, snap-rolls, Immelmanns, wingovers, chandelles, bunts, and spins—but on Jenny's terms. There were stock acrobatics, done in other airplanes, and there were Jenny acrobatics. Never were the twain alike.

Getting Jenny through a snap maneuver was a wishing game and much depended upon a buildup of the right amount of speed in the correct angle of dive and then executing the maneuver precisely as Jenny dictated. If this wasn't done, things turned into a big "whoosh." If the speed was too high, she'd slide and slither; if too low, she'd shudder, stall, and spin. Many a pilot gave up before he got the word on Jenny's stunting whims; yet some of the *artistes* of the trade could get her to cavort with an idling engine—the *pièce de résistance* of Jennying.

It is a remarkable tribute to Jenny's staunchness that these stressful maneuvers could be performed with her and that the records of Canadian and American training fields show incredibly few instances of structural failure. Today, despite fifty-three years of perfecting aerodynamics, design, materials, and stress analysis, virtually all types of airplanes currently used in student training are restricted from acrobatics. Try a snap-roll in one and you would be so encased in wrinkled aluminum that it would be simpler to bury the whole shebang.

No compendium on Jenny flying manuals would be complete without concluding it with an over-riding apothegm which was brought to student attention on every possible occasion and which was the best friend a cadet could have, not excluding his mother: "Keep the wires huming and keep out of a stall and spin. If the wires don't sing to you, the angels will."

Jenny's stubborn surmise that even without human help she could overcome everything by herself might not have been a tribute to her judgment, but it certainly produced nimble Jenny neophytes who may be excused for believing they had everything going aginst them—like crawling the wrong way on a porcupine.

Left

Not exactly bristling with armament, but nonetheless this armed Jenny is on a gunnery training flight. The twin machine-guns attached to the Scarff mount in the rear cockpit are trained to starboard. The pennants tied to each outboard strut were intended to warn other aircraft that ammunition would be flying unreliably in diverse directions. (U.S. Signal Corps)

Above

Gunnery practice with a Lewis flexible-mount machine gun at Kelly Field in May, 1918. These weapons were notorious for jamming and for a bag of surprises that sometimes made them almost as dangerous for the one firing as for the one fired at. When the author was a pilot in Navy squadron VO-4B and during a gunnery training flight, he was rear-cockpit gunner for "Spiv" Cunningham, later Admiral, who commanded Wake Island when it was captured and who wrote the revealing book Wake Island Command. While coming up the range, a warm-up burst jammed the gun; the author cleared it, and as Cunningham came abeam of the towed target sleeve, he opened up—but the charging handle hadn't been properly secured, and with the first burst, the handle hit him on the chin and knocked him cold into the bottom of the cockpit, much to the consternation of Cunningham, who thought his gunner pilot had fallen overboard. (U.S. Signal Corps)

Despite its livelier moments, flight instructing has never been fraught with the dangers attributed to it in movies and on the boob tube. In fact, the ratio of fatal and injury-causing accidents to total instructing hours flown has always been small since the airplane's advent. This has not been due and is not now due to instructors' being super-pilots; it is because a little voice in the back of their head keeps repeating: "Watch what you're doing; this organism at the controls is out to kill you."

Right
August 10, 1918. Nearing graduation, these cadets at Payne Field, West Point, Miss., are doing an excellent job of formation flying. This is especially true in view of their having only forty to sixty hours of flying by the time they received their wings. (U.S. Signal Corps)

Below
This is how Kelly Field looked in May, 1918. Cadets are waiting for instructors to come in from flights, and mechanics are standing by to take care of trouble-shooting. Note frame and chain fall on truck for crash retrieval. (U.S. Signal Corps)

However, instructing has always had unique surprises—some due to the antagonisms of nature's terrain and elements; some due to the machinations of the more evil species of gremlin, who are wont to stick their fingers into carburetor jets, drink up one's hydraulic fluid, or disrupt lift by running around on the wings with their suction-cup feet. But some of the most-hyperbollixed occurrences are traceable to cockpit trouble.

The latter was a feature of an incident at Kelly Field that almost sent an instructor * and his cadet to a noodle knocker's couch.

The point had been reached in the youth's training and in this particular flight for the instructor to use some dramatic means to get the lad over a hump of self-doubt. If successful, he would solo. If not, he was headed for the "Benzine Board" which created ex-aviators out of aspirants who got "downs" on check flights.

Fancying himself somewhat of a psychologist (although he couldn't spell it) and a practitioner of shock treatment in accom-

* This instructor, years later, became a close friend of the writer, who flew with him many times throughout Montana. "Shorty" took Lindbergh on his first barnstorming-parachuting tour. He was killed during the thirties in a bad-weather crash with the son of the late Senator W. A. Clark of Montana.

plishing his ends, the instructor, while cruising Jenny at four thousand feet, ducked below the cockpit rim and emerged holding up his control stick to indicate that Jenny was completely in the hands of the cadet, then threw it over the side and yelled: "She's all yours. Take her home."

The cadet nodded, gave a jerk and threw his own stick away. Things were now even—nobody had any elevator or aileron control, both a little more than essential to "taking her home" or anywhere else.

It was now time for both of them to have a stroke because each discovered simultaneously that things had not gone according to plan. The spare stick the instructor had hidden forward of his instrument panel was gone. The student had thought it was there because he had heard of this trick.

The pair began a frenzied and profane search of the two cockpits for some means of actuating the stick socket in preference to a scattered demise. Then Jenny flew into some "active" air and began to pitch and buck. This was step one to disaster. Step two was the finality of the discovery that there was nothing aboard that could be pried or broken loose to be used to save their lives.

They were about to say their goodbyes when the instructor whirled around and hollered: "Alf" (this was short for Alfred and its use was the first time military propriety had been breached with familiarity), "I gotta idea."

It must be explained that this instructor was not an Army officer; he was a civilian contract pilot and if his diction was not de rigueur he shouldn't be criticized because he had booted school in 4-B.

"Now, Alf," he shouted, "Don't argue. I ain't got no rank, but don't argue. This here's th' only thing that's gonna save our butts, so you gotta do just like I say or we won't live through this experience. I'd do it myself," he said placatingly, "but you don't fly so good."

After the stick-tossing gambit Alf was skeptical but he listened because almost anything was preferable to the inevitable squashing and splashing waiting below, and, besides, tension was making him airsick.

"Unbuckle yer belt, kneel on the seat facin' the tail," the man said. When Alf had complied, he continued: "Take yer fists an' bust two holes through the fabric on both sides of the turtle-back." As this was done, Alf had a feeling that something was being withheld. "Now," said the man in front, "face forward, hoist yer rump over the turtleback an' straddle it, reach through them holes you punched and hang on to them stringers."

"Like hell I will, you crazy bastard," Alf yelled back. "You're not going to . . ."

"Yer gonna get killed if you don't," was all the man said.

Alf gingerly did as he was bidden and straddled the fuselage just aft of his cockpit like he was riding a horse. He didn't dare look down, he'd upchuck if he did.

"Awright," said the instructor, "when I motion, you move forward or aft until I signal to stop. I'll take up the slack with the throttle, and by shiftin' yer weight back and forth it'll be like usin' the elevators if nothin' don't go wrong."

That last phrase shafted Alf and he tried to swear at him but the dirty words froze into hard lumps in his gullet. He felt like he'd fire ice cubes if he burped.

"When you move," admonished the coach, "don't get yer balls hung up in them stringers." He wasn't as interested in Alf's future procreation as he was in the danger that an accident of this magnitude might startle him so much he'd fall off and ruin the survival plan.

Up ahead, a captain flying a routine air inspection patrol believed he saw something peculiar about a Jenny silhouette so he turned to an intercepting heading and when he came alongside and saw Alf straddling the turtleback he went into a rage of swearing and motioning him to get to hell back where he belonged. The longer Alf and the instructor gestured to explain that this was impracticable, the more furious the captain became. He took Jenny's number, turned back to the field, and when he got to headquarters, ordered the arrest of those [profane] morons as soon as they had landed. "Turn my outfit into a [profane] circus, will they . . . the [profane] idiotic clowns. I'll send them both to the infantry." This was tantamount to consignment to military purgatory.

Meanwhile, up on the ranch, the instructor and his upstairs cowboy were progressing: not happily, none too safely, but breathing. By skidding Jenny left or right with the rudder a low wing could be brought level; drills in synchronizing the opening and closing of the throttle with Alf's fore and aft movements to raise or lower the nose had developed a degree of elevator competence, but had cost them two thousand feet of altitude. Yet somehow the descent seemed to reassure Alf, who feared the ground less when he could see it plainer.

It didn't take long to get within gliding distance of the main field and the moment of truth.

"This here's where we're goin'," said the instructor superfluously. "I'm gonna cut the gun and fer keeerist's sake, move yer butt when I signal, an' move it fast. Watch them balls. Hang on. Here we go."

The glide per se, although undulating, was uneventful except that, as the ground came up, had Alf been more than a robust twenty years old he would have died of stress.

Signals came from up front in a steady succession that taxed Alf's agility as he clawed his way in the direction ordered as fast as he could scramble. Now he was being waved aft for the leveling-off and skim to a landing. But, in his eagerness to do good work, he moved aft a little too fast and far. They were close enough to a stall that Jenny didn't balloon, but her tail skid hit the ground first, cocking and firing the bungee. As the tail flew up, the nose flew down, and when the wheels hit the bungee on the main gear shot back and the recoil zoomed the nose skyward.

Alf was pulling leather for all he was worth and had his hands as full of "them there turtleback stringers" as he could get them, but Jenny was bucking so hard they came out by the roots. This is where Alf left matters vertically, and he said later that on the way up his thoughts were: "This is going to hurt."

The instructor and Jenny went on to a clean compromise and Alf reached the infirmary as fast as the Model-T ambulance could tool it. There were no broken bones, but he did have a few yards of skid burns and a flap of his scalp was unhinged, with a dollar-sized piece missing. The doctors didn't find out what caused this, nor did they find the missing hide and hair. It was a mech who told them what happened because he found Alf's hairpiece imbedded in the leading edge of the horizontal stabilizer, which creased him behind the ears when Jenny unhorsed and ran over him.

CHAPTER TEN

Maintaining the Military Tractor

Manuals for daily inspection of Jenny and her OX-5 engine; maintenance and rigging instructions.

Those gilt-edged insurance policies, the daily and preflight inspections, had to find their way out of the thickets of ignorance as did those who designed, built, and flew Jenny. However, when she passed out of military service and into the postwar "happy-hot-dog" maelstrom, these amenities were largely neglected.

Pilots flew a JN-4D until something malfunctioned or broke. If the problem was the former, perhaps a successful pass at a pasture took care of matters. If it was the latter, and particularly if the thing that broke was a spar, longeron, or strut, the undertakers regretted the customer's shortsightedness, but welcomed his business.

Today's preflight inspection would bolster the confidence of the most reluctant "geese"—the irreverent pseudonym flight crews use to designate passengers. For example, prior to the captain's and crew's reporting aboard a Boeing 707, the flight engineer has spent a rigorous hour and a half suspiciously regarding some 140 points on the exterior of the aircraft.

When the pilots enter the cockpit they begin a twenty-five-minute preflight of eighty-three items prior to starting the engines. In this they are assisted by the flight engineer, who is an eager participant because his union is striving to keep him in the cockpit whether he is needed or not because it makes j-o-b-s, and jobs mean d-u-e-s.

157

If the average male were as meticulous before flying into matrimony as a flight crew is in checking out an airplane's parts, there probably would be fewer marital groundloops, overshoots, and undershoots.

Now contrast today's computer-oriented inspection procedures with the hopeful once-over-lightly of Jenny's days, when there were fewer parts in her whole structure, plus those in the OX-5, than there are in the landing gear alone of a 707. The material that follows is taken from *The Curtiss Standard JN-4D Military Tractor Handbook, 1918.*

IMPORTANT HINTS

1. Remember: "A stitch in time saves nine."
   [This was a medical department slogan.]
2. Always inspect the motor thoroughly before starting.
   [Why? Everything that broke was inside where you couldn't see it.]
3. Always have plenty of oil, water and gasoline before trying to start. All three are vital.
4. See that the radiator is full of water before starting.
   [Be careful when you do a loop, or it will leak out and scald you.]
5. Keep oil and gasoline clean and free from water.
6. Oil all exposed working parts daily.

Above
Ooops! Another engine failure and an overshoot. Accuracy landings under power failure have always been a problem—and were more so during World War I when flying techniques had not reached their height of perfection. Oddly enough, many cadets sustained more injuries in their haste to get out of the cockpit on these flips than in the impact. Fire was an ever-present hazard, and a student's first impulse was to trip his safety belt and get to hell out of there—usually with a badly wrenched neck from landing on his head. (U.S. Signal Corps)
Below
If a carburetor became flooded while one was trying to start a balky OX-5, the latter would invariably backfire when it "took." If the fates were meddlesome on that day, the speed with which you could jump out and run usually determined whether or not you got singed, because the chances of Jenny's catching on fire were very favorable. This is what happened to one at Love Field, Dallas, Texas, in August, 1918. (U.S. Signal Corps)

7. Be sure to retard magneto before starting; otherwise a serious accident may result.
   [Like being brained by the propeller.]
8. Turn on switch before trying to start.
9. Start the motor with the throttle only part way open.
   [If you don't want to process a mech with the propeller.]
10. Run the motor idle for only short periods; it is wasteful and harmful to run idle too long.
11. Watch the lubrication constantly, it is most essential.
12. Remember that the propeller is the business end of the motor; treat it with profound respect when it is in motion.
    [Otherwise it could be as bad as being with Custer when he had all that trouble.]
13. When the motor is hot allow it to idle a few minutes at low speed before turning off the switch. This insures the forced circulation of the cooling water until the cylinder walls have cooled considerably and also allows the valves to cool, preventing possible warping.
14. Avoid that destructive disease known as "tinkeritis." When the motor is working satisfactorily, leave it alone.
    [It was better to make a buddy of it, because if it wouldn't run, you couldn't have it court-martialed and shot.]
15. Be sure to inspect daily all nuts and bolts. Keep them well tightened.
16. Stop the motor instantly upon detecting a knock, a grind, or other noise foreign to perfect operation. It may mean the difference between saving or ruining the motor.
    [It could also mean saving or ruining a cadet.]
17. Study this instruction book at least once a week.

JN-4D

MAINTENANCE PROCEDURES AND INSTRUCTIONS

Inspections: Pre-Flight, Post-Flight, Daily, Weekly

PRE-FLIGHT: Watch for signs of trouble. A steep spiral may cause strains on the engine bearers. A flight in wet weather may cause bending stresses on the longitudinal members of the body, shrink the bungee casing, besides stretching the lift and drag wires. [About the same effects as a woman going swimming in her brassière and girdle.]

CAREFULLY EXAMINE:

All struts and their sockets, longerons, etc.

All outside wires and their attachments.

All control levers or wheels, control wires, and cables, and their attachments. The control cables should not be too tight, otherwise they will be stiff in their guides.

The control lever should be set central in the airplane body, or in a conventional position—and should give a good range of up and down elevator. Pay special attention to control wires and cables where they pass over pulleys or through guides and to all split pins; pass fingers both ways over cables to see if there is any sign of fraying [and have a supply of Bandaids to patch yourself]. Keep the pulleys well lubricated with thick oil and the guides well greased. Lift the under-carriage cables and check the stretching.

Inspect all fabric for holes, cuts, weak or badly doped places, or for signs of damage by petrol or oil.

Check the following: outside turnbuckles to see they have sufficient threads engaged and are locked; axles, wheels, shock absorbers and tyres; seats to see that fastenings are correct; safety belts for attachments; all instruments and their fastenings.

DAILY EXAMINATION SHOULD BE CARRIED OUT SYSTEMATICALLY
IN THIS ORDER:

A. Lower wings, under-carriage complete, tail planes, with all wires attached to these, tail skids and all attachments and the rudder.
B. Nacelle, bolts of lower plane, all control levers and wires.
C. Top wings, wing flaps [he meant ailerons] and wires.

POST-FLIGHT INSPECTION: EXAMINE CAREFULLY:

A. All control wires belonging to the engine and all electrical connections, wires, switches. See that both switch and throttle stop the engine.
B. Petrol and oil tanks, pipes and gauges. See that copper pipes are not crystallized and rubber ones are not perished.
   [We were almost stuck with the word "petrol," but it didn't last. However, until World War II, an airplane's altitude indicator was called an "*Alti*-meter."] Came the British for training here and we tidied our diction with their pronunciation: "Al-*tim*-eter." This lingual tutoring extended beyond aircraft, inasmuch as pilots stationed in England report that British gals didn't care what they did to them as long as they pronounced it correctly.]

C. Pay particular attention to the connection of petrol and oil pipes to see that they are tight, and to cocks to see that they are in working order.

D. Examine airscrew thoroughly to see if it is correct and that nuts are tight.

E. Test pressure pump (if any) and fill top tank.

F. Check amount of oil and petrol in tanks, and fill.

EXAMINE INSTRUMENTS FOR WORKING ORDER: Check the following, if used:

A. Tachometer

B. Clinometer °

C. Banking indicator †

D. Incidence indicator ‡

E. Altimeter

F. Radiator thermometer

G. Air-speed indicator

H. Drift indicator

I. Stabilizer

J. Clock

K. Camera

L. Bomb sighting and dropping mechanism

Standard equipment consisted of these devices: Tachometer, altimeter, radiator thermometer—with an infrequent airspeed indicator.

SUPPLEMENTAL INSPECTION AND RIGGING INSTRUCTIONS FOR THE JN-4 AIRPLANE.

No good pilot starts a flight until he has tested his motor up to speed and knows that it will give him the necessary power. The failure to know everything is right may not only mean the life of the

° Used to gauge the degree of climb and descent.

† An outline of the airplane was set level with the machine and a white bar was connected to a pendulum inside the case. When the plane was banked, the pendulum flew to the outer side of the circle and swung to the white line out of the horizontal in proportion to the radius and speed of the turn. If the bank was correct, the white line and the outline of the plane were parallel as when the plane was in level flight. If the bank was not correct, the line and plane silhouette showed whether to increase or decrease it.

‡ Clark angle-of-incidence (angle-of-attack) indicator: Fastened to a strut between the wings so the pointer and scale could be seen by the pilot. The vane was so proportioned that it remained level when the plane was in motion.

Electrical connections ran to a graduated scale on the instrument panel. The dial contained three lamps: green, red, white. When flying level no light burned; when climbing, a green light showed when the proper climb angle for best efficiency was attained. If the climb was increased to the stalling point, the red lamp lit. Should the volplane (glide) become too steep and reach a dangerous speed, the white light came on.

Whenever a complete Jenny could be encompassed by one truck, it was a certainty that some pilot had made an error. This JN-4D came to the end of the trail at Carlstrom Field, Arcadia, Fla., on August 23, 1918. (U.S. Signal Corps)

pilot, but in military matters, the loss of valuable information and the death of hundreds of troops. [This was quite true. The fate of whole divisions often rested upon the ability of pilots to accurately assay and report enemy activity.]

There are usually two mechanics assigned to each machine, one for the engine and propeller, the other for the plane and all its connections. The English call the first the Fitter and the latter the Rigger; we substitute Machinist for Fitter and retain Rigger, or plane-man for the other.

The Machinists or Fitter should thoroughly understand internal-combustion motor construction and repair, and of as many types of motor as possible. Each has its peculiarities and should be studied so as to best know how to handle it. This is particularly true of the rotary types such as the Gnome or Rhône. We have comparatively few of these in this country but their peculiarities should be known [like, don't breathe while you fill the crankcase with castor oil unless you are constipated, and for the same reason don't be downwind when

Above
Two Jennys defy gravity and each other on December 5, 1918, over a California training field. (U.S. Air Force)
Right
Jenny never seemed to become thoroughly convinced that telephone poles were here before she came and were likely to remain after she was gone. She tried her luck against this one and lost when the OX-5 died and the cadet pilot made a slipup in alignment. This embroglio took place at Osborne, Ohio, in 1917. (U.S. Signal Corps)

one is warming up], as well as how to take them down for examination and repair, and to reassemble them, for this is quite an intricate task on some of the motors of this type. The parts must go together in a certain sequence or they will not go at all, as in a Japanese puzzle. [If this naïveté puzzles the reader, remember that in these times things aeronautical were about as puzzling to most people as was that lady Adam ran into in the orchard.] Although modern airplane framework is apparently a simple arrangement of wood and wire, it will be found to contain many lessons in mechanical structures and is well worth study.

The struts, as in all built-up structures, serve to hold the framework apart and in the proper position. They are always in compression and must be held firmly but not too tight as to spring the struts out of line as they can resist very little after they are bent, but continue to bend and break under a comparatively light load.

The tension of the rigging wires is very important not only as to amount but as to uniformity, and this is one of the fine points. With these wires too tight, an undue strain is put on the strut and also on

the wire, reducing the factor of safety. With unequal tension, unequal stresses are imposed on various parts of the frame and accidents are apt to occur. For even if the strut does not break but is bent out of shape, this throws undue stresses on certain parts, shortens the distance between the surfaces it separates and otherwise disturbs the general layout of the machine.

The adjustment of the control cables is quite an art. Tension up the control cables so that when the levers are smartly moved there is no perceptible snatch or lag. Be careful not to tension up the cables more than necessary to take out the snatch.

Three OX-5-powered, and one Hisso-engined Jenny get a tuneup at Baker Field, Calif., flight-training school; an ideal primary field. 1918. (U.S. Air Force)

CHAPTER ELEVEN

The "Canuck"

Canadians adopt Jenny as their standard trainer, modify it slightly and name it the "Canuck." Winter flight-training problems. "Canuck" specifications.

Jenny's shining hours were legion in those troubled years between the mating of her J and N parents in 1914 and the close of World War I. And her star gained new luster in Canada (1917–18), where she became the aerial backbone of as gallant a group of air warriors as ever rode the mucky skies of combat.

To understand better the tremendous need for Jenny at this time, one has to know a bit about the state of the conflict in Europe during the latter half of 1916 and early 1917.

From June through October, the Battle of the Somme wrote its saga of grief on the ground and in the air. British pilots were rushed from England with but a few hours of solo and utterly no gunnery practice, to challenge a seasoned and shrewd adversary. Most of these lads could barely fly trainers and their casualty rate ran as high as one-fourth per month. A fighter pilot who lived fifteen days was likely to become a hero and an ace because he had to be extraordinary to live that long.

In the early spring of 1916, the British air units in France had been increased to 30 squadrons—flying approximately 450 aircraft. But attrition was so severe it was almost impossible to keep units up to strength. While a pursuit plane could be built in a few days it took nineteen years to bring a boy up to the point of being a potential pilot.

The filling of the R.F.C. combat gap was made additionally difficult because now the corps could no longer draw from regimental officers for pilot material. They were needed for the coming offensive by which it was hoped to relieve the tremendous pressure on the French at Verdun—that horrible massacre ground made awesome by the "Butcher Generals" * who put tears even in the eyes of Mars and which triggered the *Poilu* mutinies of 1917. Tragic, tortured Verdun, where today a man can't dig five feet down without uncovering bits of skeletons; where a magnetic compass is worthless because the subsurface is so layered with shattered weapons and the countless other shards of steel that make up the flotsam and jetsam of battle.

When the British doubled their air strength during the three weeks preceding the Allied Somme offensive, they depleted their last source of pilot material.

Until now there had not been a Canadian air force; but suddenly there had to be one because Canada alone possessed a reservoir of potential aviators.

Authority for the Royal Flying Corps, Canada, was given at a meeting held at the headquarters of the British Munitions Board, Adastral House, London, on December 21, 1916. All requisites were set in motion: recruiting offices were opened throughout the Dominion, one large air park was authorized for immediate construction, tables of organization were drafted for training squadrons.

Into the breach flew Jenny; deliveries commenced as fast as orders were telegraphed to the Curtiss plant at Buffalo. It was planned to start with a cadre of three hundred JN-3s. They would form a nucleus for a program which would provide pilots with primary flight training only. All advanced air instruction would be given in Great Britain and France along with the final stages of pre-combat flying.

The R.F.C. officers who were responsible for executing the flight program initially favored the adoption of the De Havilland D.H. 6 primary trainer because they were familiar with it and because it was adaptable to two engine types. They could not, of course, foresee that the JN-3 could and did mount an incredible assortment of a half-dozen engines spanning from 90 to 300 hp.

* 410,000 French casualties in less than four months under Generals Herr, Joffre, Pétain, Nivelle.

This is the Canuck, modified slightly from the U.S. JN-4D; however, changes were evident only to those who knew the details of the JN-4D very well. The most apparent divergence was the V-shaped pair of aileron-control struts seen at the wing tips of the Canuck. On the JN-4D the ailerons were controlled by cables. This Canuck is using a torpedo-shaped auxiliary fuel tank mounted on the center section. It increased the flight range by approximately one hour. (National Aviation Museum, Ottawa, Canada)

These men realized, however, that to get the training off to an immediate start it would be necessary to settle on the OX-5, JN-3. One of the reasons for this was that there was in operation in Toronto a small Curtiss Aeroplane and Motor Co. plant which had tooling for the JN-3. These attributes eliminated the D.H. 6.

A few structural changes in the Jenny were to be made by Canadian Aeroplanes, Ltd., under the direction of Chief Engineer F. G. Ericson. His organization ultimately reached a production peak of 120 planes a month, had a crew of 2,000, and, within 21 months from start to finish, built 2,900 Jennys valued at $14,000,000. Six hundred and eighty of them were sent here for use in Canadian and U.S. flight schools in Texas.

With Canada under deep snow, on January 26, 1917, work was begun on 15 flight sheds and other buildings for the Borden training airdrome located 70 miles north of Toronto.

During the last week of January, 1917, preparations for additional flight-training fields were begun under forced draft at Leaside, three miles north of Toronto; Armour Heights, four miles farther north; Rathbun and Mohawk, 130 miles east of Toronto.

The modified JN-3 was termed the JN-4 by the Canadians, which started one of the initial snafus of which aviation has always had a plethora. The designation clashed with that of the differently altered JN-3 built in America by Curtiss and also labeled the JN-4. The impasse was soon resolved by the oral dexterity of which aviation has also had a super abundance, when someone simply dubbed the Canadian craft the Canuck—and this stuck for all time.

The modifications which went into the Canuck involved a slight amount of skeletal and cosmetic surgery and some tinkering with the nervous system by which she was controlled. In this, ailerons were applied to the lower wings as well as to the upper. The Deperdussin controls were eliminated in favor of the stick type in both cockpits. There was a modification to the landing gear. The split trailing edge was substituted for the flattened-tubing type in the wings.

The greatest initial changes were made to the empennage. For the Curtiss wood framework, the Canadians substituted one of steel tubing but continued to cover this with fabric.

The wing spars were made of short lengths of Sitka spruce spliced with a serrated joint to provide a maximum glued surface. The one difference in wing construction was that stabilization of the former ribs was achieved by running a softwood dowel on the top and bottom of each rib between the spars.

The fuselage had ash longerons, each made up of two pieces with a glued, riveted, and wrapped splice in the bay just aft of the rear cockpit. The transverse and vertical fuselage members used both spruce and ash. Engine and cockpit cowling were of aluminum painted dark green.

The four landing-gear struts were made of Sitka spruce and shock absorption was by the conventional bungee, which secured

Above
Formation-flying training in Canucks over Canada. An unusually good photo for those times, 1918. (National Aviation Museum, Ottawa, Canada)
Below
A row of angel makers on a flight line at a Texas training field, 1918. (National Aviation Museum, Ottawa, Canada)

Canuck equipped with skis. It is believed that this was the first time aircraft were operated with this equipment. These craft were changed from wheels to skis whenever snow became too deep for regular operations. The installation was developed by the 44th Wing, R.F.C., and Canadian Aeroplanes, Ltd. The photo was taken at Leaside flight school. (National Aviation Museum, Ottawa, Canada)

the axle to the joining piece at the intersection of the main members. The joining piece was originally of laminated oak, but was replaced by an aluminum casting.

In only one respect did our Canadian friends jump the track in their zeal to "customize" Jenny, and this was when some katzenjammer board put the throttle on the right-hand side of the cockpit and the ignition switch on the aft side of the throttle-lever bracket. This latter arrangement did not make much difference, but the throttle placement did because either one had to fly with his left hand to use the right-hand throttle—or do some precarious hand shifting and crossing over at critical points in a takeoff, a landing, or when doing acrobatics.

Coverings for wings, fuselage, and empennage had always been made of linen, but German submarines were making it virtually impossible to obtain this from Ireland, which was the principal source of supply. However, it was learned that the Wabasso Cotton Co. mills in Three Rivers, Quebec, could produce cotton which, with two coats of nitrate dope, had such remarkable strength that it served admirably for Jenny's clothing.

The most commonly used auxiliary fuel tank was this one shown mounted on the center section of the Canuck's top wing. This provided from one and a half to one and three-fourths hours of additional cruising fuel. The lower wing has been cut away at the root next to the fuselage to provide for camera installation and aerial photography. (National Aviation Museum, Ottawa, Canada)

A distinctive Canuck method of securing the fuselage fabric was developed along about aircraft serial No. C 490 and was incorporated into earlier models. This consisted of lacing the fabric to the metal cowling and to a metal strip attached to the top longerons of the fuselage aft of the rear cockpit. This method was quite different from that used on British and American Jennys. It permitted a quick opening of the fuselage for maintenance or repair without cutting the fabric. Also, it had the advantage of eliminating hundreds of tacks formerly used to fasten the fabric to the longerons with each opening.

The prototype of the Canuck had small cockpits and no windshield, like the Curtiss JN-3. However, windshields were added early in the production program. The rear cockpit, from which cadets flew, was indented at the forward edge and padded to eliminate a hazard which had broken many scores of noses in minor accidents. Also, in the initial stages, the new undercarriage was added.

The top and bottom-wing ailerons were interconnected by a pair of parallel spruce struts which made a V when seen from the

front, due to having two fittings on the upper aileron and termi-
nating in a single fitting at the bottom aileron.

Most metal parts were copper-plated and covered with black
enamel. The control system and important small fittings received
a nickel-plate coat over the copper and were left unpainted. Copper rivets were generally used in the aluminum cowling. Wing
structures received a coat of sealer and the fuselage framework
was treated with spar varnish.

Jenny's propellers owed a debt to Peter the Great, Czar of
Russia. Little did either know, when in 1698 he perfected a lathe
for simultaneously making identical and multiple gun stocks, that
his almost-human machine would be modified two centuries later
by finger-wise Canadian mechanics to build Jenny's propellers.

This successor to Peter's ingenuity carved the five-ply white
oak laminated and glued blades four at a time to 1/32 inch of their
finished form. The final dressing and balancing were done by
hand. While these 8-foot 3-inch airscrews were being spun by the
OX-5 at 1,400 rpm hub speed, their tips were traveling at the
rate of 480 mph. It was a tribute to Peter and the Canadians that
the blades stayed together.

The prototype of the Canadian JN-4 was test flown at the old
Curtiss Aerodrome at Long Branch, Ontario, early in March,
1917. Its pilot, who had previously been employed by the Curtiss
school and who came north especially for this task, was Bert
Acosta, an American who subsequently carved out an illustrious
flying career. He was born on January 1, 1895, flew with Admiral
Byrd in the latter's transatlantic flight in 1927, died September 1,
1954, and is buried in Valhalla Cemetery, Portal of the Folded
Wings, Burbank, California.

To fill the demand for spares, the equivalent of one hundred
JN-4As were bought from the United States. There were more
fuselages than complete sets of wings and tails. Consequently, a
large number of U.S. fuselages were mated with Canuck wings to
produce slightly illegitimate Canadian JN-4–JN-4A combinations. Although Jenny thought they might be trying at times to
make her white corpuscles swim upstream, she took whatever
they hung onto her, and, given a tail at the rear and an OX-5 up
front, made the best of her problems.

During the winter of 1917–18, the R.F.C. moved to Texas to

The Canuck, like her sister, Jenny, not only clobbered them, but also saved them. Here is a Canuck fitted with a hinged turtleback which could be opened to take aboard a stretcher case. Many Canadian casualties regained consciousness while tucked in here en route to medical aid, and added nervous fits to whatever the plane had already done to them. (National Aviation Museum, Ottawa, Canada)

escape the worst parts of the Canadian weather, which, it was realized, would stop training for substantial intervals.

The 4th Wing was left behind at Leaside to experiment with winter flying. Wing engineers and mechanics, in conjunction with personnel at Canadian Aeroplanes, Ltd., developed skis for Jenny and she took to them like a Sourdough. So far as is known these were the first such operations.

In the winter, all petrol, oil, and water were drained at the end of the day's flying. The latter two were heated before being replaced at the start of the day. Radiators were covered over three-fourths of their surface with beaverboard lined with felt and this prevented the water from freezing in flight. Water connections were lagged with felt and fabric for insulation; and the oil line and gauge were removed from the rear cockpit to shorten the piping, which was led between the cylinders for maximum warmth.

The tail skid was enclosed with canvas where it protruded

from the fuselage to prevent snow from accumulating there due to the propeller blast on takeoff.

Rigging inspection was particularly detailed because extreme cold could set up undue stresses in tension members, but Jenny seemed born for the duty and the records do not show any accidents attributable to structural failure from this source.

Despite freezing temperatures and deep snow, flight operations were carried on under full schedules for twenty-six days in January; twenty-one in February; and twenty-five in March, 1918. Al-

CANADIAN JN–4 (THE CANUCK)

SPECIFICATIONS

Engine:	Curtis OX–5, 90 hp	
Dimensions:	Span, upper	43 feet 7⅜ inches
	lower	34 feet 8⁵⁄₁₆ inches
	Chord	59½ inches
	Gap	5 feet 2½ inches
	Stagger	10⅜ inches
	Dihedral	1 deg.
	Incidence	2 deg. 22 inches
	Tailplane span	9 feet 8⅝ inches
	Length	27 feet 2½ inches
	Track	5 feet 3¹¹⁄₁₆ inches
	Propeller diameter	8 feet 3 inches
Areas:	Wing, upper	161.2 sq. ft.
	lower	131.98 sq. ft.
	Ailerons, upper	35.5 sq. ft.
	lower	21 sq. ft.
	Center section	10.95 sq. ft.
	Vertical fin	2.48 sq. ft.
	Rudder	10.179 sq. ft.
	Horizontal stabilizer	23.72 sq. ft.
	Elevators	17.44 sq. ft.
Fuel capacity:		20 U.S. gal.
Performance:	Speed (maximum)	75 mph, approx.
	Cruise	60 mph, approx.
	Stall	45 mph, approx.
Loadings:		
	Power	21.3 lbs./hp
	Wing	6.5 lbs./sq. ft.

WEIGHT BREAKDOWN

		POUNDS	POUNDS
Power plant:	Engine, propeller, hub	435.00	
	Radiator and water	89.50	
	Piping, water	7.00	
	Piping, fuel	10.00	
			541.50
Fuel tank:			
Wings:	Upper (less sockets and wires)	124.00	
	Lower	94.00	
	Center section	12.50	
	Interplane struts	28.25	
	Wires and turnbuckles (interplane)	21.25	
	Interplane strut fittings	28.50	
	King posts	4.00	
	Wing skids	5.00	
	Ailerons	27.00	
			344.50
Fuselage:	Structure and covering	200.00	
	Controls	59.50	
	Tail skid	8.00	
	Instruments	21.50	
	Sundries	55.75	
			344.75
Undercarriage:	Struts, bracing, shock absorber	50.00	
	Wheels	42.00	
			92.00
Tailplane and elevators		37.00	
Fin and rudder		12.25	
			49.25
Fuel and oil:	Fuel, 20 gals. (U.S.)	124.00	
	Oil, 4 gals. (U.S.)	30.00	
			154.00
Crew			165.00
Passenger			165.00
Unaccounted for			44.00
TOTAL PERMISSIBLE GROSS WEIGHT:			1,920.00

though temperatures often fell to 35 degrees below freezing, instructors averaged two hours and twenty-five minutes a day in the air.

Many modifications were made in Jenny's fuselage and its appendages to fit her for the diverse training missions foisted upon her. She bore them all with remarkable fortitude and flew right along no matter what they did to her in the way of aerodynamic disruption or added weight.

An external mounting was added for a camera near the rear cockpit and, to prevent obstructing its field, a section was cut out of the lower wing's trailing edge.

For pilot combat training, a camera gun was mounted atop the center section. For actual firing practice, Vickers guns were installed and synchronized to fire between the propeller blades. One of these was on the left side of the fuselage.

The major modification, and the heaviest, was a Scarff ring installed over the rear cockpit and mounting a Lewis machine gun. This necessitated removing the aft flight controls to give the gunner mobility.

Although fitted for training to destroy, Jenny was also rigged to be merciful when her turtleback was hinged on one side so it could be opened to receive a stretcher case. Many a wounded man or training-crash victim would just as soon have died in peace in lieu of being subjected to this Jenny salvation, however, his relatives no doubt appreciated the gesture—and it may have lowered the casualty rates.

During 1918, while the war was still on, the Royal Air Force undertook several Jenny airmail flights in Canada. The first was made from Montreal to Toronto on July 24 with Captain B. A. Beck as pilot, accompanied by Corporal E. W. Mathers. In August and September a series of mail flights was made between Ottawa and Toronto by Lieutenants T. Longman, A. Dunston, and H. Burton.

On August 7, 1919, after an earlier failure, Captain E. C. Hoy took off in a Canuck from the Minoru Race Track on Lulu Island, Vancouver, at 4:13 A.M., and after flying all day with fueling and repair stops at Vernon, Grand Forks, Cranbrook, and Lethbridge, landed at Calgary at 8:55 P.M. to make the first aerial crossing of the hostile Canadian Rockies.

CHAPTER TWELVE

Combat Pilot Training

Canadian flight-training system and philosophy.

There is much recorded history covering the U.S. flight-training program in World War I. Also, the literature on Canada's activities is quite complete. However, little has been written about the close intertwining of the U.S. and Canadian systems both here and in Canada; they were, in fact, virtually one and indistinguishable. Each had its own program and then both had a much larger joint operation in which they practically lost their individual identities. Both trained their own pilots and each trained pilots for the other. For example, Canada trained several hundred of them for us at a cost of $9,660 apiece.

In earlier chapters we have detailed portions of the U.S. procedures and traced the evolution of the JN-3 into the Canuck; the next step will be to outline Canadian training methods and then join the two programs in Texas, in one of the most incredible and complex cooperative arrangements ever undertaken by two nations; and it was virtually trouble free.

Remember, this is not meant to be a history of either U.S. or Canadian flight training. It is a history of Jenny, and where Jenny went we will go.

By 1917, flight-training development in England had reached a point where elements recognized but not formerly analyzed were coming under study. The things learned from this new understanding were to be used in developing instinctive flying on the

part of a cadet. The objective was to create combat pilots, in contrast to peacetime pilots.

It was logical for the mother country to place at the Dominion's disposal all she had learned in the forced draft of war's necessities. From the British data, Canada formulated what she designated as the Armour Heights System, so-called because this was the location where details were worked out and instructors were trained in applying them.

One basic premise of the plan was that, since fear almost invariably arises from what is unknown, once the unknown is eliminated, fear should be nonexistent. This had to be whispered around Jenny, because she hated theoreticians as much as she hated overconfidence.

Training squadron of Canucks at Leaside, Ontario. (National Aviation Museum, Ottawa, Canada)

From time to time as the plan is quoted there will be irreverent interpolations by the writer, the victim of hundreds of hours of giving Navy and military flight instruction (some of it to Chinese who didn't understand English)—a victim of what often seemed like an endless coil of cadets wound around the equator waiting to get into an airplane with me and drive me nuts.

The Canadian instructor's manual began as follows:

The approach [to successful flight instruction] is by way of wiping out ignorance concerning the air and the machine, illustrating while in flight, the simplicity of those laws which are fundamental to all

Cadets, wearing overcoats, assist mechanics at a Canadian training field in fueling and inspecting a Canuck prior to flight. 1918. (National Aviation Museum, Ottawa, Canada)

good pilots and machines. [Jenny recognized but one law—gravity —Newton and the Canadians notwithstanding. What went up had to get back and it was only HOW that mattered.]

This, while simple enough, involves an ultimate strain in the Instructor [the first and last recorded recognition of this]. His pupils are limited to six, but into each he is expected to pour [beat] the sum of his knowledge and skill. He is personally responsible for their crashes. [In China I once had to pay for a cow killed by one of my students while he was practicing dive bombing.]

A crash by a pupil is due to an imperfection in training. At some stage in the course some indispensable point must have been overlooked or slighted. Hence the pupil's inability to meet the emergency.

Character, the subtle union of temperament and disposition, the increasing air sense, the delicacy of control, the spontaneous response, the nameless faculty by which the pupil becomes, as it were, welded to the machine [you were partners with Jenny like John the Baptist and Salome, or like your watch and Uncle Abe's hockshop] which in turn replies to the subconscious movement of hand and foot—the study of all these is in the Armour Heights System, which is based upon an admirable method originated at Gosport, England.

Nothing bearing the name of Gosport deserves anything but the roundest of curses. When the author was a student naval aviator at Pensacola, the hard-leather Gosport crash helmet was synonymous with a device used by the Spanish Inquisitors to shrink one's head, and the flex metal tubing attached to this as a speaking tube formed a communications system through which no one ever heard anything; it gave the instructor piles from trying to build up enough air pressure to get words through the tube to the cadet.)

The pupil is expected to do the flying, and even in an emergency the Instructor does not assume control until it is demonstrated that the pupil is literally out of his depth [or well under it and the Instructor with him].

And always [says the treatise] from the front seat the guiding voice encouraging [screaming]; reproving [pleading]; suggesting [threatening]; praising [swearing]; and probing [with a fire extinguisher]; the mental processes of the pupil.

Jenny might have said at this point: "What mental processes?" so convinced was she that those helmeted, scarved, and goggled mammals in the cockpit were only there to ruin her.

Here are a few of the most salient excerpts from a syllabus issued by the Air Ministry:

When a student makes a mistake in the air let him first exhaust his own ideas of how to put things right if height permits. [Jenny couldn't get that high and the instructor couldn't wait that long.]

Make it a point of honor to allow pupils full control except in an emergency. [Honor ended when Jenny stalled or exceeded 90 mph.]

Your greatest duty is to inspire your pupils with confidence in themselves, in their machines and you. [Winding up a class without them hating you was bonus enough.]

If the weather is too bad for instruction, you should fly yourself for the sake of the spirit it produces. [In those days, the spirit produced by such overtime flights would probably be your own and useful only for spooking empty hangars.]

Every time a pupil does something in the air he has never done before he increases his confidence.

This is arguable, like the time the writer was serving as a Navy check pilot, and when a cadet realized he had maneuvered himself into an impossible position from which to execute a simulated forced landing—the throttle was chopped—and he wet his pants. The writer is sure this didn't give Charlie more confidence in his ability to wet his pants.

To reduce it to a sentence, the system today turns out a pilot who is subdivided [Jenny was the best subdivider who ever divided a pilot; in fact, there were some who referred to her as "The Undertaker's Buddy"] so to speak into two sections. One is subjective and does the flying. The other is objective, free for pursuit or retreat, defense or attack, or any of the countless situations of aerial warfare which call for swift fearless action.

Jenny was a jump ahead of all of them, including this syllabus, in that she had declared war on the human race on the day B. Douglas Thomas and Glenn Curtiss nudged their two airplanes into becoming one. She never signed a truce—no matter what the

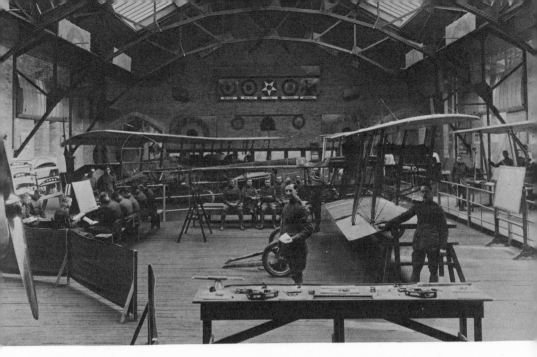

School of Aeronautics, University of Toronto, 1917. Note Allied and German airplane identification insignia on the upper portion of rear wall. Airplane at left with portion of nose in photo was an early combat model with a radial rotary engine. (National Aviation Museum, Ottawa, Canada)

Canadian government said. With her it was *huramentado* ° all the way.

By the summer of 1918 the Canadians had formulated procedures for crash investigation, with the objective of finding those key items which could be eliminated and consequently reduce accidents. Jenny was not cooperative. Whenever she was misflown by a skittish pilot, she rendered her own verdict. Yet she balanced the scales of retribution with a leavening of justice—and graven upon the consciousness of all who survived were her admonitions:

Raise not thy nose in a left turn after takeoff.

Chase not rabbits, nor livestock, nor birds, for they may smite thee grievously in the image of a tree, or a barn, or a wire.

° Moro fanatics in southern Philippine provinces believe that if they kill a Christian they will go to heaven. Periodically, one of them "gets the call" and goes *huramentado*, or berserk, with a double-edged kriss, a long rippled sword with which he will kill the first Christian he comes across.

Stall not below two thousand feet. Thy savior is altitude, prudence, and airspeed.

For I say unto thee verily, fail in my teachings and I shall rend thy butt into a hundred fragments.

CHAPTER THIRTEEN

Loaded Up with Gear

―――――――――

*Canadians impose many functions upon Jenny to enable her
to fulfill all training missions including wireless communications, gunnery, photography, and combat maneuvers.*

―――――――――

British and Canadian staffs had not overestimated the mettle of
Canadian youth. Toward the summer of 1917, cadets were applying for flight training at the rate of three hundred a month. This
soon rose to four hundred and then to five hundred, always exceed-
ing the capacities of the facilities.

No attempt will be made here to recount in detail the Canadian training system. It will merely be sketched enough for comparison with our own methods, so that later, when we go into
the merger of the incredible Texas program, its complexities will
be better understood. Furthermore, we are primarily interested in
Jenny's part. The following data are given to show the remarkable versatility of a remarkable aircraft which carried through effi-
ciently and valiantly despite those who called upon her to assume an always more important—and always more nearly
impossible—role.

Canadian enlistees were processed at a recruits' depot and
then sent to the cadet wing at Long Branch. In this establishment they were initiated into infantry drill and "buzzing," or
wireless code, in which they had to learn to transmit and receive
eight words per minute to qualify. This covered two weeks.

Next, candidates were assigned to flight centers and embarked
on what they had come for. In addition to flight instruction, they
also were taught aerial photography, gunnery, bombing, map
reading, formation, and cross-country flying.

This Primary syllabus was composed of: the instructor demonstrating the effect of the controls, flying straight and level, climbing, misuse of controls in turns, difference in controls with the engine on and off, gliding, stalling, spinning, slow flight, taking off, and landing.

After solo, these maneuvers were added: steep turns, climbing turns, side-slipping, crosswind takeoffs and landings, spot landings, forced landings and acrobatics.

In the advanced stage, the cadet would climb to six thousand feet and maneuver for fifteen minutes to note the decreased performance of Jenny and the OX-5 at that height. He would also essay flights through clouds, even though, as far as Jenny was concerned, all clouds were lined with flypaper. In this, the tyro used his compass for course indication, direction, and attitude, which was a precarious venture at best, as contemporary instrument-flying techniques demonstrate—or rather as is demonstrated by those who attempt instrument flying without being qualified to do so. Cemeteries are dotted with them, and, regrettably, with their friends and members of their families.

From the flight center the cadet was sent to Leaside, home of the Third Wing, where he received "tuition" in artillery cooperation. After ground indoctrination, the student took to the air to observe smoke puffs on target silhouettes, simulating artillery bursts. He then "wirelessed" their location to the receiving battery and directed its fire. He also reported the effects of barrage fire, located troops, hunted out barbed-wire barriers and directed scouting patrols.

If Jenny was confused by any of this, she never let on; plodding and plugging, hastening the end of the war by "damned well doing her bit for King and country" while the aces were gunsmoking each other in France, she went right on dishing up Spandau fodder—complaining little, but ever ready to clout the hapless. She was at all times a patriot, but she was also a believer

Right
Stunting over the hangar line at Camp Borden, Canadian flight-training field, 1918. Today the caption would probably read: "Bucking for a court-martial." This was a wild maneuver for a Canuck, evidently performed by someone with special skill, or who just didn't give a darn. (National Aviation Museum, Ottawa, Canada)

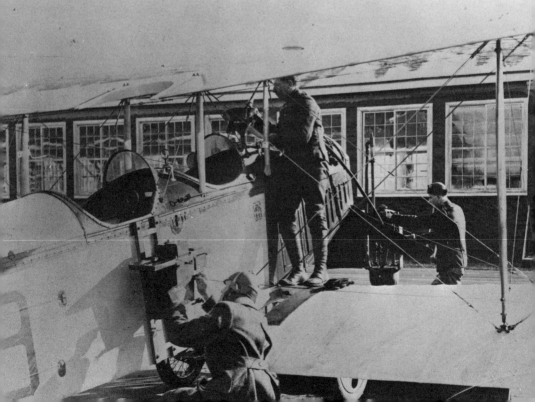

Left above
Side-mounted Vickers machine gun on a Canuck. Observer or student pilot in rear cockpit could reload and clear jams in flight. Gun created marked drag on side of airplane, and this, with the normal effects of engine-propeller torque, made it difficult for the pilot to hold a straight course. (*National Aviation Museum, Ottawa, Canada*)

Left
This is how aerial cameras were mounted on the starboard side of a Canuck's fuselage. They provided training for photographing enemy trench and artillery positions, supply dumps, and routes, and also aided in detecting significant changes in ground activity that might presage a buildup for an attack. (*National Aviation Museum, Ottawa, Canada*)

Above
One can't describe this Scarff-ring installation without being profane. The gun could be operated both horizontally and vertically. When a gunner became too engrossed in staying on the target, he often laid a burst alongside his pilot's ear. This did little for pilot-gunner rapport. The gunner was held in by a waist belt which needed considerable slack to provide mobility, and this was the worst thing imaginable if the pilot did a loop or an Immelmann in retaliation to one of those bursts alongside his ear. All the gunner could do was hang onto the spade grip of the gun for dear life, because if it got loose it would brain him. This also did nothing for pilot-gunner amicability. (*National Aviation Museum, Ottawa, Canada*)

in "finger-on-the-number," in remembering what the man said, in not corking off in a left turn, or running out of airspeed on an approach. Jenny did unto others as she was done by and to. Forget your manners and she ignored hers. The cadet was always the loser because there was always another Jenny, but his parents could not reproduce him; at least not in time for World War I.

How far Jenny was led from her original purposes by the mischief makers of World War I is a never-ending source of amazement to all who have flown her and contemporary aircraft.

With utter disdain for formulas and the warning howls of gales in wind tunnels, with contempt for all rules of common sense and an unhealthy disregard for the impossible, military people who ought to have known better and engineers who should have had the gumption to say, "Hell no," said, "Yes." As a consequence, Jenny was loaded with impedimenta she was never intended to have. For an airplane that would kill you for slightly raising her nose in a left turn after takeoff, she was expected to be docile after guns, cameras, ordnance racks, and what have you were riveted, bolted, and otherwise attached to her back, flanks, and belly. If she staggered under these impositions, the tinkerers ignored it and simply added a more powerful and consequently larger and heavier engine after elongating the fuselage, and let it go at that.

Little regard was paid to the effects on wing loading, on stabilities about the axes of pitch, roll, and yaw; on control interference, or on stresses. In short, if they had known more about what they were doing, they wouldn't have done it. Throughout these processes Jenny was aware that she was ignoring advice she frequently gave to others: "Don't stand between a dog and a fireplug."

This was the evolutionary means by which Jenny and her shirt-tail relative the Canuck became the JN-4A, the JN-4G—and the JN-4 whatever else was decided upon.

To fit her for gunnery and to keep pilots from shooting themselves down by firing into their own propeller blades, Jenny was fitted with a gun-synchronizing gear which prevented firing when a blade was in position to be struck by a bullet.

The first synchronizing mechanism consisted in part of a gear attached to the rear face of the propeller hub just forward of the

Here is a JN-4A (Canuck) getting ready to tow a gunnery target aloft. This was used for firing practice by cadets, to the consternation of many people on the ground. 1918. (National Aviation Museum, Ottawa, Canada)

radiator. Meshed with this was a second gear approximately ten inches in diameter which did the synchronizing. Since the Vickers and Browning guns were operated by their own gas generated by exploding cartridges, the synchronizing gear prevented the bolt from moving forward under the gas pressure and impinging the firing pin on the cartridge when a propeller blade could be hit.

Jenny carried one forward-firing gun attached to the center section above the person in the front cockpit. In another configuration, she mounted a machine gun on the left side of the fuselage, where the man in the rear cockpit could get at the breech for reloading and to clear jams.

To lend realism and practicality to training in single-airplane battle practice and in strafing, camera guns were utilized. These were mounted on top of the center section. When the gun trigger was pulled, the pilot shot movies instead of ammunition and this

This Canuck was stalled while making a takeoff from a Texas training field. When a Canuck stalled, it would go into a dive, controls would be largely ineffective, and, if there was insufficient altitude for a recovery, this was the result. Most crashes of this type were fatal, as was this one. 1918. (National Aviation Museum, Ottawa, Canada)

permitted him to study his flying and sighting techniques when his film was projected.

In addition, vertical cameras were attached to the right side of the fuselage with a cutout in the lower-wing trailing edge to facilitate picture taking for mapping enemy positions and for other military missions.

To complete Jenny's overburden and further confound her physics, a Scarff ring was installed over the rear cockpit to carry the "flexible" or "free" Lewis machine gun. To operate it, the pilot stood up in the open cockpit and was held in by a waist belt. To hang by this through a loop while trying to cling to the grips on the machine gun to prevent its swinging around and braining you was a quarrelsome phase of training that extended into the thirties, when the writer was flying Navy Vought 03U observation seaplanes in VO-4 squadron on the battleship *U.S.S. Colorado*. Jennymen didn't get all of the lumps.

In operation, the rear-seat gunner fired through all angles forward, to the sides, rear, above, and below, hoping not to shoot up his own airplane; but this was the best rig ever invented for shooting off one's own tail. It also figured prominently and frequently when the gunner got overenthused, stayed with the target too long, and laid a burst alongside his pilot's ear. This was always good for a difference of opinion after landing, provided, of course, they made it.

In this vein prominent signs were posted frequently about the gunnery school which said laconically: "A cadet here has many opportunities for error and usually discovers them all."

In January, 1918, all synchronized guns were moved from the side of Jenny's fuselage to the top of the center section to simulate service conditions.

In April, 1918, the gunnery school moved to its new airdrome at Beamsville, Ontario, with no sad adieus from personnel at a nearby infantry camp, who were frequently livened by a few stray caliber .30s mixing in with the day's activities. While this kept those on the ground on the qui vive with built-in, instant self-preservation reflexes, it was causing too many saloon brannigans between student pilots and the ground forces, with a dampening of morale. Anyway, the groundlings had always understood that the Hun was their enemy and they preferred to keep it that way.

In May, 1918, the gunnery-training syllabus was amended following the return of the officer in charge of Canadian Training, who had spent some time at the front in France to see how things were with machine guns. As a result, all straight shooting practice was stopped. Deflection practice became the byword, with sights rigged to simulate target speeds of 110 mph. Jenny was not about to try this rate because it would have meant stiff dives and she was not that stiff.

During June a fourth squadron was added to train observers, and this made it possible to give all cadets synchronized-gun and camera-gun training, and all rear-cockpit observers (those martyrs who lived solely upon the sufferance and professional acumen of the pilot) Lewis-gun training. The sequence was as follows—which is another fair delineation of what Jenny put up with:

1. One hour of dual camera-gun, in-flight instruction; to make silhouette pictures of a target while diving at it from behind.

2. One hour of dual firing at pictures of a target plane, with its speed simulated at 100 mph (provided for in the sight adjustment).

3. One hour of instruction in the use of synchronized machine guns, instructor in rear seat, diving at an angle of forty-five and sixty degrees (quite a Jenny caper) at silhouettes in Lake Ontario. Fire two hundred rounds.

4. One hour of dual, or at least time enough to fire sixty rounds and get a stoppage; to train cadets in jam clearance. (Depending upon the adjustment of the head space, the guns fired about six hundred rounds per minute.)

5. Dual in diving from one thousand to one hundred feet while firing into dummy trenches. (This was instant burial with the hole waiting.)

6. Five hours of refresher dual. Then the cadet repeated the syllabus while flying solo.

Both instructors and cadets were encouraged to engage in stunting; and also in "contour chasing," which was a military term for "future chasing" in that it was done by flying just a few feet over the ground and trying to follow its contours—or, in other words, trying to stay above ground while nudging it with a Jenny. An engine failure would usually terminate this phase for whoever was flying. Today, any headquarters would practically kill a pilot for "contour chasing" or its sacrilegious counterpart, buzzing. Remember earlier comments upon conformity?

Finally, using a camera gun, the near-graduate began his aerial battle practice against another pilot. This was a four-hour course, at the completion of which he had to make one spiral, two vertical banks, three loops, four Immelmanns, five half rolls and six complete rolls.

During this mélange he was in camera-gun combat with a second Jenny pilot. These maneuvers were to be used in gaining a favorable position for attacking and photographing the adversary while avoiding being photographed.

Aerial tactics were modified as rapidly as data were rushed to the training aerodromes from the cockpits of pursuit pilots in France—the latest trick, subterfuge, maneuvers of attack and withdrawal were funneled from the skies, the control sticks, and the guns of such immortals as Billy Bishop, McCudden, Mick Mannock, Ball, Collishaw, Rickenbacker, Luke, Putnam, Springs —from the enemy: Manfred von Richthofen, Boelcke, Udet, Immelmann, Voss; and from the French—Nungesser, Guynemer, Garros, Fonck—names that will ring with great clarity for all time whenever and wherever men speak of the sky battles of World War I.

A tragedy seen fairly frequently on World War I training fields. From the position of the wings, it is evident that this Canuck spun in. With few exceptions these were fatal crashes. 1918. (National Aviation Museum, Ottawa, Canada)

CHAPTER FOURTEEN

American and Canadian Cadets

Joint U.S.–Canadian training programs in the U.S. and in Canada very complex, but almost trouble-free.

Beyond doubt, the most interlaced military agreement ever made between two governments was that promulgated by the U.S. and Canada in a joint pilot-training program in Texas, which began in July, 1917.

By the time this arrangement became fully operative, it was just about impossible to tell U.S. from Canadian cadets, U.S. Jennys from Canucks, U.S. mud from Canadian mud; and whether our snafus were aimed at our own people or the Canadians and vice versa.

So intricate was the plan that it is a wonder World War One-and-a-Half didn't arise from it; but, on the contrary, it turned out to be one of the most amazingly amicable things ever done between foreign powers.

When the United States declared war against the central powers, formal communications regarding the joint flight-training program were exchanged between Ottawa and Washington. Then, all matters pertaining to organization, equipping, and training were left to one Canadian officer and a lone American colonel.

The details were as follows—and follow them if you can:

1. The R.F.C. was to train 10 squadrons for the U.S. Signal Corps, comprising 300 pilots, 144 other flying officers, 20 administrative and equipment officers and 2,000 mechanics. This was to

be commenced immediately in Canada and completed at Ft. Worth, Texas. All training equipment, aerodromes, etc., for these purposes were to be provided by the R.F.C.

2. The Aviation Section, U.S. Signal Corps, was to provide in Texas, for occupation and control by the R.F.C., two airdromes capable of accommodating 10 squadrons, and part of a third for the Aerial Gunnery School. The fields were to include all requisite buildings, water and sewer, electricity, roads, and rail spurs.

3. The Aviation Section, U.S. Signal Corps, was to provide in Texas all airplanes, spares, running supplies (oil, gasoline, etc.) office and barrack fixtures and other airdrome equipment. The R.F.C. was to furnish gunnery, wireless, and all other ground instructional equipment.

4. Each service was to provide its own pay, clothing, and transportation, and draw rations in repayment of balances during their stay in each other's country.

5. The R.F.C. would supply all medical services for us in Canada and we would provide them here for the Canadians.

6. The Imperial Munitions Board in Canada would lend its experienced assistance in Texas by establishing a purchasing staff.

To summarize the bewildering interrelation, consider the following and wonder why it didn't start a separate war:

The United States owned the buildings, but the R.F.C. used them and was responsible for their upkeep.

There were R.F.C. squadrons beside U.S. squadrons being trained by the R.F.C. but administered by U.S. authorities.

Airplanes, engines, tools, and supplies were furnished by the United States, but the R.F.C. directed flying, repaired and re-

Jenny had the nose of a bloodhound (in fact, some thought she was a bloodhound, she spilled so much of it) and she would get you no matter where you were. An ambulance was not a sanctuary, as we see here. Jenny looks like she might fly again, and perhaps the ambulance might run again; but the driver said he might as well take his chances in a Jenny as get mauled by one while on an errand of mercy. This happened at Camp Rathbun, Ontario, 1918. (National Aviation Museum, Ottawa, Canada)

built planes and engines, drawing the necessary spares from U.S. stores.

The Aviation Department of the Imperial Munitions Board transacted R.F.C. affairs as though in Canada and with equal facility.

Canadian and American cadets and enlisted men were being received continuously in American or Canadian units, trained, and returned to their own country's organizations.

American railroads honored transportation warrants redeemable in Ottawa, and Canadian rail lines honored ours, redeemable in Washington, D.C.

R.F.C. medical officers quarantined R.F.C. camps that were half filled with Americans.

Weekly trainloads of Canadian-made OX-5s and Canucks arrived, came under U.S. control, and were immediately placed in service by the R.F.C.

The truly astounding feature of the foregoing is that this whole program, involving millions of dollars and hundreds of thousands of men—and a complex training mission containing builtin troubles of a high degree—was noted on the back of a business-size envelope, signed by one Canadian and one U.S. officer, and was carried out without a major dispute.

The relationship was not without bobbles, however. Early in July, Canada received from the United States 1,400 enlisted men and cadets to be trained. A U.S. Signal Corps colonel described this contingent as "underofficered, underorganized, unpaid, without records, and with many lacking uniforms." [This remarkable military system remains unchanged—like the time the Navy lost three Jepp Carriers and the Army lost a whole trainload of Sherman tanks.]

On September 24, 1917, Canada's advance party left for San Antonio, Texas and they came to wish they had stayed home. The group was made up of four U.S. officers and fifty men, four R.F.C. officers and thirty-four men, constituting a wing headquarters and a fatigue party. They arrived on September 26 and proceeded to their headquarters. They learned that there were three flying fields located north, south, and west of the city, named locally Hicks, Benbrook, and Everman, but designated by the Signal Corps as Camp Taliaferro, Fields 1, 2, 3.

"Construction had been delayed," wrote a Canadian officer. "Barracks and airdromes were incomplete. At one field, buildings had been barely started; water, light and sewers were not installed. It was nearly three months before this was corrected."

Before the first Canadian-trained American pilots had completed their flight course, they were moved to Texas. Back in

1918. This cadet didn't mind his instructor and let his Canuck stall on a landing approach. Note comparatively small damage to wings. The building absorbed most of the impact and undoubtedly saved the cadet's life. While the writer was a student naval aviator at Pensacola, a classmate did this same thing in a primary seaplane and landed in the midst of a crap game on the top floor of a Marine barracks. The only bloodshed resulted from a free-for-all when one Marine picked up all the money and headed for the stairs. (National Aviation Museum)

their own country again and for the first time since starting training, they were flying over flat, timberless terrain. There were now sufficient Jennys for them and their northern colleagues, and the standard of flying was good. In fact, it was so good that it became "a thing" for almost-graduated cadets to loop a formation of Jennys, and it was not uncommon to see as many as five do this and maintain good position.

When an occasional "norther" moved in on Ft. Worth the temperature would drop as much as fifty degrees in two or three hours. In between these, there would be "wet" seasons. None of the flying fields had subdrainage and they often became quag-

A cadet stalled this Jenny about fifty feet above the field. Before the nose dropped and put him in nose-first, he hit—and so hard it broke the fuselage at the rear cockpit. The Jenny was just turning right in an incipient spin, as will be seen from damage to the right wing outer section. (U.S. Signal Corps)

mires in which landing gear and propellers were the losers. On one particular morning, forty propellers were broken from mud-stuck nose-ins. The average breakage was 10 percent a day.

Although our men got on well with the Canadians, we often went out of our way to bushwhack them (and our own people too). This tended to make our guests believe they were being led by a bunch of pie-eyed pipers. For instance, a Canadian unit posted to Hicks Field arrived in a cloudburst after a ballup in their train routing had kept them in day coaches an extra forty-five hours, during which their only rations consisted of what they could afford to buy from depot-platform vendors along the way.

This is an example of what happened when inclement weather hit Texas. The cadet who made this forced landing due to engine failure would have been all right if he had had solid ground underneath him. Note the "curl" on the propeller. (U.S. Signal Corps)

They were disembarked at a shelterless siding three miles from Hicks and got drenched while waiting an hour for trucks. When they arrived at the field at 3:15 A.M., it was discovered that because of another snafu they were assigned to barracks which had no doors or windows, toilets, water, electricity, heat, or sleeping gear.

Their hangars were congested to the roof with crated Jennys and there wasn't a tool in sight. Yet, within eight days, the crates had disappeared, and every Jenny was flying long before the amenities had been installed in the barracks. This was accomplished with partially trained men.

Also on the plus side, during 1917 and a fraction of 1918, the Engine Repair Park overhauled thirteen hundred OX-5s. This required an average of three hundred man hours apiece. During 1918, the park began the manufacture of almost every OX-5 part and was so successful that only twenty out of several dozen individual units had to be purchased. Bench workers were paid 50 cents an hour and machinists received $1 an hour for these tasks.

The Aeroplane Repair Park began activitities on February 23, 1918. Its work consisted of rebuilding not only every crashed machine but also every one which had completed its allotted four hundred hours of flying time between overhauls. In addition to this and salvaging damaged Jenny parts, the unit had also to repair instruments, tires, tubes, metal fittings, and radiators.

In summary, the Texas operations accumulated 67,000 flight hours between November 17, 1917, and April 12, 1918. During this time, 1,960 pilots were trained for the U.S. and R.F.C., in addition to the many hundreds trained for the U.S. and Canada in

This kind of short-cut landing was recommended only for hummingbirds and other hover types—and not for novitiate pilots. One reason was that it was a long climb down and a person could get hurt if his foot slipped. Its next most important drawback was that it griped the mechanics who had to climb up and retrieve the Canuck. However, if a person was tired of military flying this was as good a way as any to get a long, long rest. [To me, this is the greatest airplane photograph ever made. How the pilot got it into those trees is beyond comprehension. Furthermore, the Jenny is damaged very little] (National Aviation Museum, Ottawa, Canada)

Canada. Besides these, 669 nonflying aviation officers and 4,150 enlisted men were trained.

Jenny took immense pride in the fact that, despite an unbelievably high crash rate, in-flight fatalities were only 1.88 percent of the total pilots trained in the fourteen months of operations; nonetheless, there were lots of funerals.

Despite snafus, crashes, and the grim mission of preparing young men for combat, life at this large complex of Mars was occasionally punctuated with events that served to take the troops' minds off their joint predicament.

A corporal was the author of one of these, and the whole production was worthy of a much higher rank.

On a bright and about-to-become noteworthy day, matters at the affiliated airdromes were progressing in a regulation manner and all was about as well as could be expected, when our corporal-mech started down a line of Jennys swinging props for cadets who were about to engage in their daily adventure.

"Up, on and off?," asked the mech. "Up, on and off," assured each cadet. The prop was yanked through. "Cough, cough," went the OX-5 and then it belched blue smoke, choked, cleared its throat, and settled down to a mildly dependable 800-rpm idling speed. Wheel chocks were pulled and that ship joined the column taxiing out for takeoff.

This was normal enough and it probably would have stayed that way had not the corporal been thinking about the fuselage of a girl he had dated on his last leave. So engrossed was he in her aerodynamics that he muffed his signals when the cadet in the next Jenny said: "Hold off a minute," climbed out of the cockpit, and headed for the latrine for that last nervous draining before joining the doubts overhead. So intent was the corporal on his personal piping that he neglected to turn off the ignition switch.

The corporal-mech swung the prop and in a moment the OX-5 came to life. He turned his back on it and went to the next Jenny, still ruminating over the anatomy of the girl.

Throttles in Jennys were a part of her overall militancy, and they crept. This one was no exception, and as the OX-5 warmed to its task, the throttle inched forward until it was almost to cruising, then Jenny jumped her chocks and bolted toward freedom. Since she was parked only twenty degrees out of the wind, she handily weathercocked. Within a few rods the throttle had reached the stop and the OX-5 had reached 1,450 rpm. This was takeoff power and take off she did.

The ensuing events will take many more minutes to describe than they took to happen because minutes like these are very nimble. Afterward everybody agreed they had been the liveliest minutes that had been encountered in that end of Texas, not excluding the Alamo.

Jenny was now airborne, and with no one at the controls she was heading here and there willy-nilly in whatever direction she was nudged by the whims of vagrant convection currents. They raised one wing and then the other, turning her this way and that, then tilting her nose upward a piece or dropping it a mite in a shallow dive. All things considered, she wasn't doing much worse on her first solo than lots of cadets were doing on their first dual.

Things might have been calmer had the officers of the day of various units let bad enough alone, but, mindful of what Congressmen would say if a runaway Jenny creamed a building full of cadets, they lighted the switchboards throughout the establishment with the warning that a maverick was loose overhead. For several thousand active young men that sufficed. They began bulging at high velocity from all kinds of buildings.

One American cadet detachment had been quarantined for smallpox, and when they tried to get out of their compound nearby Canadians told them to keep their damned red spots to themselves so other people wouldn't lose their passes because of being quarantined. Thus began one of the fastest-growing mass fights between friendly powers that took place during World War I. Most Americans and Canadians who were on the outskirts of the argument didn't know what they were fighting for, but it seemed to be the vogue to select someone from the other country and bust him one.

Meanwhile, the officer of the day, a captain, jumped aboard his motorcycle without waiting for his driver and went wide open toward headquarters for orders. A major had had the same

210

If there are those who believe that Jenny didn't have guts, let him study this situation. It is hard to tell whether the man at the right rear is saluting the Canuck or the engine; in any event, Jenny did her best—she stopped the train and so abruptly that the engineer had to sift coal dust for twenty minutes to find his false teeth. There is no accounting for what goes on in the mind of a student pilot—but what comes out is seldom dull. Nineteen eighteen was a vintage year for Canadian training crashes. (National Aviation Museum, Ottawa, Canada)

impulse. They rounded a barracks and the two sidecars hooked. People remarked that this was the farthest they had ever seen a major and a captain thrown without explosives.

By this time a brigadier general, known to the garrison and in the Army in general, as "Old Muzzle Blast," stepped out of headquarters to make a personal estimate of the situation. His highly agitated adjutant was at his heels.

"Sir, had we better turn out the guard to clear the area and then send up a gunnery plane to shoot it down?" he asked.

At that instant, a lieutenant said to another one, "Just wait until Old Muzzle Blast gets his bore blown; he'll tear up the whole damn place and every officer in it."

This evaluation of the general was not without a basis in fact, since he was known throughout the military as a poor man with whom to tangle. Extraordinarily brilliant and capable in his profession, he was the most iron-pantsed disciplinarian in khaki memory. In fact, not only was this a military reputation but also a legislative one, because at a couple of Army appropriations and policy hearings he had chewed up Senators and Congressmen like they were Feenamint.

But Old M.B. didn't combust. He said to his fidgety adjutant through a bemused grin: "Damn, Lieutenant; look at them go." This was in reference to whole units running one way while other units ran another as Jenny alternately dipped and pirouetted toward them, dived to roof level, climbed, turned, and thoroughly enjoyed her freedom. At long last she was doing her own flying.

Once in a while Old Muzzle Blast let out a snort followed by uncontrolled laughter. Between paroxysms he managed to say to the adjutant: "Life has been pretty dull around here, but it isn't today. Look at them go."

Just then a .45 automatic cracked as an officer drew a bead to kill or at least wound Jenny's engine. His aim was good: the slug hit something solid and ricocheted. It came belching across the field and whacked a bulletin board about ten feet from the general, who let out another roar of laughter and yelled to his apoplectic adjutant: "The damn thing is shooting back."

Then a gunnery class at the target butts opened up with a dozen caliber-.30 Lewis guns. Instantly the switchboards lighted up again and a frantic voice from a nearby crossroads village shouted from the phone: "Fer Chrisakes, quit shellin us, youall."

When this was reported to the general he said: "Good. They're nothing but a bunch of damn squatters, anyway."

Luckily the gunnery class ran out of ammunition. But they still had several drums secured to four guns mounted on the bed of a truck which attempted to simulate firing from a moving gun platform at a moving target. This contraption took off under the theory that it could track Jenny and pick her off at a propitious time before she dived into a barracks, or, worse yet, flew into town and tore up something civilian.

Meanwhile Jenny had headed off in a broad circle, then was pointed back at the field by convection currents. When she reached midfield, the four lads on the careering truck opened fire. "Somebody's going to get killed sure as hell this time," the general said, laughing. "Lieutenant," he said to his wide-eyed adjutant, "you better take cover. I'll let you know what goes on."

A strong air bump tilted a wing and abruptly changed Jenny's heading. The driver, with his eyes on Jenny and not on the foreground, essayed a high-speed sharp turn which might have worked had he not run into a pile of wheelbarrows. This flipped the truck. The kids on the guns didn't have anything else to hang on to on such short notice so they kept on hanging on to their triggers. As the truck rolled, it had the net effect of creating a Gatling gun six feet in diameter, and that's a lot of diameter when it is considered that each gun was spewing six hundred rounds a minute; multiplied by four, that gave this wreck quite a fire power.

A navigation instructor had just written on a blackboard: "When going from a true to a compass course, subtract easterly variation and deviation." He started to put a period after it, but a caliber-.30 round came over his shoulder and did it for him. "J-e-e-e-zus," he said.

By this time the environs of headquarters was teeming with officers and suggestions. A major said: "General, what are your orders? What should we do?"

"Don't do a damn thing. Don't spoil this," the general bellowed through his laughing.

Then Jenny stuck her nose into a downdraft. She dipped and in a moment her wheels glanced off the roof of a classroom to which about two hundred cadets had returned. A bomb dead center couldn't have blown them out faster, or to the greater merriment of the general, who by now was holding his sides, with tears running down his cheeks: "Damn . . . damn," he kept snorting. "Look at them go. This is the greatest thing that has ever happened in the Army."

Jenny was not through. The roof deflected her upward sharply, where she hung for a moment. Then, just before she stalled, her nose settled and she flew off to the east, maintaining a fairly steady course, to the dismay of Old Muzzle Blast, who wished something would turn her around and stir things up some more.

Soon Jenny was well away from the field, and while her watchers were wondering who, where, when, and what she would terrorize next, the OX-5 expired abruptly and she nosed down.

The first to arrive, followed by a speeding cavalcade of staff cars and trucks, was Old Muzzle Blast. Before him lay Jenny, wounded but not dead. When the engine had quit she had slowly eased into a mushing glide and was proceeding according to the manual until a gust raised her right wing. This swung her left a bit and she met the ground in a skid but with the nose fairly level. The running gear collapsed on the second bounce, just as the manual said it would. The loop under the port wing tip crumpled and let the tip dig in. The propeller splintered when a tip hit the ground. The fuselage slid along on the curved underside and did no more damage than sanding off the aluminum and fabric.

A left lower wing tip, new landing gear and prop, and fabric on the fuselage were all the bandaging she needed to let her go back to the training wars. The engine had a bruise on a corner of the crankcase, where the near-spent .45 slug had whapped it—and—you guessed it—what killed the OX-5 and brought Jenny down was that the c-a-m-s-h-a-f-t broke.

The garrison waited with taut apprehension for Old Muzzle Blast to fire his shrapnel, crack heads, rip off bars and chevrons and issue penalties by the gross. "He had his fun," a colonel observed. "But that old this-and-that is too much of a ramrod to let this one pass. He's just letting us sweat out the executions."

At the instant the colonel was predicting, the general was seated at his desk writing to a West Point classmate: "Dear Joe,"

*Alas, poor Bossy. She stopped the Jenny, but she in turn was also stopped—permanently—the victim of a camshaft. At any rate the camshaft is what started this tableau. When it broke, the hapless cadet headed for this field and then—*MOOOOOO! *(National Aviation Museum, Ottawa, Canada)*

he began. "You'll never believe half of what I'm going to tell you, but last week a corporal set the whole place on its ass. It was even better than when that ornery old bastard, General —— got pitched by his horse at the President's review."

The last paragraph said: "All these commissioned 90-day-wonder lunkheads are waiting for me to bust them, but I figure that worrying about what I'm going to do will upset them more than what Regulations will let me do, so I'm not going to do anything. You know, Joe, in the 20 years we've been in the Army, we've taken a lot of crap, civilian and military, with never a chance to get even. But now I've got a chance to screw the whole goddam

Army; I'm having that ill-conceived, misbegotten Corporal made a Lieutenant."

Jenny was not at all squeamish about her illegal flight or about the jitters she had wrought from corporal to colonel, because she was indifferent to status. She had never subscribed to the credo, "Whose bread I eat, his song I sing." She would just as soon drink one man's gasoline as another's. But don't get the impression from this that she ever bucked for Bum-of-the-Month. It was simply that repeated indignities and demands fobbed off onto her person had convinced her that both civilians and the military were people with birds on their aerials.

However, at introspective times and in the intuitive way the funny mind of a woman works, hers would penetrate the strivings and the rumbling of war to sense the tribulations of her opponents whom she was sending overseas. Also, she could perceive the anxiety of parents, wives, children, and a long-forgotten Latin proverb would spell out the mood:

"Dulce Bellum Inexpertis"—"War is magnificent for those who have never tried it."

CHAPTER FIFTEEN

Graduation

*Cadets graduate from flight-training and
are ready to go overseas.*

Primary training had been completed. American and Canadian cadets were now officers. The ceremonies ended at 10 P.M. and those who were shipping out tomorrow for Europe were in their bunks. Vaguely from a distance came the music of a Victrola in a Rekki Hut: "Tipperary," "Mr. Zip," "K-K-K-Katy," "Over There," "My Buddy."

Cadet Smith, now Lieutenant Smith, found sleep fugitive, and he lay there thinking about his parents, his brothers and sisters, and his dog back home in Manitoba. He saw his mother in the kitchen preparing dinner over the hulking black range with its redolent odors of crackling pine, simmering vegetables, roast browning, and the cinnamon smell of apple pie.

Red, his big Chesapeake, would be behind the living-room stove, dozing with his snout on his paws—wondering where his companion had gone. Lieutenant Smith saw him there and he had a huge urge to pet him.

Dad sat in his rocker beside the table, where he read in the evening. The kerosene lamp flickered occasionally as some vagrant air current disturbed its flame and changed the lighting across the features of this big, kindly man whom the lieutenant admired and loved so much—and who had done his bit "for King and Canada" in the infantry.

Then his mother called: "Dinner." Annette and Charles made a

217

grownup thing of helping Dad to his feet because, you see, he had lost a leg at the Marne.

Lieutenant Smith tossed and wondered as the night wore on—going back over the things that had started his sleeplessness from the moment he lay down.

Had he learned all of it? Was he good enough? Did he have what it would take? What was it really like in the air with a Hun?

In a nearby barracks a combat-toughened instructor tossed in his bed, too. Had he taught his kids every skill he possessed? More important, had he imbued them with the guts and determination they'd have to have in overwhelming quantities; had he given them every bit of confidence their spirits could contain without making them carelessly overconfident?

Who would get killed first? Not that blond kid from Montana —no—no favorites now—none of them would get killed; but he knew that from the law of averages, barring an act of God, most of them at this stage of the war would be dead within three months. What a rotten, putrid world! So he tossed and rolled and time and time again cussed the aching arm that a Hun had shortened with a Spandau.

Out in the hangars Jenny was pensive. Was she up to the over-burdens placed upon her? Did she have the right characteristics to make a lad fly by instinct—to weld his bottom to fifteen hundred pounds of Spad, Sopwith, Nieuport so firmly that the two became one—just the one needed to blast any enemy they closed with, fair, square, but final?

At other U.S. fields, and at those in Britain, France, Italy, Canada—and in Germany—other cadets were graduating into the insatiable maw of combat. Like Smith, they were restless too, as they lay in their bunks waiting for tomorrow. A tomorrow they hoped to see every day until, well—until it was over.

Then across the moon-swept and snow-light Texas airdrome, over the backs of the hangars humped like elephants with their rumps pointed upwind, came the soldier's benediction—"Taps"— the plaintive close to a warrior's day that tells him he is still alive and can dream another night.

The soft notes that draw lonesome men to a barrack window came through the trees, swept over the flying field with a loveliness that touches the heart and makes one better for having served under this soldier's hymn; his symphonette, his faith, his salvation—or his requiem:

> Day is done, gone the sun
> From the lakes, from the hills,
> From the sky;
> All is well, safely rest, God is nigh.
>
> Fading light dims the night;
> And the stars gem the sky,
> Gleaming bright;
> From afar, drawing nigh,
> Falls the night.
>
> Go to sleep, go to sleep, go to sleep, soldier boy,
> Go to sleep. . . ."

And then the last fading notes blended with the wind, the snow, the moon, and the hopes: Canadian, Yank, Frenchman, Briton and German; Spad, Fokker, Sopwith—and Jenny slept. Tomorrow would be another day.

CHAPTER SIXTEEN

Aces

America's aviation strength when Armistice is signed.
Jenny pilots who became aces.

When the signing of the Armistice ended World War I, American pilots were flying 1,005 aircraft in the Zone of Advance in France. Of these, 740 were in actual combat. (In World War II, there were a number of bomber raids containing in excess of 2,-500 aircraft.) They consisted mainly of French Spads, Nieuports, and Salmsons, and British Sopwiths. In front-line squadrons there were also the 196 dubious U.S.-built De Havillands, only a few of which took a look at the enemy.

On November 11, 1918, we had in America 40 flight-training schools; 8 balloon-training establishments; 3 radio, 3 photography, 5 military-aeronautical centers; 14 aircraft depots. At the peak, there had been 2,000,000 square feet of factory floor area, and 18,000 men and women building Jennys and OX-5s.

When the war ended, orders were canceled for 61,000 U.S.- and Allied-built airplanes and 20,000 U.S.-built engines. Thus fell our paper air force. Of the cancellation orders, 4,450 were for Jennys, but as has been mentioned earlier, 2,317 were manufactured anyway; never have so few manufacturers owed so much to so many taxpayers.

In terms of waste and mistakes, every airplane we sent to France cost $1,000,000. In terms of today's money, this represented the cost of one of our most expensive combat jets.

Demobilization, or demoralization, of the Air Service began

immediately, and by June, 1920, out of its 200,000 men, fewer than 10,000 officers and enlisted men remained in uniform. Ninety percent of the aircraft industry was liquidated by the end of 1920.

Deployed across the nation at the various airdromes we retained were 1,100 De Havillands,* 1,500 Jennys; 179 British SE-5 pursuits, the type Lindbergh flew when he was a flying cadet at Kelly Field. We also had 12 Martin MB-2 bombers, a craft we would hardly need unless we had to arbitrate another Mexican presidential election.

What did Jenny accomplish for us?

Her fledglings acquitted themselves with honor and many of the accolades for this go to her, because she bore the brunt of our inexperience, our unpreparedness, and our lack of foresight. For one of the world's largest nations to hurl itself into a tremendous war and base its entire air participation upon one airplane, and not meet disaster, was miracle enough.

Compensating for lack of research facilities, for a dearth of instructors and experienced aviation administrators, Jenny—as unlovely and as unwarlike as she looked—was as true a daughter of Pallas Athene as ever consorted with Mars. Her winged offspring did her credit in combat—that unrelenting crucible which tries men beyond all else; and when it was over, after a brief and terrible nineteen months, most of America's eighty-three aces owed a tremendous debt to Jenny.

On the following pages are listed the names of these men. Captain Eddie Rickenbacker, our ace of aces with twenty-six victories, is not included—simply because he did not train in Jennys. This is also true of twenty-seven others who entered British and French aviation before we declared war and did not, as several others did, transfer to our Air Force in 1917.

These valiant men were from 39 American squadrons serving in France when the Armistice ended the war. The units were made up of 18 pursuit, 12 corps observation, 3 Army observation, 1 night bombardment, and 5 reconnaisance squadrons. Assigned to these units were 1,402 pilots and 769 observers. Using day

* How did the old airplanes do in this postwar reshuffling? There were 330 military crashes between July 1, 1920, and November 30, 1921, with fewer than 600 pilots on the active list.

The omega of Jenny's military career and the marking of a new civilian life took place with this Armistice Day peace-celebration flight over San Diego, California. Wherever Jennys were stationed, they participated on November 11, 1918, in observations which were heralded as the finish to "the war to end wars." (U.S. Signal Corps)

bombers and pursuits, they flew 150 bombing sorties and dropped 275,000 pounds of bombs. Squadrons engaged in more than 2,100 aerial combats during 12,830 pursuit flights and 6,672 observation flights.

The aces, and many of the pilots who shot down fewer than five enemy, accounted for 927 German aircraft and balloons destroyed between early March and November 11, 1918. Our losses in both categories were 316, which gave us a victory ratio of three to one.

These achievements were attributable mostly to Jenny's protégés.

	PLANES	BALLOONS	TOTAL	HOME
Luke, Frank, Jr., 2nd Lt.	4	14	18	Phoenix, Ariz.
Vaughn, George A., Jr. 1st Lt.	12	1	13	Brooklyn, N.Y.
Kindley, Field E., Capt.	12		12	Gravette, Ark.
Springs, Elliott W., Capt.	12		12	Lancaster, S.C.
Landis, Reed A., Capt.	9	1	10	Washington, D.C.
Swaab, Jacques M., Capt.	10		10	New York, N.Y.
Putnam, David E., 1st Lt.	10		10	Boston, Mass.
Baer, Paul F., 1st Lt.	9		9	Ft. Wayne, Ind.
Cassady, Thomas G., Capt.	9		9	Spencer, Ind.
Wright, Chester E., 1st Lt.	8	1	9	Cambridge, Mass.
Hamilton, Lloyd A., 1st Lt.	6	3	9	Burlington, Vt.
Clay, Henry R., Jr., 1st Lt.	8		8	Ft. Worth, Tex.
Coolidge, Hamilton, Capt.	5	3	8	Boston, Mass.
Creech, Jesse O., 1st Lt.	8		8	Washington, D.C.
Erwin, William P., 1st Lt.	8		8	New York, N.Y.
Hunter, Frank O'D., 1st Lt.	8		8	Savannah, Ga.
Jones, Clinton L., Jr., 2nd Lt.	8		8	San Francisco, Cal.
Meissner, James A., Major	7	1	8	Brooklyn, N.Y.
White, W. W., Jr. 1st Lt.	7	1	8	New York, N.Y.
Biddle, Charles J., Major	7		7	Andalusia, Pa.
Burdick, Howard, 1st Lt.	7		7	Brooklyn, N.Y.
Chambers, Reid McK., Major	6	1	7	Memphis, Tenn.
Cook, Harvey Weir, Capt.	3	4	7	Toledo, Ohio
Holden, Lansing C., 1st Lt.	2	5	7	New York, N.Y.
Larner, Gorman DeFreest, Capt.	7		7	Washington, D.C.
Robertson, Wendel A., 1st Lt.	7		7	Ft. Smith, Ark.
Rummel, Leslie J., 1st Lt.	7		7	Newark, N.J.
Schoen, Karl J., 1st Lt.	7		7	Indianapolis, Ind.
Sewall, Sumner, Capt.	5	2	7	Bath, Mo.

* An official list of those persons who had received victory credits during World War I was published by the Air Service in 1920, revised by the Air Corps in 1931, and amended by order of the Secretary of the Air Force in 1960. That list, which shows the number of victories credited to each man, includes victories won by members of the U.S. Air Service while attached to British, French, or Italian organizations for duty but does not list victories gained by Americans while in the service of foreign nations. The USAF holds this list, as revised and amended, to be the authoritative statement of victory credits for U.S. Air Service of World War I. (The reader will recall that the above list of aces is limited to those who trained in Jennys.) This list was taken from *USAF Historical* 73.

	PLANES	BALLOONS	TOTAL	HOME
Stovall, William H., 1st Lt.	7		7	Stovall, Miss.
Vasconcelles, Jerry C., Capt.	5	1	6	Denver, Colo.
Beane, James D., 1st Lt.	6		6	Concord, Mass.
Brooks, Arthur, Capt.	6		6	Framingham, Mass.
Campbell, Douglas, Capt.	6		6	Mt. Hamilton, Cal.
Curtiss, Edward Peck, Capt.	6		6	Rochester, N.Y.
Esterbrook, Arthur E., 1st Lt.	6		6	Port Flagler, Wash.
Guthrie, Murray K., 1st Lt.	6		6	Mobile, Ala.
Hammond, Leonard C., Capt.	6		6	San Francisco, Cal.
Hayes, Frank K., 1st Lt.	6		6	Chicago, Ill.
Knotts, Howard C., 2nd Lt.	6		6	Carlinsville, Ill.
Lindsay, Robert O., 1st Lt.	6		6	Maderson, N.C.
McArthur, John K., 2nd Lt.	6		6	Buffalo, N.Y.
Ponder, William T., 1st Lt.	6		6	Mangum, Okla.
Porter, Kenneth L., 2nd Lt.	6		6	Dowagiac, Mich.
Stenseth, Martinus, Capt.	6		6	Tevin Valley, Minn.
Tobin, Edgar G., Capt.	6		6	San Antonio, Tex.
Vernam, Remington DeB., 1st Lt.	3	3	6	New York, N.Y.
Badham, William T., 1st Lt.	5		5	Birmingham, Ala.
O'Neil, Ralph A., 1st Lt.	5		5	Nogales, Ariz.
Bair, Hilbert L., 1st Lt.	5		5	Ft. Wayne, Ind.
Bissell, Clayton L., Capt.	5		5	Kane, Pa.
Buckley, Harold R., Capt.	4	1	5	Agawam, Mass.
Cook, Everett R., Capt.	5		5	San Francisco, Cal.
Furlow, George W., 1st Lt.	5		5	Rochester, Minn.
George, Harold H., 1st Lt.	5		5	Niagara Falls, N.Y.
Gray, Charles G., Capt.	4	1	5	Chicago, Ill.
Haight, Edward M., Capt.	5		5	New York, N.Y.
Healey, James A., Capt.	5		5	Jersey City, N.J.
Knowles, James, Jr., 1st Lt.	5		5	Cambridge, Mass.
Luff, Frederick E., 1st Lt.	3	2	5	Cleveland, Ohio
Owens, J. Sidney, 2nd Lt.	5		5	Baltimore, Md.
Ralston, Orville A., 1st Lt.	5		5	Lincoln, Neb.
Seerley, John J., 1st Lt.	5		5	Chicago, Ill.
Strahm, Victor, Major	5		5	Evanston, Ill.
Thaw, William, Lt. Col.	4	1	5	Pittsburgh, Pa.
Todd, Robert M., 1st Lt.	5		5	Cincinnati, Ohio
Williams, Rodney, 1st Lt.	4	1	5	Everett, Mass.
Wehner, Josef F., 1st Lt.	0	5	5	Boston, Mass.

CHAPTER SEVENTEEN

Barnstorming

World War I ends, Allies dump surplus airplanes in the U.S.; Jennys sold at extremely low prices and become virtually the only airplanes used in the fabled barnstorming era.

The close of the war sparked the opening of a veritable Pandora's Box, from which emerged all of the ills that could accompany the release into mostly unqualified hands of hundreds upon hundreds of Jennys. True, there was, as in the legend, hope at the bottom of the box—and this was the hope that America would run out of Jennys before she ran out of men.

Jenny went on sale at a large number of Army fields and factories. She could be had for $500 brand new, and abused for as little as $100.

The British immediately formed a company here to handle the disposal of their surplus aircraft, which not only included hundreds of Jennys but also Avros, Sopwiths, and almost anything else that flew with a British accent.

France began exporting (dumping) to us and before we caught on we were flooded. Those two nations, now that the war was over, no longer needed our friendship and, to get even for all real and fancied grievances, swamped us with airplanes. They were also shrewd enough to enact embargos to keep us from exporting unwanted planes to them. By the time we woke up there were about four Jennys for every garage. It was indeed a backward cow pasture that did not have a brace of them.

Most of Canada's surplus Canucks were acquired by F. G. Erickson, of Toronto, who set up outlets in the United States,

227

where most of them were sold. The company developed a "three-passenger" Canuck by removing the front seat and installing a board on which two very narrow-bottomed people could sit if they were that foolhardy.

When Camp Borden was closed, the Canucks there were sold to Bishop-Barker Aeroplanes, Ltd., of Toronto, who also entered the "dump-them-in-America" business.

On the Canadian west coast, Hoffar Brothers, looking for new Jenny fields and unsuspecting customers to conquer, converted some Canucks into seaplanes. Most were sold in Canada, but three were exported to the Phillipines, and some came here.

Not to be outdone, the Yarrow Co. of Canada developed a twin-float Canuck which floated better than it flew.

Canucks by the swarm featured prominently in most postwar Canadian and U.S. barnstorming. The largest operator and flight-school owner was the J. V. Elliott Co., of Hamilton, Ontario. Some of today's most senior pilots on Trans-Canada Airlines received their training from the company.

Ultimately the Wright Aeronautical Co. obtained injunctions to halt the avalanche and had an assist from General Billy Mitch-

ell and others in helping fight the surplus war against our erst-
while colleagues in combat.

By 1920, Jenny dealers were advertising vigorously. For example, De Luxe Air Service, Inc., of Ashbury Park, New York, listed
"Jennys: Practically new. Overhauled OX-5 engines, New wings
—$500.00. A-1 Ships, Used—$250.00."

Because of the deluge of supplies, owners found it more
economical to replace airplane and engine parts with new ones

Left
*Canuck fitted with twin floats for water operations. Because
of the increase in weight over conventional wheel landing gear,
or over a single float, this one floated better than it flew.
(National Aviation Museum, Ottawa, Canada)*

Below
*This single-float installation was developed for the Canuck by Hoffar
Brothers of Canada. This was superior to the twin-float type
because it was much lighter. The use of this, wheels, and skis, gave
Jenny a triple utilization, and now she could not only mash you,
but she could also drown you. (National Aviation Museum, Ottawa,
Canada)*

than to make repairs. It was much cheaper, as these advertised prices indicate: newly covered wings, $30; newly covered ailerons, rudder or elevator, $2.50 each; uncovered wings, $15; new copper-tipped propellers, $15; complete and just-overhauled OX-5s, $75.

Companies like Sperry, Sikorsky, Martin, and others developed "high-lift" monoplane wings for Jenny. These bettered performance by introducing airfoils with more lift and less drag. For example, the Sperry-wing Jenny was 10 mph faster than its biplane counterpart, and it landed at only 35 mph.

Clipped-wing Jennys next came into vogue and flourished until their uncertainties began clipping too many pilots. Before long Jennys were so scrambled that hundreds of them began losing their original model identities, as the parts of different models, in every conceivable conglomeration, became combined in a single craft. These, quite logically, were called "Combination" Jennys, and so they were: the combination of too much enthusiasm and not enough knowledge. For the pilot of this miscegenation, the odds were plenty to one.

Engine modifications also came on the market. "Millerized" * OX-5s put more colts into the old stable. "Toothpick" propellers came out which produced a few more revolutions per minute with the same power input. Blueprints and drawings were available showing how to install Hall-Scott, Duesenberg, Thomas, and other engines.

Jenny was very apprehensive about these rampant experiments put together by entrepreneurs more concerned with chasing the dollar than with giving her and her purchasers an even shake amid the risers and sinkers of life upstairs. Her kaleidoscopic evolution had given her an unusually keen perception. At times, some attributed this to clairvoyance or extrasensory perception; but Jenny preferred to call it simply a "woman's intuition."

It was through this keen sensitivity that she became aware of and worried a great deal about Murphy's Law, which states: "If something can be put together or operated improperly or otherwise screwed up, it eventually will be put together or operated improperly or screwed up."

* See pages 240–42 for "Millerizing the OX-5."

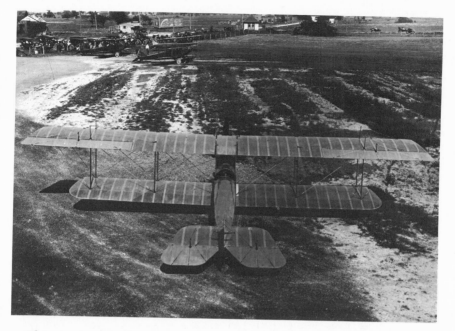

This was a typical passenger-hopping day. The crowd is undoubtedly being exhorted to "see the country from the air." The center section on this JN-4B does not have the cutout used later to facilitate cockpit access. (Curtiss Aeroplane Co.)

In the prophetic wisdom of this cogent homily, as experiment was piled upon experiment, Jenny sensed a continually recurrent chance of being prematurely bumped off the running board of existence.

It was not long until America literally swarmed with Jennys, of an always proliferating mongrel breed, and as the postwar years progressed she bred a clan of men who were to aviation what cowboys and Indian scouts (some add cattle rustlers and claim jumpers) were to the frontier. This was a restless breed who always rally around rebellious occupations. They were and are the men who will not stay put in the eight-to-five world and ask only that life get out of the way and stay out of it.

These men were the original barnstormers, and the pure, 100 percent warp and woof of this phylum did it in Jennys. They were as itinerant and as gypsy as their imagination and the capabilities of the craft would let them be: making it from here to

there without benefit of airports, air maps, radio, navigation devices or instruments—running away from winter, dodging storms,
chasing the sun from cow pasture to alfalfa field, hauling passengers in plush towns for $20 a head, once around the field; or for
$2 if they had skipped a meal or two in the previous town.

These knighted wanderers usually slept out with a propped-up
gunny sack for a windbreak and hay for mattress and pillow.
They were not men to get downwind of during a long tour.

As has been noted in Jenny's vital statistics, the wing fabric
was treated with nitrate dope. Cows dearly loved it. Many an ex-
hausted barnstormer, bedded down in a pasture, wakened in the
morning to find that cows had put him out of business by licking
the dope off the wing covering so it hung down between the
spars and ribs like Mrs. Murphy's drawers. However, a few dollars' worth of dope, some warm, dry days, and many profane
hours of labor restored airworthiness and Jenny got out of there
—or the cows did.

This was but one of the reasons pilots became fabric workers
and mechanics; at least, those who didn't were soon buried somewhere along their route or were shipped home so their relatives
could handle the after-life amenities.

No county fair up to 1925 was complete without four idiots
and two Jennys to stage—as the six-sheets phrased it—
"STUPENDOUS, SPINE-CHILLING, DEATH-DEFYING ACTS, THE LIKES OF
WHICH HAVE NEVER BEFORE BEEN SEEN IN JERKVILLE." And, oddly
enough, the six-sheets were right. It was during these aerial
Roman carnivals that America tingled to wing walking, breath-

Above
Looks like his head is caught in something, but it isn't. He is standing
on it while the JN-4D pursues its indifferent way. This man could make
quite a mark for himself if he fell off. This Jenny was so recently out
of the Army that its painted-over military insignia is still visible.
(R. S. Robin)

Below
"Look out below!" What a helluva way to earn a living; what a way
to go for an airplane ride! This man could make quite a splash in his
profession. There he is with his high tan boots pointed at heaven with
every prospect of reaching it. Convection bumps didn't seem to reg-
ister on these people. (R. S. Robin)

catching mid-air plane changes, "loop-the-loops," et cetera, et cetera. . . .

With these pieces of meal-getting insanities there were also parachute jumps, and mighty spectacular they were, too. The chute then was on a par with Jenny; and gravity had a whammy on both. The chute either worked or it didn't, and no matter how much the crowd pulled for the jumper, if it didn't it was messy.

During one short-lived period, a short-lived genuine Sioux Indian with hair three feet long used to swing by it from the landing-gear spreader bar. With his hair tied to the bar, he was flown aloft in a tube attached to the bottom of the fuselage. As Jenny cruised past the grandstand, Mr. Indian would wriggle out and let himself be suspended by his long, black locks—until one day someone must have greased them. Then the pilot got a new act.

There was another stunt that always "oohed" and "aahed" the crowd. A chap would crawl out of the rear cockpit and onto the top wing. Holding onto a rope bridle he would stand erect, hook his feet into stirrups and then with mock sangfroid and shaking knees wave to the crowd as the pilot executed a low-altitude loop. The main trouble with this act was that it got increasingly harder to talk a friend into replacing a predecessor.

Still another spectacular was carried out by a man on the top wing changing to another Jenny flying above by grasping a rope ladder attached to the top ship's landing gear, climbing up to where he could make it onto the lower wing and then into the cockpit. The catch in this act was the same as in the one above.

It wasn't the "oohs" and "aahs" of the crowd that were so great

Above
If this Jenny thought she had had it rough during her war-training days, she was in for a shock when peace broke out—because in her league, there was no peace, only people crawling over, under, and on top of her—and hanging all over the place without benefit of good sense. (R. S. Robin)
Below
How he got out there isn't as important to him as whether or not he will get back to that comfortable JN-4D front cockpit which he left for the purpose of spreading goose flesh among the spectators with this transient piece of idiocy. State and county fairs seemed to bring out the worst in the Jenny devotees. (R. S. Robin)

during these brannigans, however. It was the wonderful little
boys who came in droves. I have known hundreds of them during more than thirty-five years of Air Corps, Navy, and civilian
flying and they are the greatest crop America ever had.

These were the kids who became the backbone of the airmail,
of military and naval aviation—the heroes of World War II and
Korea. These were the same little guys—wistful dreamers and
hopers, with sucker-smeared faces jammed tight against the
fence, eyes bulging, hearts pounding—who later ripped hell out
of Tarawa, Regensburg, Guadalcanal, Ploesti, Leyte, Hamburg,
Chosin, Pusan, and a hundred other raw pauses on the way to
the wobbly peace of two wars.

As Jenny traced her unlovely profile across America's pioneer-
ing skies, she was sketching the foundation for today's fabulous
aviation, in which anything that flies less than a thousand miles
an hour is a sissy. She was the craft whose descendants would, in
forty years, shrink the world to the travel-time size of a single
U.S. state.

By 1920 there were 88 commercial companies operating Jennys (or was she operating them?). These soon increased to 125,
and before the close of 1925 there were 425 separate Jenny, or
part-Jenny, operators.

During the period 1918-26, three events took place which, considering the primitive state of the art, make one wonder whether
certain of man's conduct ought to be attributed to his restless
spirit, or to some abhorrent haste to make it to the next world.

On September 28, 1918, when radio was 99 percent static, a
pilot in one Jenny maneuvered another Jenny and pilot solely by
radio control. This was over Langley Field, Virginia.

Above

*Things were not wacky just in civilian life; it was nuts in the Army, too,
and here Sergeant Wells proves it in a JN-4H Hisso Jenny at Post
Field, Okla., June 25, 1922. If a present-day pilot requested permis-
sion to engage in a caper like this, the psychiatrists would have him
in a strait jacket. The fun is all gone. (U.S. Air Force)*

Below

*Lt. Omar Locklear, America's first and one of her most daring wing
walkers. Photo made on March 22, 1919. A parachute was not worn.
(U.S. Air Force)*

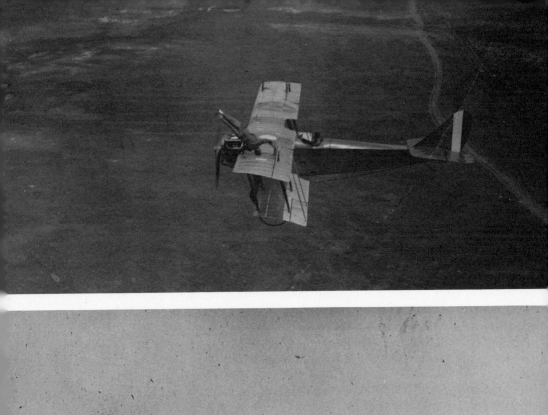

Jenny did not approve. In fact she disapproved vehemently because while being manipulated by radio she had the same sensation as if she had been under hypnosis, inasmuch as she was completely under the influence of invisible forces coming at her through the air. Like most women she rebelled because she had a skeptical reservation about relinquishing her control.

As for hypnosis, despite its practitioner's claim that no woman can be induced to do anything under its influence that she wouldn't do willingly otherwise, Jenny took this with a pinch of gas and summarized her opinion by saying: "If I am going to do wrong, I want to be there."

Yet Jenny was not a prude, and she had a bit of the philosophy of the cat in Don Marquis' rheumy-eyed classic of the twenties *Archy and Mehitabel.* She often expressed herself somewhat as did mehitabel to her alter ego, Archy, the cockroach: "What the hell, Archy; what the hell. There's life in the old dame yet. Toujours gai!." Or if in sedate company she phrased it more conservatively: "Dum vivimus—vivamus"—"While we live, let us live"; or "But let each be Captain of his fate." She simply didn't want to be led astray by a string of dits and dahs.

On August 25, 1926, the pilot of a Jenny that carried a stowed parachute with its shroud lines attached to the plane's structure climbed to 2,500 feet over the Fleet Air Base at San Diego, shut off the OX-5, took a deep breath—his last for a while—and pulled the rip cord.

Above
Although Jenny was a glutton for punishment, she must have shuddered at these shenanigans and the many other indignities foisted upon her by the restless barnstormers who toured the county fairs after World War I and well into the late twenties. (R. S. Robin)

Below
Four idiots and two Jennys spelled c-o-u-n-t-y f-a-i-r *anywhere in America from 1919 through 1927. Here we see half of a team proving that life can be as precarious as you want to make it. The character aft seems oblivious of the fact that his 160 pounds multiplied by a lever arm of eight feet gave him a weight of 1,280 pounds as far as this Jenny's center of gravity was concerned. This is why the pilot has full down-elevator—to keep the tail up and to support that nonproducer behind him. (R.S. Robin)*

After the chute had opened, the pilot's role changed to nonparticipant, because he had no control over anything including his bladder. On the way down, things weren't going so good and he wished he were not a party to this thing. As the situation went from worse to still worse, he was inclined to chop the shrouds and let gravity have the whole thing. At least he would know then what was going to happen. This way he didn't. In the latter stages the suspense nearly killed him. So did the landing. In time he flew again. The Jenny didn't.

On November 15, 1921, presaging a rash of endurance flying in which pairs of pilots stayed aloft for weeks without landing, there occurred the first air-to-air refueling—the hard way.

On that date, Wesley May, riding in a Lincoln Standard flown by a rational and later world-famed pilot, Frank Hawks, tied a five-gallon can of gasoline to his back, crawled out onto a wing and grabbed the wing-tip skid of a Jenny flown by Earl Daugherty, of Long Beach, California, equally all right. May next clambered onto the Jenny's wing, made his way to the fuselage, dumped the gasoline into the tank, and then crawled into the front cockpit.

Anybody for refuelling?

A few years ago, a group of pioneer airmen formed a national organization called the OX-5 Club, whose membership is limited to those who flew behind these engines, 90 percent of the time probably in a Jenny. The group's purpose is to commemorate such events as the above three and to prolong memories of the organizations and individuals who operated this equipment.

Survivors of the OX-5, Jenny, and four controlled panics referred to as OX-5 conventions * have said that one or two more of these whiskey klatches will probably liquidate the last of the Jennymen.

"MILLERIZING THE OX-5"

One of the lads who used to sneak out of bed to read whatever aviation literature he had been able to find was Leslie G. Miller, a farm boy.

* On October 8, 1965, the OX-5 Club held a convention in Chicago, Illinois, with Major General Benjamin Foulois, U.S.A.F. (Ret.), now deceased, as guest of honor.

After various bouts with gliders and tiffs with gravity, he acquired a cracked-up pusher biplane, which he rebuilt; whether
he flew it is moot—and Miller regards this as personally classified
information. Be that as it may, by then he was hooked, and when
he became old enough for service in World War I he enlisted as
a flying cadet and learned to fly at the Army Air Corps field in
Lawton, Oklahoma. He soloed in a Hisso Jenny. The untimely (to
him) end of the war kept him from becoming an ace.

His next few years were hectically occupied with making a living flying at county fairs and in race meets and in "hopping" passengers in OX-5 Jennys and in Standards and Canucks. In the
1919–25 period there were very few other craft flying in America.

When the Laird Swallow came out in the mid-twenties it immediately became the hot ship of the times. It was more facile in
acrobatics and it was faster than the others. To beat it in a race,
opponents had literally to shave the paint off the pylons in turns.
Miller saw in this airplane an opportunity to clean up. However,
right on its empennage came the Waco 9, Travelair, K. R. Chal-
lenger, and the Eaglerock.

All of these airplanes mounted an OX-5 because it was the
only affordable engine in its class. Since the new craft were
about equal in performance, Miller decided that any racing or
acrobatic advantage would have to come through improvement
in the engine—and if in the process one could cajole the camshaft
into not breaking, his retirement prospects would be materially
bettered. This he proceeded to do, and before he had finished, an
airplane owner flying a Millerized OX-5 was like today's cat with
a pink Ferrari.

The first improvement was an intake control, which was built
in a blacksmith shop in 1923. It was produced with crude tools,
but it gave Miller the speed edge he needed to win most of the
races he entered. "The OX-5," he says with fatherly pride, "performed with the speed of a bachelor making an emergency bailout from a married woman's bed."

The thing that ultimately lent impetus to Miller's foregoing his
monopoly was the low purses offered at air meets. This was synonymous with poverty. However, the relinquishment proved to be
a Janus because the same economics that bushwhacked him into

selling his intake control to other pilots destroyed his advantage and soon had the pack flying neck-and-neck again. This not only cut Miller's revenue, but it put the boys back to cutting pylons, which was not good; hit one, and no more races—no more airplane—no more pilot. *Alles war kaput!*

After a few bad times at the pylons, Miller decided there must be a better way of earning a living flying, so he developed his Miller rocker arm. This came out of a welding shop and again with crude tools—but by 1925 it had put him ahead of the pack, and he could move out a respectable distance from the pylons and still come in first. He entered the famed New York-Spokane race in 1927 against some good airplanes with the wonderful new Wright J4 engine, and won. The prize money financed the Miller Airplane Products Company in Los Angeles.

The complete Millerization of the OX-5 began at this point, and before it was finished it included silver-bronze bearings; three-ring, high-compression pistons; perfect-circle piston rings; Bosch or Scintilla magnetos; replaceable valve guides and seats; Rich valves and the Miller Overhead with intake controls; roller rocker arms; grease-tight and fail-proof (it was about time) intake rocker arms and pins.

From 1927 to 1931 approximately 3,800 complete conversion kits were sold and the OX-5 never had it so good. Even the camshaft quit breaking now that it had less arduous duties; power increased and reliability improved so much that one could fly without having to pick his way from one forced-landing site to another. This helped navigation, too, because now a pilot could fly by compass instead of by cow pasture.

CHAPTER EIGHTEEN

Requiem

Jenny reached the end of her runway and was "shot down" by General Order. Requiem.

In 1927, progress took a hard, analytical look at Jenny and, with one subjective and one objective eye, studied her turbulent and ambivalent career: born by transmutation, brought to her zenith by synthesis—warrior and civilian—courageous in achievement, but now bereft of contemporary science. A monument to her time—yes; but the times were getting old.

Her restless wings had crossed millions of sky miles; she had sent thousands to fame, to posthumous glory, and to oblivion. She was the vanguard of America's entry into aerial war, the seven-league boots of its first civilian air strides, the incubator for a reservoir of pilot ability and engineering technology that went on to build the airmail and civil air transport and develop the crews and the sky weapons for another world war; and next, the jet, the missile, and the satellite age.

Jenny was the springboard of our aerial knowledge because she was the first airplane spurred along by the pressure of great need, an ample diversity of intelligence and sufficient funds to apply it. She was the launch pad of our visions and our dreams for peace as well as for progress. She was the drive behind the little kids hanging onto the airport fence who became the men who have done it all—and she developed them.

Now Jenny was on trial, but mind you, she was not charged with an offense or with malfeasance—just with being old. Her longerons were arthritic, her bungee had lost its fight, her wing curve was lumpy, and she had but one field of vision—toward the past.

Jenny didn't compromise with her detractors; she fought for her life, pitting her performance against that relentless inconoclast—AGE—that arbiter of the past, present, and future; the limiter of all things that live with time; the implacable foe that has dulled the greatest intellects, pulled down massive temples, and destroyed civilizations.

For the first time in a fight Jenny was alone; none of her thousands were there to plead her case before the tribunal of obsolescence. None rose to recite her valor and request a reprieve. There were only Jenny, the court, and the velvet flak.

On a table rested 397 sheets of blueprints, two cases filled with change orders, several volumes of her accomplishments, log books recording hundreds of thousands of flights. But these were mute. They were not the articulate, pugnacious, kultus, gung-ho Jenny; the free spirit, the untamed madam or madonna, saint or sinner, friend or foe, vulpine Jenny.

Now, with life and flight running out and no consul to win a stay, she stood steady, proud, and hopeful for a last-minute mission—any mission. But none was ordered:

On June 1, 1927, her own Air Corps shot her down with General Order AG 452.1:

a. After July 1, 1927 whenever replacements have been furnished or whenever JN airplanes are no longer needed in carrying out the approved training program, JN-type airplanes may be salvaged at the discretion of the local Commanding Officer.

For a few fleeting moments on June 29, 1957, Jenny recaptured her past glory. In a demonstration of the deep affection flying men held for her, this reconstructed JN-4D was "recalled to active duty" to honor General Nathan Twining, outgoing U.S.A.F. Chief of Staff, just designated by President Eisenhower as Chairman of the Joint Chiefs of Staff. Jenny is flying past the reviewing stand, not only in salute to General Twining, but also to receive the salutes of the officers and men of Andrews Air Force Base, Maryland, on behalf of the United States Air Force, the U.S. Navy, the U.S. Marine Corps, and America's entire civil aeronautics complex. (U.S. Air Force)

b. All JN-type airplanes remaining on hand Sept. 1, 1927, will be salvaged regardless of their condition or flying needs and none of this type plane will be flown after that date.

c. Parts not salvaged will be rendered unserviceable and disposed of.

d. The airplane to be salvaged will be dismantled insofar as is necessary to mutilate all component parts beyond the possibility of future use for aircraft purposes.

e. Commanding Officers of each station will appoint an officer who will personally witness the destruction of this property.

Lutz Wahl
Brigadier General
Acting The Adjutant General

Jenny would fly only once more in uniform and this would not be for thirty years, when she flew in review on June 27, 1957, to honor General Nathan Twining, outgoing U.S.A.F. Chief of Staff, just promoted to Chairman of the Joint Chiefs of Staff by President Eisenhower.

History doesn't tell us all that happened that day when Jenny stood trial and lost, but when the grounding orders were signed, this is what should have happened:

From the top of the highest mountain, the best bugler in the Army Air Corps should have sounded Taps loud and clear. Then, when he had finished, from the top of another mountain, the next best bugler should have sounded the echo, sad and sweet and not too loud—just loud enough to be heard in Valhalla to tell all the old-time pilots there that Jenny was gone forever.

APPENDIX

General construction of the JN-4D.
Overhauling the Curtiss OX-5 motor.

GENERAL CONSTRUCTION OF JN4-D

(A) PANELS

The contour of the wing curve is cambered according to the type known as the Eiffel No. 36. The chord for the general wing curve section is 59½ inches. The upper plane is built in three sections; one central engine-section panel, and two side sections; one on each side of the engine section. The lower plane is built in two sections; one on each side of the fuselage. The engine section is designed for the width of the fuselage. In both the upper and lower panels, adjacent to the engine section and fuselage respectively, the rear portion of the panels are cut away to a smooth ogee-shaped curve, to enlarge the range of vision above and below. The engine section extends to the rear beam only, and has no overhang beyond the rear beam.

(B) INTERNAL TRUSSING OF PANELS

The internal truss system of the panel is composed of tension diagonals and compression struts. The tension diagonal members which are designed to take the stresses induced in flight are in duplicate. All fittings for fastening these members are so attached to the beams, which form the transverse members of the internal truss, that the failure of the attachment of one such member or diagonal, does not cause a loosening or failure of the attachment of the duplicate member. The diagonal members taking the stress due to landing are single members. The adjustment of the tension in all the diagonal members is accomplished by means of turnbuckles, fitted to the end of the member. The turnbuckles fitted to the duplicate arranged members are so disposed that one wire is adjusted at the front beam and its duplicate member is adjusted at the rear beam. The turnbuckle on

247

the diagonal members taking the landing stresses are generally located at the front beam terminals. The internal compression members
conform to the cross sectional contour of the panel. These members
are solid in section and not lightened. Cap-strips passing over the
upper and lower surfaces of the front and rear beams securely maintain all truss (solid) and intermediate (lightened) ribs longitudinally
in alignment. All ribs conform to the cross sectional contour of the
panel.

(C) COVERING

The main panels are covered on the upper and lower surfaces with
fabric. This covering is machine-sewn at the seams; this being of the
type known as the lap seam. In this construction each strip is lapped
over at the edge to be sewn. The two strips are so brought together
that the lapped edges meet; thus in the upper strip the lap is folded
upward. The thread passes through three pieces of linen in sewing
the seam.

The fabric is carefully stretched over the framework of the panel.
The tension applied to the linen, as necessary for smooth covering, is
directed parallel to the span of the panel. Care is taken not to apply
this tension in the direction of the chord, so that when the dope in
the linen contracts, it does not alter the wing curve.

In laying the linen covering on the panel the seams are placed diagonally to the fore and aft direction. The fabric is hand sewn on the
two sides to the panel frame.

For sewing the fabric to the ribs, Andover No. 7 harness-maker
thread, properly waxed, is used. This thread is taken around each rib,
each stitch being properly locked with a knot. The stitches are 4
inches apart.

The fabric is tacked to the frame at those points around the side
hinges and similar locations where it is impossible to fasten by sewing.

After the fabric has been sewn to the frame, a strip of aeroplane
linen, 2¼ inches wide, with the threads frayed at the sides ⅛ inch, is
doped over the stitches.

(D) INTERPLANE TRUSS

The bracing between the upper and lower panels consists of two
transverse trusses in the planes of the front beams and rear beams respectively, and continuous from the fuselage to the outer ends of the

panels. The vertical members are designed for compressive stresses; the diagonal members for tension stresses. The diagonal members are aligned in opposite directions to withstand any reversal of stresses. The front beams of the upper and lower panels constitute the upper and lower chord members of the front truss. The rear beams similarly constitute the chord members of the rear truss. The trusses are symmetrically disposed with respect to the longitudinal plane of symmetry of the aeroplane. The trusses are crossbraced with tension diagonal members attached to the panel (strut) points.

Flying wires between the wing posts are in duplicate. Their attachments and fittings to the front and rear beams are also in duplicate. Each wire and its attachment is of sufficient strength to take the whole designed load with the factor of safety.

The landing wires between the wing posts are single.

The engine section wires are designed for their full load at the given factor of safety.

The transverse wires between the upper and lower planes are single cables in both directions.

Drift wires to both the upper and lower planes are single cables. The front drift wire is attached at its forward terminal to the nose of the machine and at its rear terminal to the lower socket plate of the front intermediate wing post. The rear drift wire is attached at its front terminal to the nose of the machine and at its rear terminal to the upper socket plate of the rear intermediate wing post.

Mast wires, both front and rear, inner and outer, are single cables.

All these cables are galvanized, non-flexible, 1/19 strand.

The sizes of these cables are in accordance with the Wing Wiring Diagram, C.A. Co., Dwg. No. 15180.

All interplane wires have a turnbuckle fitted to one end and a shackle at the other end, or directly attached to the head of an eyebolt. The connections of the shackles to the fittings are made by means of pins which are locked by cotter pins.

(E) AILERONS

Ailerons are fitted to the rear beam in the recessed section of the upper panels, at their outer ends. The trailing edge (integral with the outer end edge) of the aileron is parallel to the leading edge. The end edge of the aileron is continuous in the same line with the panel outer end edge.

The cross sectional contour of the aileron conforms to the lines of the wing curve from the rear beam to the trailing edge.

The control braces of the aileron are equipped with hard wire guys to free them from any bending stresses. These braces are securely bolted to the ailerons. The guy wires are fitted with turnbuckles.

The ailerons are fitted at their trailing edge with suitable steel clips, bolted in place, for the attachment of the elevator brace guy wires.

(F) FUSELAGE

The fuselage consists of two side trusses, continuous from the nose of the machine to the tail. The vertical web members are designed for compressive stresses; the diagonal members for tension stresses. The diagonal members are aligned in opposite directions to withstand any reversal of stresses. The longerons constitute the upper and lower chord members. The upper longerons are horizontal and parallel to the line of thrust, from the point of maximum depth of the truss to the tail. The alignment of the lower longerons is curved to conform to the required streamline formation.

The side trusses are symmetrically disposed with respect to the longitudinal plane of symmetry of the aeroplane and gradually taper towards this plane, meeting at the tail post.

The trusses are braced in a horizontal plane at the upper and lower longerons. The members of this bracing, perpendicular to the longitudinal axis, are designed for compressive stresses. The diagonal cross members are designed as tension members and aligned in opposite directions to withstand any reversal of stresses.

The main trusses are further braced at each panel point abaft the pilot's seat by crossed diagonal tension members in a vertical plane perpendicular to the plane of symmetry.

From the nose of the fuselage to the station abaft the pilot's seat the diagonal tension members are non-flexible cable. Abaft the pilot's seat all diagonal tension members in both the vertical and horizontal planes, and cross bracing are single members of hard wire. The diagonal tension members are connected to the fittings on the longeron which receive the compression struts. These tension diagonal members are attached to the fittings by either a turnbuckle or a shackle.

The compression members are solid struts framing between the longerons. The cross section of these struts is generally square.

(G) TAIL ASSEMBLY

The horizontal stabilizer, vertical stabilizer, rudder and elevators are assembled in accordance with the C.A. Co.'s Dwg. No. 11842.

The horizontal stabilizer is mounted at the rear end of the fuselage with its lower surface resting on the top edge of the upper longerons. It is further braced and anchored to the fuselage in a fore and aft direction by a system of struts arranged from the under side of the stabilizer to the lower longerons and tail post.

The vertical stabilizer is mounted on the upper centerline of the horizontal stabilizer to which it is anchored by suitable clips and tie-down cables.

The rudder is suspended from the end edge of the vertical stabilizer and tail post of the fuselage. The guy lines from the control braces to the trailing edge are so arranged as not to foul the elevators for any position of operation. The upper edge of the rudder is in a continuous line with the leading edge of the vertical stabilizer.

The elevators are mounted on the trailing edge of the horizontal stabilizer. The inner edges of the elevators are arranged to permit operation of the rudder through an arc of at least 30 degrees each side of the fore and aft center line.

Covering and doping is the same as for the panels.

(H) LANDING GEAR

The landing gear is of the "V" type cross-braced construction. It consists of two trusses, suitably separated and cross-braced. The lower ends of the members of each side truss terminate in the fittings of the continuous cord shock absorber bridge. The landing gear is fastened to the lower longerons with suitable fittings.

The axle is properly streamlined. The bridge is so aligned vertically as to permit an upward and downward movement of the landing gear axle.

The shock absorbing bridge is of the type known as the continuous rubber cord shock absorber.

The shock absorbing unit of the bridge is a continuous built-up rubber cord covered with fabric. This cord is securely wound around the axle saddle which passes through the steel bridge and rests over the axle on both sides of the struts.

The bridge proper is a lightened steel member with a slotted arrangement to permit the vertical movement of the axle. This guide for controlling the vertical movement is curved in a transverse direction to accommodate the vertical rotation of the axle about one wheel in case of a side-landing.

(I) CONTROL SYSTEMS

The three-directional control of the machine is centered in each cockpit, and arranged to operate as an interlocked system. The directional controls in the two cockpits are identical, with the exception that the aileron quadrant, mounted on the tubular fore and aft axis between the two cockpits, is located in the rear only. Under normal conditions of flight, the controls are arranged to operate in the standard and universally accepted directions: a forward movement of the stick beyond the neutral point will cause the elevators to drop and the machine to dive; conversely, rearward movement of the stick beyond the neutral point will cause the elevators to rise, and the machine to mount. The sticks are connected by a horizontal tubular link. From the rear stick aft, there extends another link that terminates in a universal ball and socket joint with the lever which operates the axis on which the elevator control "walking-beams" are fastened. The elevators are direct connected to these walking beams by means of flexible cable.

The movement of the stick to either side of the fore and aft axis operates the ailerons. The stick in each cockpit is permanently fastened with respect to any lateral motion to the main fore and aft tubular axis of the control system. At the rear end of this shaft or axis, is permanently fastened the aileron-control-quadrant. Any side movement of the stick causes an equal angular movement in the quadrant. The aileron control lines are looped around and fastened at one point to the quadrant.

The rudder is operated by the foot-bar type control which is direct-connected and operating.

The ailerons, rudder and elevators are all equipped with control braces. These braces are located at or near the hinge line of the member. The braces are equipped with sufficiently large bases to distribute the compressive stresses developed in this member. Sufficient hard wire guy lines run from the upper end of the control braces to the trailing edge of the member to be controlled.

These braces are made of sheet steel, hollow construction and so arranged that the axis of the control column is approximately normal to the direction of pull. The control braces are arranged in pairs on opposite faces of the member to be controlled, and are fastened to the member and to themselves in pairs, by bolts which pass simultaneously through the members and the bases of the control column.

The top or upper end of the braces are reinforced. The cross-section of these braces are of a general streamline shape.

The general arrangement of the control lines to operating surfaces is shown diagramatically in the C.A. Co.'s Dwg. No. 16195.

LANDING GEAR ASSEMBLY TO FUSELAGE

The landing gear is assembled by mounting the wheels on to the axle, and bolting the wheels in place with bolts No. 4172 and accompanying nuts and cotters. The fuselage should now be elevated to receive the landing gear. This may be accomplished in one of two ways —either by tackle, or by shims and blocking.

(a) If block and tackle are used to raise the fuselage, pass a line under the engine bed supports or sills (Part No. 11741; just to the rear of the radiator. To this line attach hook of block. Do NOT ATTACH LIFTING DEVICE IN ANY OTHER MANNER, TO AVOID DAMAGING OR CRUSHING SOME PART. With the fuselage now resting on blocking location under the fuselage, just ahead of the tail skid, and under a vertical member of the fuselage side-trussing, lift the front end until the lower longeron clips for attachment of landing gear struts clear the landing gear. These clips on the lower longeron for connecting the front struts of the landing gear are found at Station No. 3. The clips on the lower longeron for connecting the rear struts are found at Station No. 5. The short bolts, with lock-washers, nuts and cotters are found in the clips attached to the bottom longerons at Station No. 3 and Station No. 5. The lock-washers are put under the head of the bolt, and when the clips on the longerons line up with the clips on the ends of the struts of the landing gear, these bolts are passed down through the holes thus aligned. This places the nuts on the down side of the connection, thus facilitating assembling and inspection of connections. The castellated nuts are then put on the bolts and drawn up tight, until the drilled hole in the bolt is visible through the castle of the nut. Then insert cotter pin and spread the two leaves backward, and in opposite directions, over the nut. This locks the nut in place. When the landing gear has been completely assembled to the fuselage, the tail of the machine should be elevated and supported by a horse and blocking under Station No. 10, until the upper longeron is level. This can be determined by placing a spirit level on the upper longeron, between Station No. 10 and No. 12, at the tail.

(b) The other method that may be employed for raising the front end of the fuselage, to assemble the landing gear is the following: remove the shipping blocking and front flooring of shipping case from under the fore part of the fuselage. Insert a block under the bottom longerons at Station No. 4, thus coming ahead of the point on which the fuselage is resting, as shipped. This blocking should be aligned under the vertical strut. The flooring to the rear of the blocking should now be removed. By lowering the tail, the nose of the machine is elevated, the above mentioned blocking serves as a fulcrum. Block up under nose of machine, placing blocking under RADIATOR BRACKET, AND NOT UNDER RADIATOR. If the tail of the machine be now lifted, this nose blocking serves as a fulcrum, and the fuselage at Station No. 4 will clear the blocking at that point. Block up again with wedges under Station No. 4 until blocking is tight against lower longeron. By depressing tail of machine, the nose will again be elevated so that blocking there will now need to be increased. By this alternating method of changing the fulcrum point and increasing the blocking, the nose of the machine can ultimately be blocked up sufficiently high (with tail of machine on the ground and blocking at Station No. 4 removed) that the landing gear may be assembled to the fuselage. A horse placed at Station No. 10, while the nose blocking is in place, will permit the removal of the blocking under Station No. 4, and allow the placing of the landing gear under the fuselage.

HORIZONTAL STABLIZER

After the upper longeron is leveled up, the horizontal stabilizer is assembled to the tail of the fuselage. The disposition of the member is shown. Each upper longeron has one U bolt and one special bolt to fasten down the horizontal stablizer. The U bolt is just ahead of Station No. 10, passing under the longeron with the legs pointing upward. These bolts extend through the stabilizer and are fastened by means of nuts, serving as a means for holding the leading edge of the stabilizer.

At the tail of the machine, two special bolts are arranged so that they extend through the horizontal stabilizer, at Station No. 12, one on each side of the vertical stabilizer. These bolts also extend through a small metal, L-shaped piece on each side, which is fastened to the vertical stabilizer, thus fastening both vertical and horizontal stabilizers to the tail of the fuselage. These two bolts are flattened on their lower ends so that they rest against the tail post and are held to it by one bolt running through, and two screws, one on each side. All nuts are castellated and secured with cotter pins.

Vertical Stabilizer

The vertical stabilizer is now fastened to the horizontal stabilizer:

(1) By means of the bolts which pass through the forward and after parts of the horizontal stabilizer, and

(2) By means of the hard wire stay lines running from the top of the vertical stabilizer to the upper surface of the horizontal stabilizer. The forward bolts pass through the clip at the lower front point of the vertical stabilizer. The bolts which are fastened to the tail post of the fuselage, and engage the after end of the horizontal stabilizer, also engage the lugs fastened to the bottom edge of the vertical stabilizer at the rear. Draw the nuts up tight and lock with cotter pins. The hard wire lines attached to the vertical stabilizer, and turnbuckles are used to align and tie down the vertical stabilizer.

Rudder

The control pylons or braces are first attached to the rudder. These braces are so placed that the upper tips point toward the hinge line. In this fashion the holes will match up. The bolts and nuts for securing braces to the rudder are shipped and fastened to the braces. Before mounting the rudder the vertical stabilizer should be checked up, so that it is in plumb alignment with the tail post. This check is absolutely necessary to insure the absolute alignment of the hinges in the vertical stabilizer and the tail post. The rudder is now mounted onto the tail post and vertical stabilizer by means of the hinges. The hinge pins are now inserted in the hinges, and cotter pins passed through the drilled holes in the bottom of the pins. The cotter pins should be spread backward as usual.

Elevators

These are first equipped with the control braces, which, with the accompanying bolts, nuts and cotters, are found in the Wing Panel Packing Box. The position of the base of the control brace is indicated on Drawing No. 11842. These braces are also arranged so that the upper tips point toward the hinge line. The elevators are mounted to the horizontal stabilizer by means of the hinges and hinge pins.

The hinge pins are kept in their bearings by the cotter pins, inserted through the drilled holes in the bottom of the hinge pins. The position of the elevators is shown on Drawing No. 11842.

Panel Assembly

The panels are now to be assembled. Before the main panels can be connected to the fuselage, the engine section panels must be erected.

ENGINE SECTION PANEL (Part No. 14798): The engine section struts are first set into place into their sockets on the upper longerons. These posts are found packed in the "Panel" box. The forward posts (Part No. 11967) are approximately held in place by the flexible wire lines to be found coiled up and temporarily fastened under the cowl in the motor compartment. The rear struts (Part No. 12733) are approximately held in place by the flexible wire lines leading from lower longeron, Station No. 7, and to be found tied to the control stick in the front cockpit. The engine section panel is now mounted on the struts, after the front transverse bracing, between the posts, is approximately trued up. The engine section panel posts and wires are then trued up prior to further erection. This condition is obtained by adjusting all "mated" or similar wires to the same length.

Main Panels

The main panels are now to be assembled to the machine. There are two methods for accomplishing this:

(a) Assemble panels, struts and wires, before attaching to fuselage.

(b) Assemble the upper plane to the engine section, and complete assembly.

The first method is the most advantageous, since it permits the setting of the main panels at the approximately correct stagger and dihedral, and does not require as much subsequent adjustment as the second method.

(A) FIRST METHOD—Wings Completely Assembled

All the main struts will be found to bear a number. These numbers run from 1 to 8. The method used in numbering the posts is as follows: Starting at post No. 1, with the outer post on the left hand side of the pilot, as he faces his direction of travel, the front posts are numbered successively from No. 1 to No. 4: Nos. 1 and 2 being on the left side and Nos. 3 and 4 being on the right side. The rear posts are similarly numbered from No. 5 to No. 8: Nos. 5 and 6 being on the left and Nos. 7 and 8 being on the right. This system of numbering does not include the engine section struts.

The system of marking also insures that the struts are not inverted in their sockets. This is accomplished by painting the number on the strut so that when viewed from the pilot's seat all numbers can be read; i.e., the numbers are painted on that side of the strut intended to face the fuselage, as diagramatically shown. If a strut be inverted by mistake, it can thus quickly be detected.

(1) The upper left wing panel is first equipped with the front and rear masts by inserting the masts into their sockets on the upper surface of the panel. The mast wires are then connected to the anchor plates, located on the upper surface to the right and left of the mast socket. Adjust the tension in these wires, by means of turnbuckles, until the front and rear wing beams become straight, in a vertical plane.

(2) Stand the upper left wing panel and lower left wing panel on their "leading," or "entering" edges, properly supporting the panels in cushioned blocks to prevent damage to the nose. Space the panels apart, approximately equal to the length of the struts.

(3) Next connect up the diagonal cross wires. These must be loosely connected up (by loosening up the turnbuckles), to permit the easy entering of the posts into their sockets. The wires are connected before the posts or struts are set in place, since, with the latter in place, the connecting of the wires to the lugs of the sockets is accomplished only with difficulty. After these wires are thus connected, insert the posts and bolts into place.

(4) Connect up loosely the "landing" (single) wires and "flying" (double) wires of the outer bay to hold the wings together as a unit. The outer bay is thus completely wired, though but loosely.

(5) The posts that are used for this left side are No. 1, No. 2, No. 5, and No. 6 according to the diagram. No. 1 is the outer front; No. 2 is the inner front; No. 5 is the outer rear; No. 6 is the inner rear.

(6) The wings, as above assembled, are now erected to the fuselage. Extreme care should be exercised in transferring the wings to the fuselage, not to strain or break them. In carrying the wings, use wooden boards placed under the wings, and block up under the wing beams (which can be easily located by the line of fittings attached) so

that these take the strain of the load. Do not attempt handling assembled wings using the posts as carriers, or by attachments to the trailing or leading edges. Fig. 15 shows a good manner in which the panels may be shifted.

The wings should be firmly supported temporarily by a suitable sling at the upper outer post point (not beyond this point), or by a horse, properly blocked under lower wing at outer lower post point (not beyond this point), during fitting of wing to machine. See Fig. No. 16 for arrangement. The wings will have the approximate stagger if assembled as above, since the posts are in place and the tension cross wires are adjusted to almost correct length when shipped. Insert the hinge pins through the hinges, located at (1), Fig. No. 16, as now coupled up.

Adjustment for Dihedral

(7) The fuselage must now be leveled up transversely and longitudinally. A spirit level placed across the top longerons will determine the transverse condition. With the level placed fore and aft on the longerons aft of Station No. 5, the longitudinal level is established.

(8) Adjust the tension on the flying and landing wires until the dihedral of one (1) degree is established, also to make the leading and trailing edges parallel and straight. The amount of lift for the one (1) degree dihedral is 2¾" in 13'6" (distance from the inner edge of the panel to the centerline outer post). An easy method for checking the correct adjustment of the dihedral is to place a block 2¾" high on the upper surface of the lower wing, at the extreme inner edge. A straight edge resting on this block and on the upper surface of the wing (straight edge kept parallel to the front or rear beam) should be level.

This may also be checked by using a light spirit level, suspended from a string stretched over the given range. If a block 2¾" high be clamped to the inner edge of the panel, and a line pulled taut from this block to the centerline of the outer beam, the level suspended next to the block will be sufficiently sensitive to determine the required degree of dihedral.

If the outer end of the wings is too high, the landing (single) wires are too short and the flying (double) wires are too long. Hence, loosening up equally on the inner and outer, front and rear flying (double) wires, will correct this condition. If the panels are too low (dihedral not up to one degree), reversing the above method corrects this condition.

Adjustment for Stagger

(9) The tension in the longitudinal cross wires is now adjusted for stagger. The distance between a plumb line dropped from the leading edge of the upper wing and the leading edge of the lower wing should be 16 inches. If the amount is less than 16 inches, the line leading from the lower wing front socket to the upper wing rear socket is too long. Hence, drawing up on this line and lengthening out on the cross line will correct this condition. If the distance is more than 16 inches, reverse corrections of wire lengths.

(10) Check up the dihedral to see if this has been disturbed while setting the stagger. Also check up with eye the alignment of the front and rear beam, and parallelism of leading and trailing edges. If these are not parallel, adjustment of the landing (single) wires in the inner bay (next to the fuselage) will generally correct this condition.

(11) The wing skids on the under side of the lower wing should now be fastened to the sockets, directly under the outer posts.

(12) Bend all cotter pins out.

(13) The other side of the machine (right side) is then assembled in the same manner. Examine the left side to see that its adjustment has not been disturbed.

(14) Lock turnbuckles with safety wires. This latter is accomplished by first passing a soft wire through the eye of one shank of the turnbuckle, then winding the wire four or five times about the shank, the shorter, loose end of the wire being wrapped under the windings; then pass the free end through the small hole in the center of the barrel, then through the eye of the opposite shank, wrapping this free end around this shank and wire. This effectively locks the turnbuckles.

(B) SECOND METHOD OF ERECTING PANELS

The following outline method is given; the details of handling and adjusting of wires is identical with the details given for the first method:

(1) Insert masts (Parts Nos. 5092, 5093) into sockets and connect mast wires to anchor terminals. Adjust tension of mast wires until beams are straight.

(2) Connect upper panel to engine section and bolt upper ends of struts into fittings.

(3) Jack up wing tip of upper panel so that lower panel can be connected.

(4) Connect lower panel to fuselage.

(5) Connect cross diagonal wires.

(6) Bolt lower end of struts into fittings on lower wing.

(7) Connect landing (single) wires.

(8) Connect flying (double) wires.

(9) Proceed in like manner with other side of machine.

(10) Remove jacks and level fuselage longitudinally and transversely.

(11) Adjust tension on landing (single) and flying (double) wires until the dihedral is one degree; leading and trailing edges are parallel and straight.

(12) Adjust tension on diagonal wires until stagger is 16 inches.

(13) Attach wing skids.

(14) Bend cotter pins and safety wire turnbuckles.

Aileron Adjustment

Attach both ailerons (one on each side of machine, after having mounted control braces to ailerons) and fasten pins of hinges with the necessary cotter pins. Temporarily support ailerons so that their trailing edges are one (1) inch below the trailing edges of the upper panels. Then connect up the flexible tie-in that, passing over the top of the upper wings, through fairleads, is connected at the center by a turnbuckle, and, passing through pulleys attached to the upper surface, front beam, is attached (by shackle and pin) to the upper control brace of the aileron. This "lead" is allowed, so that when in flight, the force of the lift will somewhat raise both ailerons and bring their trailing edges on a line with the trailing edges of the panels. Now lead the end of the aileron control line attached to sector through the hole in each side of the fuselage (between front and rear seats). Uncoil the connecting line which passes over the pully attached to the lower surface of the upper wing, near the front outer post. Attach shackle and pin end to lower control brace of aileron, and attach turnbuckle end to loop of aileron control lead attached to control sector in fuselage (and which passes through side of fuselage). In making this last attachment, the leads should be so arranged (by moving the stick of the controls) that the lengths projecting through the fuselage are equal.

Rudder Control Adjustment

Uncoil the lines attached to the rudder bar, to lead out through the upper surface of the rear end of the fuselage cover, and, keeping the rudder control bar at right angles to the longitudinal axis of the machine, fasten the ends to the control braces. Next take up the slack of the lines, by means of the turnbuckles, adjusting the tension equally in each set; the rudder control bar (foot control bar) should remain at right angles to the longitudinal axis, when the rudder is neutral (or in a vertical plane through this fore and aft axis).

Elevator Control Adjustment

Temporarily maintain the elevators in the plane of the horizontal stabilizer (Neutral position). Move the stick forward until the distance between the instrument board and the nearer surface of the tube of the stick is nine and one half (9½) inches. By fixing this distance from the instrument board or dash to the tube of the stick, a slight lead is given to the control, for the greater range for raising the elevators. Now uncoil the wires leading from the clips attached to the walking beams of the stick control, and coiled up aft the pilot's seat. Pass the wire attached to the lower end of the beam out through the side of the fuselage, through the lower of the two vertical holes, aft of the pilot's seat. With the control stick lashed, or fastened to the nine and one-half (9½) inch position, connect this wire to the lower control brace of the elevator. Repeat operation for the other side of the machine.

Similarly the wire attached to the upper end of the walking beam is passed through the upper hole in the fuselage side, and attached to the upper control brace of the elevator. Drawing Nos. 16195, 16196 shows the general arrangment of the controls. Adjust tension in these wires, by means of turnbuckles, so that all lines have the same degree of tautness. The elevators will then be neutral for the position of the bridge.

GENERAL

All connections having now been made, carefully go over each shackle, pin and turnbuckle, and see that all pins are properly in place, all nuts on bolts tight, and all cotter-pinned. Try out all controls for action and freedom of movement. See that no brace wires are slack, yet not so taut that, when plucked they "sing."

Attach nose wires leading from nose of machine to intermediate posts, front and rear. The lower wire connects up with the lower front socket, on the upper surface of the lower panel; the upper wire connects up with the upper rear socket plate on the under side of the upper panel, after the panels are attached to fuselage, with the stagger and dihedral properly corrected.

OVERHAULING THE CURTISS OX-5 MOTOR
Nicholas-Beazley Airplane Co., Inc. Marshall, Missouri.

The Curtiss OX-5 motor has been conceded to be by far the most practical and reliable motor on the American market for light aircraft. Our stock of these motors is sufficient to take care of the needs for several years. We have an enormous stock of parts for OX-5 and OXX-6 motors. They are new and in perfect condition.

PRICE LIST
(Subject to change without notice)

OX –5	90 hp	brand new	$1000.00
OX –5	"	Govt. overhauled	600.00
OX –5	"	Used, serviceable: Write for prices	
OXX–6	100 hp	brand new	1250.00
OXX–6	"	Overhauled	750.00
OXX–6	"	Used, serviceable: Write for prices	

CHAPTER 1: DISASSEMBLY OF THE CURTISS MOTOR

WHAT SHOULD BE DONE BEFORE DISASSEMBLY: Inspect engine as a whole to determine general layout and consider best order of removal of parts. Notice any fractures or signs of trouble or heating.

Determine direction of rotation of motor. This is done by turning the engine over and carefully watching the operation of the valves of any cylinder, remembering the fact that in the proper operation of a four-cycle motor the inlet valve will open at the same time or immediately after the exhaust valve closes. If the motor were being revolved in the wrong direction, this order of operations would be reversed.

Check valve clearances after making sure that they are at neutral point. All valve clearances should be roughly checked in taking the motor down, as this affords an opportunity to detect a bent or sprung rocker arm. (In taking clearance measurements, the tappets must be held away from the valve stem with one hand to get the full measurement.)

Check timing of valves by piston distance. (Exact method will be described later.)

Check timing of motor as hereinafter described.

Removing minor assemblies—Remove high-tension ignition wires and spark plugs. Be sure to immediately fill spark-plug holes with

263

plugs of soft wood or some other material that will not chip, to prevent cotter pins or other foreign bodies from dropping inside of the cylinders.

Remove carburetor and duplex manifold as one unit after disconnecting water tubes.

Remove inlet water manifolds, breaking the hose joint which is next to the water pump.

Removing rocker-arm assemblies, manifolds, and pump—Next remove rocker-arm assemblies complete by removing two nuts on top of each cylinder and two at the base of the tie-down straps. In releasing the tie-down straps, tension may very conveniently be taken off the nuts while unscrewing by placing the jaws of a monkey wrench above the tie-down straps and around the hollow push rods. Very slight pressure downward on the wrench handle will make it bind and hold down the spring without doing any injury to the push rod. The inlet manifold assemblies complete may be removed next, care being taken to save and not injure the gasket.

Next the pump and timing gear end plate should be removed.

Removing magneto—The magneto and base plate may now be taken off and the magneto sent to the electrical repair room for overhauling.

Removing cylinders—Nothing remains on the top of the crankcase now but the cylinders. If, after all nuts have been removed, the cylinders stick, a slight tap of the hand will release them from the case. They should then be raised carefully, first making sure that the gaskets are coming up complete with the cylinders. When the cylinders are being raised clear of the pistons, make sure that someone is holding the piston so that in case the wrist pin bearing is free the piston will not fall over and hit its skirt against the connecting rod. Pistons falling over in this way may become at least dented outward or cracked.

Care must also be taken not to bend outward the cylinder tiedown rods. In order not to do this, the cylinder must be raised to the top of the stud and held there while the four nuts are unscrewed over the thread at the top of the studs.

Revolving crank case; removing sump and connecting rods—Now the motor may be turned upside down. (WARNING: Make sure that the motor is tightly bolted to the revolving stand by all four legs, and that oil has been drained.) First remove the oil pump and connecting pipe, then the face plate on the hub end of the crankcase, then after removing all bolts the entire sump may be lifted off. Here again care should be taken not to destroy the paper gasket that runs under the

Above

Top view of an OX-2 engine. There was lots of walla-walla when all those parts got to jumping around. Plainly visible here are many things to give a pilot fits. The rocker-arm mechanism for valve actuation, push rods and springs, to say nothing of electrical, fuel, and water systems were nobody's friends.

The battle of weight-per-horsepower was being fought in this pioneer wilderness, and at this stage of the art weight was ahead. (Curtiss Aeroplane Co.)

Below

The bottom of an OX-5. This is the part that dragged along the ground when the landing gear folded up. (Curtiss Aeroplane Co.)

sump. The strainer may now be removed from the sump and washed with gasoline or kerosene, and the whole sump carefully examined for cracks.

The connecting-rod bearings and the main bearings are now exposed. Remove all cotter keys. The caps of the connecting-rod bearings may now be removed, care being taken to hold each rod so that it will fall through when the nuts are released. Each cap should be replaced on its own connecting rod, and all nuts must be released with a proper fitting socket wrench.

Removing, examining, and handling of crank shaft—Before removing the crank shaft, examine clearance between cam gear and crank shaft gear in order to determine whether or not the bearings will have to be raised. Then the crank shaft may be taken out. In removing the bearing cap nuts, a socket wrench should always be used and should be carefully fitted so that it will never slip.

When nuts are removed, the caps can best be lifted with the use of a special tool in the form of a lever with a fulcrum attached. Caps should not be pounded with any kind of hammer to free them. Before raising the crankshaft out of its bed, pieces of rubber tubing should be placed over the bearing studs, in order to prevent the shaft from scraping against the threads when it is being lifted out. This is very important, because the threads are much harder than the shaft, and the least touch can cause a nick in the journal.

If the bearing has shims between the halves, it is well to prepare a board with nails for the nuts and shims. In laying the shaft down on the bench, care should be taken to rest the shaft on its side on a flat board so that it will get bearing surface at more than two points, giving an equal distribution of the weight of the shaft.

If the shaft is laid down resting on the gear and thrust bearings only, it will almost always bend a few thousandths out of true. The crank shaft should now be thoroughly washed with kerosene, special care being taken to blow out all oil passages. This may well be done by squirting kerosene into the different holes with a grease gun. Shaft should now be very carefully examined for signs of wear and crystallization, which is noted by a peculiar flaky appearance of the steel. If there is any sign of crystallization, the shaft should be discarded. Early crystallization is due to the incessant hammer-like blows delivered to the shaft by the connecting rods, as *the engine runs at full speed all the time.*

Removing the cam shaft—All of the motor has now been taken down except the cam shaft. First, all of the bearing set screws should be removed. Then a special Curtiss can gear puller should be fitted to the gear, and the whole shaft and bearings may be easily drawn out. Very light tapping on the sides of the bearings with a piece of fiber or and a hammer will ease out the bearings if they bind at all. Before removing the bearings from the shaft, it should be noted whether they are numbered, so that they may be put back in the same order. The cam shaft should now be carefully cleaned, both inside and out, in the same manner as the crankshaft. Then the crank case may be thoroughly washed out and examined for cracks.

Chapter 2: Assembly of the Motor

Preparatory inspection—In building up the motor, the greatest care must be used in the inspection of the parts. The least crack of any kind should be sufficient to condemn the part. Before assembling, all parts must be very carefully cleaned with kerosene or gasoline, and after becoming dry, all bearing surfaces must be covered with a coating of oil. This because, if the motor be assembled dry, it may be forced to run for some time before the pump is able to circulate oil to remote parts of the engine.

Fitting cam-shaft bearings—As the cam shaft was the last part to be removed from the engine, so it is the first part to be replaced. First, examine the cam gear for wear in the teeth, then examine the shaft. It should be tested in a lathe for straightness if it binds in any way. The split bearings must be screwed together tightly without shims and should not have over 0.0015 to 0.002 of an inch clearance on the shaft. These may be tried before replacing the shaft. The bearings, if all right, should be removed from the shaft and tried in their proper location. The cam-shaft bearings should fit in their casings with an extremely light driving fit. If loose, new bearings should be procured. Remove these bearings, slip shaft into position, then replace bearings around the shaft in a position adjacent to the casing which is to retain them. Great care must be shown in determining that the oil holes in the bearings properly register with the holes in the webs and also with the holes in the shaft. Notice the small shoulder on the front bearing and see that this is guided properly into its place. Set up retaining set screws. It should now be possible to rotate cam shaft easily with one finger on the gear.

Inspecting and checking the crank shaft—The first operation in fitting the shaft is to cover the journals with a very thin coating of prussian blue and then lay it in its bed to get a preliminary marking. The thrust bearing should also be blued; and it may be noted here that this bearing should have been carefully inspected, especially to see that all balls have a perfectly smooth surface, scars indicating a future break. After rocking a few times, the shaft is removed and all markings examined carefully. Not much can be said on paper about the proper method of fitting bearings, but the following bits of advice and warning should be heeded: First, do not do any scraping until you have considered the markings on all bearings in conjunction with each other, and have decided the effect that the removal of metal from one spot may have on other bearings farther down the line.

When it has been decided to scrape a spot, use a long stroke which will lift the tool off the surface while it is still moving forward; that is, do not stop the stroke of the tool in such a manner that it will leave a nick. Scrape a spot a little larger than that actually covered by the blue spot, as this surrounding area will undoubtedly mark blue on the next trial, and tie will be saved by removing this at first.

The bearing surface should not be carried entirely up on the sides of the linings, a two-thirds surface being sufficient. When this is procured on the five bearings, attention must be paid to thrust bearing and gear. Both should be loose and bear no part of the weight. With the end bearing cap screwed down tight, it should be just barely possible to rotate the thrust bearing with the fingers. There should always be a clearance between the cam and crank shaft gears. This can be "felt" by hand as well as seen with a clear eye, and should be between 0.001 inch and 0.003 inch, measured parallel to the circumference of either gear. On no condition should a cam gear be filed to give more clearance; and if there is tightness here or at the thrust bearing, the trouble is that the bearings are too low and these should be removed.

Placing new bearing shells—If it is found necessary to put in new bearing linings, these should be pressed into place with the use of a jig, and held while retaining screws are being inserted. It is well also to allow the edge of the lining to extend about 0.0005 inch above the surface of the casing on both sides, so that when the two halves are clamped together the bearing lining may be further and more completely seated. If no new bearing linings are at hand and the shaft must be raised, 0.002-inch shims may be placed under the bearing linings. This is not good practice, however, and is not to be commended. If shims are used, they should be cut to cover the whole surface with the exception of oil holes, and should furthermore extend above the surface about 0.0005 inch in order to be pressed down properly into place. If bearings are shimmed, it will be found necessary to scrape a little off the sides of the linings, as the action of the shims makes the horizontal diameter of the bearing 0.004 inch less, while it decreases the vertical diameter only 0.002 inch.

Aligning and fitting the main bearing caps and shells—Having obtained a proper bed for the shaft, the caps must now be considered. These should first be fitted to the case to insure a true surface with no tendency to rock. Then all should be set up in place and motor turned over so that the shaft will rest on caps. A marking with bluing should be made in this position, and high sections cut away as was done in the other half. Then allowance should be made for the clearance of 0.0025 inch in the following manner: A piece of 0.002-inch shim stock should first be laid in the bottom of each bearing under the shaft. These pieces should run the whole length of the journal, but should be only about one-half inch wide. By this method, the shaft is raised up a trifle over 0.002 inch and the caps may be fitted until they are a very snug fit. This is done in the same manner as the lower caps, only one at a time. They should be scraped until there is a two-thirds bearing surface, and until the shaft may be turned only with considerable force by hand when the cap is completely screwed down.

In screwing down bearing cap nuts, great care must be taken not to strain the threads. It is very easy to put too much power into a well-fitting large socket wrench and this seriously strains the threads. Moreover, only a socket wrench should be used in screwing up these nuts.

When each cap has been fitted, shims are removed, and all caps screwed down, after first covering the bearing surfaces with a coat of oil. The shaft should then turn quite freely, and thrust bearings and gears should have proper clearance. In case there is too much clearance, the caps must be filed down. This may be done by drawing the ends of the cap back and forth over a strip of crocus cloth placed on a surface plate. Care must be taken to keep the surface true.

The "end play" of the crank shaft—Nothing yet has been said about the end-play adjustment of the crank shaft. This is determined entirely by the thrust bearing. It will be found that with no thrust bearing, there will be allowed about three sixty-fourths inch of end play to the shaft by the webs of the crank case. If the motor is to be used as a tractor, as is usually the case, this end play should be adjusted so that two-thirds of the space is toward the forward end of the motor. This is done so that the forward pull of the shaft will cause the throws to center themselves between the webs as wear appears in the thrust bearing. If it is necessary to set the shaft to the rear, this may be done by introducing a thin shim between the thrust bearing and the shoulder on the shaft. If the shaft must be set toward the front, it is necessary to put the shaft in the lathe and take a very fine cut from the shoulder on the shaft. No shims can be placed between the thrust bearings and the case.

Safety locking bearing nuts—In regard to the proper placing of cotter pins in the bearing nuts, there is much argument, but the following points stand out preeminent:

First   No nut must be turned backward or loosened to make the cotter-pin holes line up. If it cannot be turned forward to the next slot in the castellations without straining the threads, the nut should be removed, and the bottom surface filed a very small amount. This process should be repeated until the nut will turn nicely up to a slot in the castellations.

Second   The cotter keys must completely fill the holes in the stud bolt.

Third   The cotter keys must not be bent over with a hammer, but should be bent with a pair of round nose pliers. Bend one side of the cotter key up over the nut and the other side downward, unless in particular cases it is found to be distinctly better to bend both sides of the key around the nut.

Preparing the piston assembly—The next operation in assembling the motor is to be assured that the piston assemblies are in proper condition. First, try the wrist-pin bearings. These should be, when cold, quite stiff, so that the pistons will not rock over with their own weight, but will require a fair amount of pressure with the hand. It must be remembered that when the bearings become hot, the alluminum pistons expand considerably more than the steel wrist pins and the bearings become sufficiently loose. If it is necessary to remove a wrist pin, the set screw is loosened and the pin pressed through.

Next, see that the set screws holding the wrist pins in the connecting rods are screwed up firmly and properly locked with wire. It is very important that this wire be perfectly tight—cannot be moved with the fingers. All carbon should be scraped from the inside of the piston as well as the outside, taking care to use no instrument that will scratch the aluminum. Examine connecting rods for possible cracks.

Next remove the piston rings and carefully clean out the grooves. Do not pry ring out of groove if stuck, but put piston in hot water and ring can easily be removed. The rings may best be removed by inserting under them three or four pieces of hack-saw blades, the teeth ground off, and carefully sliding the rings from the piston. They should not be sprung more than is absolutely necessary. If the rings show signs of wear and do not have perfectly true surfaces, they should be renewed. If a new ring is found to be too thick to slip easily into the slot, it may be dressed down slightly by rubbing the top surface on a piece of fine emery placed on a surface plate. The bottom surface of the ring must never be dressed in this manner, as this is the surface that comes in close contact with the slot in the piston, and the true factory-ground finish should be left intact in order to assure a perfect fit between the piston and the ring. It should be noted that the factory trade mark is always stamped on the bottom or the most perfectly finished surface of the ring. This will be found in very small markings at the point where the two ends of the ring come together. Any roughness on the pistons must be dressed down with a fine stone, and the pistons may finally be polished with Dixon's graphite, but no free flakes must be left on the surface.

Fitting the connecting-rod bearings—Now that the piston assemblies have all been completed, attention can be paid to the connecting rod bearings. These are fitted much in the same way as the main bearings, except that each is done independently of the others. First, the lower halves should be scraped to a proper fit with two-thirds bearing surface. Then the caps are screwed on and the bearings fitted so that there will be a clearance of not over 0.002 inch. It will not be necessary to determine this clearance with the use of shim stock. The clearance may be determined by grasping the connecting rod in the hands and rocking it from side to side, taking care that the rod does not slip on the shaft.

A clearance of two thousandths may be easily determined in this manner after a small amount of practice. Another highly important point in the fitting of connecting rods is their perpendicularity. The best way to check this is by measuring the distance between two ends of mandrels in wrist-pin and connecting-rod bearings, but much may be determined with the use of a square laid against first one and then the other side of the piston, and resting on some true part of the case.

The bolts and studs should now be firmly cotter keyed, as in the case of the main bearings. In placing the connecting-rods on the shaft, it must be pointed out that there is a difference between the two sides of each bearing—the side of the bearing toward the adjacent connecting rod is finished off squarely, while the outside of each pair of rods has a rounded edge on the babbitt lining. While fitting the connecting-rod bearings, and in all subsequent work until the pistons are on, great care must be taken not to let the pistons fall over from one side to the other, in case the bearings are loose enough to allow them to do so. Also, when the shaft is revolved or the motor turned over, the same care must be taken with each connecting rod. This is very important, as the weight of a falling piston or rod is sufficient to bend or scar the piston. All nuts and cotter keys in the crank case must now be inspected for looseness. The surest way to accomplish this is to place the fingers on each nut, feeling for any looseness or lack of a key.

Preparing to mount cylinders, grinding valves, and testing springs —The next unit to be added to the assembly is the cylinders; but first these must be inspected and the valves ground in. No serious trouble is likely to have happened to the cylinders unless the motor has become dry and they are scored. They should, however, be examined carefully for signs of this, and all carbon should be taken out by the use of a scraper that will not injure the cylinders. The valves should next be removed by pressing the cylinder against a forked piece of iron or the jaws of a vise which will compress the spring so that the key may be removed. All valve springs should be tested for tension. The proper data are as follows:

Exhaust valve spring, 35 pounds at a length of 1⅝ inches.

Inlet valve spring, 16 pounds at a length of 1⅝ inches.

While testing these, the intake pull-down springs may be tested. This type of spring should test 40 pounds at a length of 2¾ inches. It is very necessary that the springs test very closely to the required amount, otherwise there will be vibration during operation. If a spring tests only slightly below the correct amount, the defect may be eradicated by the introduction of washers under the spring. It is highly important that these washers be placed under the spring and not out on the stem, for if placed at the latter point, they would increase the weight of the valve and change the operation.

The valve-grinding process—After grinding the valves, notice must be taken of the valve-stem guides. There should not be any noticeable looseness here, or air will rush in on the intake stroke, ruining the mixture. The valve seats should be inspected next to determine whether there is need of grinding at all. Very small pits may be disregarded, but large ones should be ground out as follows:

a. Place a small amount of fine grinding compound on the edge of the valve and insert valve into its seat, taking care not to get any of the compound on the inside of the cylinder walls.
b. Grasp the end of the valve stem with a valve-grinding tool which resembles a tap wrench.

c. Rotate the valve upon its seat.

d. Use very short strokes and lift the valve off its seat, at the end of every stroke.

e. Very little pressure must be exerted, but the compound must be renewed after a very small amount of grinding.

f. The valve must not be pounded down onto its seat. It must be borne in mind that fresh compound continually redistributed on the surface by lifting the valve will accomplish a much quicker and better job than much rubbing under heavy pressure. Moreover, this latter method will cut grooves or rings in the valve seat.

g. When it is considered that the valve has a tight seat, the cylinder and valve must be thoroughly wiped with gasoline to remove all traces of the compound, and the valve replaced with its spring for testing. Rubbing the valve around in its seat at this point with a little pure oil on it will usually produce a tighter fit.

h. Test by introducing a small amount of gasoline in the manifold and watching inside the cylinder to see if any of it seeps through inside.

Port-side view of an OXX-3 engine. Somewhere in there lurks a camshaft, the nemesis of Jennymen. Propeller hub is at the left. Black unit is the magneto. Carburetor at lower right. There were more things that could go wrong with this than a mechanic could remember. (There was very little difference externally between an OXX-3 and an OX-5.) (Curtiss Aeroplane Co.)

A perfectly seated valve should hold the gasoline without showing any signs of leaking. If the pit holes are very deep, coarser compound may be used in the beginning, but in this case, the valve should be finished off with the finer compound. In placing the cotter keys in the valve stem, care should be taken that the ends are bent around far enough so that they will not interfere with the action of the springs, and at the same time that they are not loose.

Mounting cylinders—The next point before placing the cylinders on the motor is to see that the gaskets at the bottom are in good condition. Shellac should be used to hold the gasket on the cylinder, and it is of the utmost importance that no edge of the gasket is bent over, for if this is the case, the whole cylinder will be forced out of line, oil will leak out at the gasket, and the intake manifold will not fit without straining something. In placing the cylinders, great care must be taken not to break or injure the rings. These should be compressed with the hands and the cylinder should be rocked sideways gently until it slides down easily. Just after passing over the rings, however, the cylinder must be held while the four cylinder nuts are screwed on over the top threads on the long cylinder tie-down studs. If the cylinders are dropped all the way down, the nuts cannot be put in place without springing the studs outward, which will tend to crystallize the metal.

Again, before bolting the cylinders down in place, a thin coating of graphite should be placed on the under side of the gaskets. This will seal the joint tight, but will not seize it like shellac and tear the gasket when the cylinder is removed again.

Just as the cylinder nuts are about to be tightened down, the intake manifold should be placed on the intake ports of the four cylinders and screwed up in order to line up the cylinders with the manifold. Then the cylinder bolts should be tightened down gradually and together. The cylinder nuts may be locked with the use of lock washers with a flat washer under each to prevent the sharp edge of the washer from cutting into the aluminum of the crank case. The tie-down spiders should next be put in place, but the nuts should not be screwed down as yet, and the center nuts should not be put on at this time, as they will have to be removed later in order to put on the water manifolds.

Placing the valve-operating parts—The cam followers should now be placed in position. Each should be examined carefully to make sure that the set screw is not so long that it binds the exhaust cam follower. Also, if a flat surface has been pounded on the bottom of the followers, they may be very carefully ground off by hand on a fine stone until the surface is round again. At this point, the end play of the cam shaft should be checked, if this has not already been done. There should be practically no end play to the cam shaft, just enough so that it will turn free, and it should be so placed that the cams fall exactly under the center of the holes in the case for the cam follower guides. If the cam shaft is out only a little in this respect, there will be danger that the exhaust follower will ride on the intake cam, or rub against and break down the edge of it.

The cam follower guide nuts, like the cylinder nuts, should be locked with lock washer and flat washers. Next, the magneto base may be put in place with a lock washer under each screw.

Mounting the intake manifolds—The intake manifolds should next be put in place, after first examining them carefully for cracks and for trueness along the ports. The gaskets must be carefully picked over, and if the life is gone from them, new ones should be used. Care must be taken, however, that the gaskets used on one side are of the same thickness as those on the other so that the manifold will screw down tightly without springing. The gaskets in this case are put on dry.

Mounting the rocker-arm assemblies—While some of the men are working on the manifolds, others should be inspecting the valve-operating mechanism. Quite frequently, exhaust rocker arms are found bent or sprung. In this case, they should be renewed and not rebent. The rocker-arm bearings, if improperly oiled, will wear quite badly and become loose. Bearings in this condition should be taken down and reworked in the machine shop. Possibly it will be necessary to make new pins. Very careful attention should be paid to the small bearings on this part of the motor. The small water gaskets on this assembly should not be overlooked. They must be shellacked to the rocker-arm assembly, but should be coated with graphite grease on the side next to the cylinders. These gaskets must be cut so that they extend out to the sides around the studs.

All moving parts must be properly oiled and special attention paid to the small oil holes in the rocker arms. These become easily clogged with dirt, and this condition is the cause of a great deal of wear that so often takes place at this point.

The two center nuts holding the water leads are now tightened, as these cannot be tightened later without throwing out the valve clearance. Then the four outside ones may be set up, and safely locked with cotter keys on account of the excessive vibration on them. The nuts holding the tie-down straps must be safely locked with lock washers. As the nuts located on the tops of the cylinders are fastened down, the cam shaft should be revolved so that there will be no strain on the rocker arms when the nuts are being set up.

Valve timing—Everything is now ready for the timing of the valves. On the Curtiss OX-5, the exhaust valve should close 10 deg. past top center. All valve clearance should average 0.010 inch. If a timing disc is available, this clearance should be set on No. 1 cylinder and the gears meshed so that the exhaust valve is just closing at this point. This may be determined by placing a 0.001-inch or 0.002-inch thickness gauge under the rocker arm, the moment that this is released being the moment at which the valve is seated. If the gear teeth do not mesh at this point, the cam shaft should be moved so that the timing will be later rather than earlier, but not by an amount that would be in excess of 5 deg.

After No. 1 cylinder is correct, each succeeding cylinder should be placed at 10 deg. past and the timing checked up. Any small variation may then be corrected by changing slightly the valve clearance. If a timing disc is not available, the engine may be timed by piston distance, though this is not so accurate. In this case, the piston should be allowed to drop one-sixteenth inch below top center and No. 1 exhaust valve timed at this point. The remaining clearances should be set at ten-thousandths, as this method is not accurate enough to correct by clearance.

Preparing the magneto for mounting—The magneto should now be installed, but first it should be checked up in the following respects: The breaker-box cover should be removed, and small parts examined for wear or burning. The distributor head should be removed and the distributor wiped out carefully with a dry cloth. If the contacts are black, they may be burnished with very fine sandpaper, but if the surface is badly rough, it must be faced off in a lathe. After the surface has been made smooth and clean, it should be wiped over with a rag moistened in oil to give it the most polished surface.

The magneto should be rotated by hand quickly to see if a spark can be produced across the safety gap. If no spark is obtained, the magneto should be sent to the electrical room for repairs. The magnetoes will not be further disassembled than above mentioned without being sent to the repair room. Whenever a magneto is removed from the engine, the distributor must be removed also and not left attached to the wires.

Timing the magneto with the engine—If the magneto is found to be all right, it is placed in position on the motor. The timing of the magneto on the OX-5 is 32 deg. before top center; of piston distance, about seven-sixteenths of an inch. The motor is accordingly placed in this position with respect to No. 1 cylinder. The magneto is then turned over until the distributor brush is in contact with the segment to be connected to No. 1 cylinder, and then adjusted until the breaker is just on the point of opening. The magneto is then slipped forward into position, great care being taken in meshing the gears not to turn the magneto armature over out of the position in which it has just been set. Very little oil is put on the magneto, just a few drops in the oil holes for each main bearing. The timing should be checked up with two or three other cylinders.

Finishing up the gear end of the engine—After the magneto, the timing-gear cover plate should be put in place, the gasket being shellacked underneath and graphited on top, with due care that it is not doubled under at any point. The screws holding this should be "safetied" with a wire running through all, and drawn tight. This wire must be so run through the successive screws that, if any one of them were to start to loosen, it would immediately draw the wire tighter. Next, the split plate at the rear of the magneto gear should be replaced. After this plate is in place, the motor is ready for the water pump. The pump should be taken apart to see that the vanes are in good condition and not rubbing on either side of the housing. If they are, the blades must be shifted on the pump shaft and shimmied. This shaft must be very smooth under the packing and all rust must be carefully removed, otherwise it will wear the packing out rapidly and cause the pump to leak. The packing is a wick, and a piece about eight inches long is required.

In taking the pump apart, the housing opposite the coupling will slide off after the nut is removed, but it frequently comes very hard, so care must be taken to not bend it or injure the gasket between the two halves. The gasket should be covered with shellack on one side and graphite on the other. The screws holding the pump together may be "safetied" with lock and flat washers. After the pump is in place, the air pump is added, if one is used. This is a simple plunger pump, the bearings of which should be looked over for excessive wear.

Placing the sump—It is now necessary to turn the engine over in the stand and put on the sump. This should be carefully cleaned, including the strainer, and examined throughout for cracks. The gasket must be complete and perfect, shellacked to the sump, but covered with a coat of graphite on the other side. The bolts must be run up from the under side with a flat washer, lock washer, and nut on the top. When this is secured, the end plate at the thrust bearing may be put on and the retaining nuts wired. The oil pump bearing may be put on and the retaining nuts wired. The oil pump should be opened and examined, although there is little chance of trouble here. It should be perfectly clean, however. In dropping the pump into place, it will be necessary to rotate it until the square end drops into place, in the square socket in the bevel gear.

Placing the carburetor and miscellaneous connections—The motor is now turned back right side up, and the carburetor, water pipes, and small oil pipes added. The plugs in the bottom of the carburetor should be removed and the carburetor flushed out to make sure that it is clean. The float mechanism should be examined to make sure that it will function properly. A good combination of jets to use for average conditions is: main 120, comp. 110. This is affected more or less by the quality of the gasoline and the condition of the atmosphere. It is highly important to have good tight-fitting fiber gaskets under the jets. Lock and flat washers may be used in "safetying" the carburetor nuts.

In putting the inlet water pipes on, new gaskets should be used unless the old ones are in good condition. All rubber hose connections in the water system should be coated inside with shellac. The clamps should be screwed tight, but not tight enough to cut into or injure the hose. As an additional precaution against leaks, the hose may be taped with friction tape and another coating of shellac placed outside. This shellac will seize or stick to the rubber, but may usually be broken away by grasping the hose in the hand over the joint and twisting it.

The few remaining parts are now added and the motor is complete.

An inspection—Undoubtedly, the most important part of airplane motor work is the inspection, so that now the motor must be given a very thorough and rigid inspection. It is well to feel of each nut with the fingers, as in the case of the crank-case nuts.

Ignition wires should be looked over for possible chafing. They should be checked over again to see that the right lead goes to the proper plug, and that the ends of the leads are not weakened by the breaking of a number of the strands of the wire. This is a point that is quite important and one which is often overlooked by the mechanic in the field.

Regarding spark plugs—The proper cleaning of spark plugs should be demonstrated before these are replaced in the cylinders. Several plugs should be taken apart and the correct method of installing porcelains or gaskets taught. The proper setting for the spark plug points is 0.025 inch. In fastening and tying down the high-tension leads, make sure that they touch no moving part.

SPECIFICATIONS, OX-5 ENGINE

Type—90 deg. V
Cooling—Water
No. Cylinders—8
Bore—4.0 Inches
Stroke—5.0 Inches
Comp. Ratio—4.92:1
H.P.—90
Fuel consumption, Gal. 1 hr.—9.0
Oil consumption, Gal. 1 hr.—.035
Oil circulation—Full force gear pump

INDEX

Numbers in italics indicate illustrations.

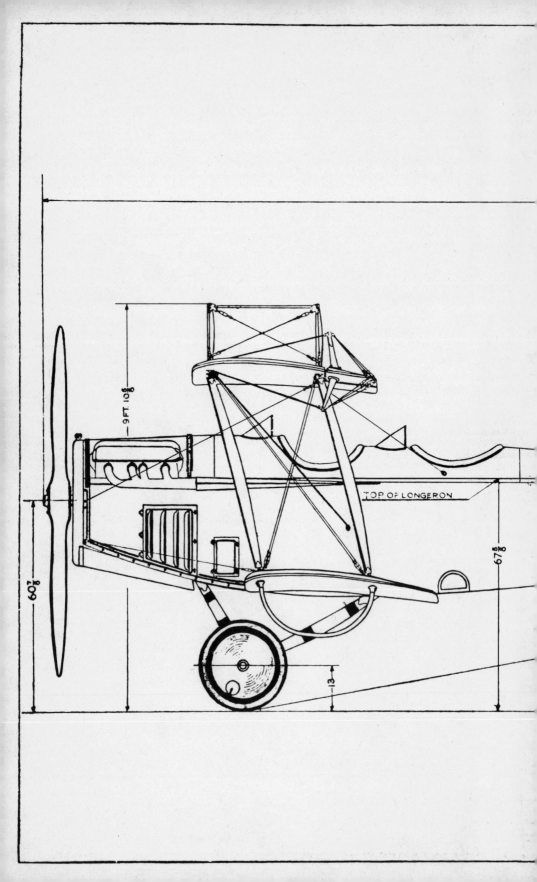

9FT. 10⅝

TOP OF LONGERON

67⅝

60⅞

13